W9-BSF-520

BACKGROUND FOR RADICAL RECONSTRUCTION

TESTIMONY OF THE TIMES:
SELECTIONS FROM CONGRESSIONAL HEARINGS

John A. Garraty, General Editor

BACKGROUND FOR RADICAL RECONSTRUCTION

Testimony taken from the Hearings of the Joint Committee on Reconstruction, the Select Committee on the Memphis Riots and Massacres, and the Select Committee on the New Orleans Riots — 1866 and 1867

Edited by
HANS L. TREFOUSSE
Brooklyn College, City University of New York

LITTLE, BROWN AND COMPANY *Boston*

LIBRARY OF CONGRESS CATALOG CARD NO. 78–119816

FIRST PRINTING

Published simultaneously in Canada
by Little, Brown & Company (Canada) Limited

PRINTED IN THE UNITED STATES OF AMERICA

Contents

Part Two

CONDITIONS OF WHITES IN THE SOUTH

Part Three

EFFECTS OF JOHNSON'S PLAN OF RECONSTRUCTION

INTRODUCTION

The era of Reconstruction was one of the most fateful periods in the history of the United States. To bring to a conclusion a great civil war and at the same time to provide for the integration into society of almost four million former slaves was a staggering task, which President Andrew Johnson sought to accomplish by relying in effect upon the existing power structure in the South. The radicals in Congress, considering his policy to be mistaken, proposed to undo it. Whether they were justified has remained a matter of dispute among historians.

Andrew Johnson's plan was simple. Believing himself to be following in Lincoln's footsteps, on May 29, 1865, the new President issued a proclamation in which he promised amnesty to almost all former insurgents except a number of high Confederate officials and persons owning property worth more than $20,000, a large sum in 1865. All that former rebels had to do was to take an oath of allegiance to the United States. In separate proclamations, the President appointed provisional governors who were to call upon loyal and amnestied voters to reestablish regular state governments. Although he let it be known that he expected the former Confederate states to nullify the secession ordinances, ratify the Thirteenth Amendment, and repudiate the Confederate debt, his scheme was so mild that it did not take long for the former ruling circles in the South to recover a good measure of control. That Johnson rarely refused pardons to those exempted from the amnesty facilitated this process. None of the states extended the suffrage to even the most qualified Negroes, several passed drastic Black Codes remanding the freedmen to a condition barely removed from slavery, and many elected former leading Confederates to high office. By the time Congress met in December, 1865, all the seceded states except Texas were ready to resume their places in the federal Union. But the leaders of the Republican party were unwilling to accept these arrangements. Refusing to admit the Southern members-elect to their seats, the dominant faction in Congress served notice on the President and the South that certain additional safeguards were required. And although most Republicans were at first willing to come to some sort of an agreement with Johnson, they improvised their own solutions when this did not prove feasible — first the Fourteenth Amendment and then the four radical Reconstruction Acts. Thus the ex-Confederate states were finally remanded to military rule two years after the war had ended.

Was this radical policy justified? Was it even necessary? The answer depends in part on conditions prevailing in the Southern states, and the following excerpts from the hearings of three Congressional committees [1] are designed to throw some light on the state of affairs in the former Confederacy in 1865 and 1866.

The first and most important of the Congressional inquiries was conducted by the Joint Committee of Fifteen on Reconstruction. Often considered a device conceived by the radicals to procure greater influence within a small body than they could muster in Congress as a whole, the Joint Committee was the result of two Republican caucuses held on December 1 and 2, 1865, shortly before Congress convened. Totally unwilling to adopt Johnson's plan without change, a number of party leaders, among whom Thaddeus Stevens of Pennsylvania was especially active, agreed not to accept the credentials of any of the Southern Congressmen-elect until the matter should have been considered by a joint committee. Accordingly, a resolution to set up such a committee was introduced and passed in the House of Representatives on December 5, amended by the Senate on December 12, and finally passed by both Houses by December 13. It stated:

> Resolved by the House of Representatives (the Senate concurring), That a joint committee of fifteen members shall be appointed, nine of whom shall be members of the House and six members of the Senate, who shall inquire into the condition of the States which formed the so-called Confederate States of America, and report whether they, or any of them, are entitled to be represented in either House of Congress; with leave to report at any time, by bill or otherwise.

Congress also gave the committee power to call for persons and papers, and stipulated that all papers concerning Reconstruction be referred to the committee.

Armed with such powers, the committee became an exceedingly important arm of Congress. William P. Fessenden of Maine, James W. Grimes of Iowa, Ira Harris of New York, Jacob M. Howard of Michigan, and George H. Williams of Oregon became the Republican Senate members; Reverdy Johnson of Maryland represented the opposition in the Upper House. The House Republicans, including Thaddeus Stevens, were John A. Bingham of Ohio, Henry T. Blow of Missouri, George S. Boutwell of Massachusetts, Roscoe Conkling of New York, Justin Morrill of Vermont, and Elihu B. Washburne of Illinois; Henry Grider of Kentucky and Andrew J. Rogers of New Jersey were the Democratic members. Of all these, Howard, Williams, Stevens, Boutwell, Conkling, Morrill, and Washburne were radicals; the remaining Republicans were generally considered moderate.

[1] The references are: (1) *Report of the Joint Committee on Reconstruction*, H. R. No. 30, 39 Cong., 1 Sess., 1866; *Memphis Riots and Massacres*, H. R. No. 101, 39 Cong., 1 Sess., 1966; *New Orleans Riots*, H. R. No. 16, 39 Cong., 2 Sess., 1867.

The committee soon resolved itself into four subcommittees. Grimes, Bingham, and Grider took testimony on conditions in Tennessee; Howard, Blow, and Conkling became responsible for North Carolina, South Carolina, and Virginia; Harris, Boutwell, and Morrill took charge of hearings concerning Alabama, Arkansas, Georgia, and Mississippi, while Williams, Washburne, and Rogers dealt with Florida, Louisiana, and Texas. The hearing led to a lengthy report condemning conditions in the South, which the Democrats refused to sign; in addition, the committee reported what finally became the Fourteenth Amendment to Congress. At the time of the hearings, the amendment was still in a rudimentary stage — a proposition to deduct all persons disfranchised on account of race and color from the total to be counted for representation. Soon after the close of the testimony, however, the committee hammered into shape a version which was passed by the House and amended by the Senate to read as it now stands. It finally became the committee's most enduring monument.

The testimony taken by the committee has often been denounced as partial, biased, and exaggerated. "The four subcommittees meeting to hear evidence, formed a great American Court of Star Chamber sitting for the conviction of the South in an *ex parte* case," wrote Howard K. Beale in *The Critical Year*.[2] Beale pointed out that most of the witnesses were committed to points of view the committee wanted to hear, that the members had made up their minds before the hearings began, and that the evidence was "patently useless." That the majority had definite opinions about the South is true; that it wanted to see the freedmen protected is equally true. But it does not follow that the evidence uncovered is worthless. As Eric L. McKitrick has pointed out, "To say that the testimony consisted of lies would be dubious; one does not get nearly the impression of flamboyance in reading it that one gets in reading about it." [3] Eyewitnesses saw facts, and the facts, when properly assessed, were of great significance.

What follows is an attempt to select from the mass of testimony,[4] meaningful items, and from the many persons who were summoned, witnesses who had something to say. The men who appeared before the committee were of varied origin; if the members *preferred* radical witnesses, they nevertheless called a number of ex-Confederates and conservatives. By combining the testimony of all these, a coherent picture can be established. Men of differing backgrounds gave testimony about the five topics selected — conditions of blacks in the South, conditions

[2] Howard K. Beale, *The Critical Year: A Study of Andrew Johnson and Reconstruction* (New York: Frederick Ungar, 1958), pp. 94–96.

[3] Eric L. McKitrick, *Andrew Johnson and Reconstruction* (Chicago: The University of Chicago Press, 1960), p. 330.

[4] Minor changes from the original documents have been made to modernize spelling and punctuation.

of whites in the South, effects of Johnson's plan of Reconstruction, the problem of Negro suffrage, and the need for Congressional interference. Native Unionists, Northern white settlers in the South, blacks, Southern leaders, provisional governors, members of the armed forces and officers of the Freedmen's Bureau, travelers, and others of conservative, moderate, and radical background all had their say, and properly weighted, their testimony helps to present a rounded picture of conditions.

The committee's hearings were held between January and May, 1866. Even before they were concluded, a riot took place at Memphis, and in July, another disturbance occurred in New Orleans. Because of the pertinence of these disorders to the problems of Reconstruction, selections from testimony before the committees investigating these riots are also of significance.

The first of these disorders was the Memphis riot. Feeling in the city had been running high for some time. The lower classes, especially the Irish who tended to predominate in the police force, resented the Negro troops, and when on May 1, 1866, an altercation occurred between black soldiers and the police, the latter reacted with a total lack of restraint. The result was a massacre lasting several days, during which an infuriated mob killed, plundered, and maimed defenseless Negroes. Congress acted promptly; on May 14, on the motion of Thaddeus Stevens the House passed a resolution to establish a committee of three to investigate. The speaker thereupon appointed Elihu B. Washburne, John M. Broomall of Pennsylvania, and George S. Shanklin of Kentucky. Washburne became chairman; Broomall generally cooperated with him, as both sympathized with the radicals, while Shanklin represented the Democratic opposition and finally submitted a minority report. The committee took testimony at Memphis from May 22 until June 6, 1866.

The New Orleans riot was even more sensational than the disorders at Memphis. Its origins may be traced to the determination of the radical faction in Louisiana to recall the convention of 1864, a resolve that met with resistance from the conservatives. Seeing themselves outvoted and discriminated against, the radicals were anxious to enfranchise the Negroes and to disfranchise certain former Confederates. The latter were determined to prevent these changes, and the riot was the result. A mob invaded the convention hall, members were killed and maimed, and a procession of Negroes supporting the gathering was set upon and massacred. When Congress met in December, it appointed an investigating committee headed by Representative Thomas D. Eliot of Massachusetts. Samuel Shellabarger of Ohio and Benjamin M. Boyer of Pennsylvania were the other members. The first two were radicals, the third, a Democrat. Taking testimony in Washington and New Orleans between December 1866 and February 1867, the committee heard a variety of witnesses ranging from federal officers to prominent supporters of the former Confederacy. Again, the minority member submitted a separate report, but the testimony merely strengthened the impression that Johnson's policies had not been successful.

In assessing the testimony taken by these committees, the personalities of the questioners must be kept in mind. Because of their great interest in radical measures, Howard, Boutwell, Williams, Washburne, Shellabarger, and to a lesser extent, Conklin, Morrill, and Broomall, were anxious to bring out the injustices perpetrated under Johnson's plan. Bingham, Grimes, Harris, and Blow were interested in discovering shortcomings of the President's arrangements, but were less radical in their outlook. The Democrats, Grider, Rogers, Shanklin, and Boyer, were not only anxious to emphasize the President's successes but also to discredit the radicals.

One of the most active of the investigators was Senator Jacob M. Howard. A founder of the Republican party in Michigan, he had represented his state in the Senate since the beginning of the war. He had been bitterly opposed to General George B. McClellan, had taken a hand in framing the Thirteenth Amendment, and generally acted with the radicals. A large handsome man with hazel eyes and a dark, olive complexion, he was a Latin and French scholar who had published a translation of the *Memoirs* of the Empress Josephine.

George H. Williams was another prominent member of the Joint Committee of Fifteen on Reconstruction. Appointed Chief Justice of Oregon Territory by Franklin Pierce, he later practiced law in Portland and in 1864 was sent to the United States Senate as a Republican. He was an active radical, who, after serving on the committee, played an important part in preparing and introducing the Tenure-of-Office Act and in framing Reconstruction legislation. He was also one of the managers in the impeachment trial of President Johnson. After his defeat for reelection in 1871, President Ulysses Grant first named him one of the High Commissioners to negotiate the Treaty of Washington with Great Britain and then appointed him Attorney General. In 1873, Grant nominated Williams Chief Justice of the Supreme Court, but because of widespread criticism, the nomination was withdrawn.

George S. Boutwell, the most active member of the subcommittee on Alabama, Arkansas, Georgia, and Mississippi, was also a radical. Elected Governor of Massachusetts in 1850 as a result of a coalition between Democrats and Free Soilers, he later became one of the founders of the Republican party in the state. After establishing a reputation as Commissioner of Internal Revenue under Secretary of the Treasury Salmon P. Chase, in 1862 he was elected to the House of Representatives, where he served until 1869, consistently favoring radical measures. He played an important role in the framing of the Fourteenth and Fifteenth Amendments as well as in the impeachment of Andrew Johnson. In 1869, President Grant appointed him Secretary of the Treasury, an office in which he pursued conservative financial policies. In 1873, he went to the Senate where he remained until 1877. Toward the end of his long life, he served as President of the Anti-Imperialist League. Often considered a fanatic, he nevertheless possessed great ability.

Elihu B. Washburne and Thomas D. Eliot, the chairmen of the Memphis and New Orleans investigating committees, were both radicals who had long served in the House — Washburne since 1853 and Eliot since 1859. Washburne, who represented a district in northern Illinois, was at first best known for his activity of watchdog of the Treasury, although he later became famous as the political mentor of General Grant, whose fellow townsman he was. After Grant became President, Washburne briefly served as Secretary of State; then he went to Paris as American minister to France. While not as prominent a radical as some of his colleagues, Washburne nevertheless sympathized with radical measures. Eliot came from New Bedford, Massachusetts; during the war he had introduced the Second Confiscation Act which provided for the freeing of all slaves held by rebels. His support of radical legislation was consistent.

Finally, there were a number of members of the various committees who played minor roles in the questioning. James W. Grimes was one of the best-known Republican Senators in Washington. Originally radical, as time went on, the Senator from Iowa became more moderate, and finally voted for the acquittal of President Johnson. Samuel Shellabarger was a radical from Ohio who was interested in framing Reconstruction legislation, and Henry T. Blow, a Missouri businessman, had been minister to Venezuela in 1861–1862 before his election to Congress. He was a member of the House from 1863 to 1869 and was generally considered a moderate. The Democratic members of the various committees were less well known, but they ably represented their party and their questions were useful to balance those of their opponents.

The witnesses appearing before the three committees highlighted some of the outstanding problems facing the South during the period of Presidential Reconstruction. The testimony showed that in the minds of many, there was some question about the security of Union men in the former Confederacy. It also raised the problem of the treatment of the freedmen, the contumacy of the ex-Confederates, the difficulties encountered in carrying out Johnson's plan, and the almost universal resistance to Negro suffrage. Finally, the witnesses brought to the attention of observers the existence of violence in the region to be reconstructed. Although this problem had been publicized earlier by the press and other media of information, its reiteration by witnesses before Congressional committees was effective. It is not surprising that Congress became convinced that more stringent measures were needed to protect both black and white Republicans in the South and safeguard the gains of the Civil War. Radical Reconstruction involving black suffrage and military rule was the result.

BACKGROUND FOR RADICAL RECONSTRUCTION

Part One

CONDITIONS OF BLACKS IN THE SOUTH

1 TESTIMONY OF BLACKS

Testimony of Oscar J. Dunn

Oscar J. Dunn was one of the most notable leaders during the period of radical Reconstruction. Born a slave, he ran away from his master and eventually bought his own freedom. Because he was active as a radical Republican in his native New Orleans long before his election as Lieutenant Governor (1868–1871), his testimony before the committee investigating the New Orleans riot is of great interest.

The Chairman: Where do you reside? — A. I reside in New Orleans; I am a native of the place and have always resided here.

Q. What is your age? — A. About forty-one; I was born in 1826. . . .

Q. State whether you have any knowledge of the feelings and opinions of the colored citizens here. — A. I know them to a certain extent; I have been with them a great deal. The feeling among them is that there is no security for them under the present municipal government; that there is no justice for them. They have occasion every day to be satisfied of that fact.

Q. State, in your own way, what reasons bring you to this conclusion. — A. We are insulted on every occasion, whenever they have an opportunity. In going through the streets it is a common thing to hear them say, "These Negroes think they have their own way now, but they are mistaken; the President is with us, and we will soon drive the Negroes and their Yankee friends off." I have frequently seen them point out Negroes as belonging to the Union central committee, and say, "As soon as we get things in our own hands we will manage the matter."

Q. State whether you are a member of that committee. — A. I am the treasurer, and was one of the founders of it.

Q. Is it a committee of colored persons alone, or colored and white? — A. No, sir; colored and white. Mr. Durant was formerly president of it.

Q. In what way, other than by speech, does this feeling of which you have spoken show itself? — A. I have known instances in which they tried to pick quarrels with us. They very seldom do it with only one alone, but when there are three or four along they will do it. If a colored man goes along genteelly dressed they will rub against him and try to pick a quarrel with him. They seem to have a deep-seated hatred against loyal people, without regard to color — against the whole loyal community.

Q. Has there been a branch of the Freedmen's Bureau here in the city? — A. Yes, sir; and I have had occasion to send a great many freedmen to it. The planters, in many portions of the state, would make arrangements with them and fail to perform their part of the contract. There have been many instances the present season where planters have employed laborers at $15 a month. The contract specified that the planter should be allowed to retain one-half the monthly salary; they would retain it in that way until the cotton was picked, and then manage to get into a quarrel with them and drive them away without paying them. I have had several come to me with such information, and some of them I have taken to the Freedmen's Bureau. This is a common thing through all the parishes. The Freedmen's Bureau is a great eyesore to the planters; they do not like it at all; and I am sorry to say that in many instances agents in the parishes do not act exactly just towards the freedmen.

Q. What do you attribute that to? — A. I have the facts from freedmen coming to me and writing to me, reporting that they have made application to the bureau agents, but could get no redress whatever, and generally when they come down here with their complaints I refer them to Mr. Stickney, the agent.

Q. Is there a general feeling in the community against the colored people? — A. In many instances the planters have undertaken to raise crops without sufficient means, and have not paid the hands because they have not had the money. They have drawn pretty extensively from the merchants, and their crops have not been sufficient to extricate them from their liabilities.

Q. Are you speaking now of facts within your own knowledge? — A. Many of them are within my own knowledge; many of them have told me themselves that they were not able to pay in consequence of the failure of their crops, and I have known others who did not pay their hands because they would not.

Testimony of Alexander Dunlop

Alexander Dunlop was a blacksmith who had been free before the Civil War. Despite the disabilities from which free Negroes suffered in antebellum Virginia, because of his thirst for knowledge he had learned to read. During Reconstruction, he was a leader of his community and served as a trustee of the First Baptist Church in Williamsburg.

Mr. Howard: How old are you? — A. Forty-eight years.

Q. Where do you reside? — A. In Williamsburg, Virginia. I was born there.

Q. Have you ever been a slave? — A. Never, sir.

Q. Are you able to read and write? — A. No, sir; I can read some. That was not allowed me there.

Q. Can you read the Bible? — A. Yes, sir.

Q. Do you belong to a church? — A. Yes; I belong to the First Baptist Church of Williamsburg. I am one of the leading men and trustees.

Q. About how many are included in the church? — A. Our minutes show seven hundred and thirty-six.

Q. Do you own the church building? — A. We do.

Q. Are you a delegate to the President of the United States? — A. Yes, sir; I was sent by my people convened at a large mass meeting.

Q. For what purpose? — A. My purpose was to let the government know our situation, and what we desire the government to do for us if it can do it. We feel down there without any protection.

Q. Do you feel any danger? — A. We do.

Q. Danger of what? — A. We feel in danger of our lives, of our property, and of everything else.

Q. Why do you feel so? — A. From the spirit which we see existing there every day toward us as freedmen.

Q. On the part of whom? — A. On the part of the rebels. I have a great chance to find out these people. I have been with them before the war. They used to look upon me as one of the leading men there. I have suffered in this war; I was driven away from my place by Wise's raid; and so far as I, myself, am concerned, I do not feel safe; and if the military were removed from there I would not stay in Williamsburg one hour, although what little property I possess is there.

Q. In case of the removal of the military, what would you anticipate? — A. Nothing shorter than death; that has been promised to me by the rebels.

Q. Do they entertain a similar feeling toward all the freedmen there? — A. I believe, sir, that that is a general feeling. I ask them, sometimes, "Why is it? We have done you no harm." "Well," they say, "the Yankees freed you, and now let the Yankees take care of you; we want to have nothing to do with you." I say to them, "You have always been making laws to keep us here, and now you want to drive us away — for what?" They say, "We want to bring foreign immigration here, and drive every scoundrel of you away from here." I tell them that I was born in Virginia, and that I am going to die in Virginia. "There is but one thing that will make me leave Virginia," I say, "and that is, for the government to withdraw the military and leave me in your hands; when it does that, I will go."

Q. Has your property been destroyed by the rebels? — A. I had not much, except my blacksmith's shop. I carried on a large business there. The rebels and the Northern men destroyed everything I had; what the one did not take, the other did; they did not leave me even a hammer.

Q. Have you a family? — A. Yes, sir; a wife, but no children; I bought my wife.

Q. How much did you give for her? — A. I gave four hundred and fifty dollars for my wife, and seven hundred dollars for my wife's sister. After I bought my wife, they would not let me set her free. I paid the money, and got the bill of sale.

Q. What hindered her being free? — A. It was the law, they said. She had to stand as my slave.

Q. How extensive is this feeling of danger on the part of colored people there? — A. I believe, sincerely, that it is the general feeling.

Q. Did you ever see a black rebel, or hear of one? — A. I must be honest about that. I believe that we have had some as big rebel black men as ever were white.

Q. Many? — A. No, sir; they are "few and far between"; but I believe that any man who, through this great trouble that we have had, would do anything to stop the progress of the Union army, was a rebel. When Wise made his raid into Williamsburg, I just had time to leave my house and make my escape. They broke up everything I had; they took their bayonets and tore my beds all to pieces. All they wanted was Aleck Dunlop; they wanted to hang him before his own door. One day, since the fall of Richmond, I met General Henry A. Wise at Norfolk. He spoke to me, and asked me how I was. I said, "I am doing a little better than could be expected." Said he, "Why?" Said I, "Them devils of yours did not catch me; I was too smart for them that morning." "Do you think," said he, "they would have hurt you?" "No," said I, "I don't think so, but I know it; they had orders to hang me."

Q. Did Wise admit it? — A. He did not say so; but he turned and went off. The day that Wise's men were there, my wife asked them what had I done that they wanted to hang me in preference to anybody else? They said it was because I was a Union man. I had worked for the rebels from the time the war broke out until General McClellan moved up; and then they concocted a scheme to get me to Richmond; but when I saw the wagon coming for me, I went off in the opposite direction. When General Hooker and General Kearney came there, they sent for me, within three hours of their arrival, and asked me about the country, and what I knew. I gave them all the information I could; that, through a colored friend, got to the secessionists and embittered them against me. The next Union officer who came there was Colonel Campbell, of the 5th Pennsylvania cavalry; and I believe he was as great a rebel as Jeff Davis. He was governor there for a long time. They captured him, and carried him to Richmond.

Q. The rebels never caught you? — A. They have never caught me yet.

Q. How do the black people down there feel about education? — A. They want it, and they have a desire to get it; but the rebels use every exertion to keep teachers from them. We have got two white teachers in Williamsburg, and have got to put them in a room over a colored family.

Q. Do the black people contribute liberally to the support of their own schools? — A. They are not able, sir. The rebels made many raids there, and destroyed everything they could get their hands on belonging to colored people — beds and clothing.

Testimony of Richard R. Hill

Richard R. Hill was a former slave who lived in Hampton, Virginia, where he had been acquainted with ex-President John Tyler. Able to read and write, Hill was a keen observer of events and was free from animus against the former slave owners.

Mr. Howard: Were you ever a slave? — A. Yes, sir.

Q. When did you become free? — A. When the proclamation was issued. I left Richmond in 1863.

Q. Did you serve in the rebel army? — A. No, sir.

Q. Or in the Union army? — A. No, sir.

Q. How do the rebels down there, about Hampton, treat the colored people? — A. The returned rebels express a desire to get along in peace if they can. There have been a few outrages out upon the roadside there. One of the returned Union colored soldiers was met out there and beaten very much.

Q. By whom was he beaten? — A. It was said they were rebels; they had on Union overcoats, but they were not United States soldiers. Occasionally we hear of an outrage of that kind, but there are none in the little village where I live.

Q. What appears to be the feeling generally of the returned rebels towards the freedmen; is it kind or unkind? — A. Well, the feeling that they manifest as a general thing is kind, so far as I have heard.

Q. Are they willing to pay the freedmen fair wages for their work? — A. No, sir; they are not willing to pay the freedmen more than from five to eight dollars a month.

Q. Do you think that their labor is worth more than that generally? — A. I do, sir; because, just at this time, everything is very dear, and I do not see how people can live and support their families on those wages.

Q. State whether the black people down there are anxious to go to school? — A. Yes, sir; they are anxious to go to school; we have schools there every day that are very well filled; and we have night schools that are very well attended, both by children and aged people; they manifest a great desire for education.

Q. Who are the teachers; white or black? — A. White, sir.

Q. How are the white teachers treated by the rebels down there? — A. I guess they are not treated very well, because they have very little communication between each other. I have not heard of any threatening expression in regard to them.

Q. Did you ever hear any threats among the whites to reduce your race to slavery again? — A. They have said, and it seems to be a prevalent idea, that if their representatives were received in Congress the condition of the freedmen would be very little better than that of the slaves, and that their old laws would still exist by which they would reduce them to something like bondage. That has been expressed by a great many of them.

Q. What has become of your former master? — A. He is in Williamsburg.

Q. Have you seen him since the proclamation? — A. Yes, sir.

Q. Did he want you to go back and live with him? — A. No, sir; he did not ask me to go back, but he was inquiring of me about another of his slaves, who was with him at the evacuation of Williamsburg by the rebels.

Q. How do you feel about leaving the State of Virginia and going off and residing as a community somewhere else? — A. They do not wish to leave and go anywhere else unless they are certain that the locality where they are going is healthy and that they can get along.

Q. Are they not willing to be sent back to Africa? — A. No, sir.

Q. Why not? — A. They say that they have lived here all their days, and there were stringent laws made to keep them here; and that if they could live here contented as slaves, they can live here when free.

Q. Do you not think that to be a very absurd notion? — A. No, sir; if we can get lands here and can work and support ourselves, I do not see why we should go to any place that we do not want to go to.

Q. If you should stay here, is there not danger that the whites and blacks would intermarry and amalgamate? — A. I do not think there is any more danger now than there was when slavery existed. At that time there was a good deal of amalgamation.

Q. Amalgamation in Virginia? — A. There was no actual marrying, but there was an intermixture to a great extent. We see it very plainly. I do not think that that troubles the colored race at all.

Q. But you do not think that a Virginia white man would have connection with a black woman? — A. I do, sir; I not only think so, but I know it from past experience. It was nothing but the stringent laws of the South that kept many a white man from marrying a black woman.

Q. It would be looked upon as a very wicked state of things, would it not, for a white man to marry a black woman? — A. I will state to you as a white lady stated to a gentleman down in Hampton, that if she felt disposed to fall in love with or marry a black man, it was nobody's business but hers; and so I suppose that if the colored race get all their rights, and particularly their equal rights before the law, it would not hurt the nation or trouble the nation.

Q. In such a case do you think the blacks would have a strong inclination to unite with the whites in marriage? — A. No, sir; I do not. I do not think that the blacks would have so strong an inclination to unite with the whites as the whites would have to unite with the blacks.

Testimony of William Thornton

Unlike Richard R. Hill, the Reverend William Thornton, who had also been a slave and also knew how to read and write, painted a gloomy picture of conditions in and about Hampton, Virginia.

Mr. Howard: What is your age? — A. Forty-two, sir.

Q. Where were you born? — A. In Elizabeth City County, Virginia.

Q. What degree of education have you received? — A. My education is very narrowly limited; I have not had the advantages of a first-rate education.

Q. You can read and write? — A. Yes, sir.

Q. Can you read the Bible? — A. Oh, yes, sir.

Q. Can you read ordinary newspapers? — A. Yes, sir.

Q. Can you write a letter on business? — A. Yes, sir.

Q. Were you ever a slave? — A. Yes, sir.

Q. When were you made free? — A. I was made free under the proclamation.

Q. Where do you reside? — A. Hampton, Elizabeth City County, Virginia.

Q. How do the old rebel masters down there feel toward your race? — A. The feeling existing there now is quite disagreeable.

Q. Do they not treat the colored race with kindness down there? — A. No, sir.

Q. What acts of unkindness can you mention? — A. I was asked the other day if I did not know I was violating the law in celebrating marriages. I did not know that that was the case, and I went up to the clerk's office to inquire; I said nothing out of the way to the clerk of the court; I only asked him if there had been any provision for colored people to be lawfully married. Said he, "I do not know whether there is or not, and if they are granting licenses you can't have any; that is my business, not yours." After I found I was violating the law, I went to the Freedmen's Bureau and stated the case. A provision was afterwards made in the bureau granting licenses, and authorizing me to marry. Some days after that an old gentleman named Houghton, a white man living in the neighborhood of my church, was in the church. In my sermon I mentioned the assassination of Mr. Lincoln. Next day I happened to meet Houghton, who said to me, "Sir, as soon as we can get these Yankees off the ground and move that bureau, we will put you to rights; we will break up your church, and not one of you shall have a church here." Said I, "For what? I think it is for the safety of the country to have religious meetings, and for your safety as well as everybody else's." "We will not have it, sir," said he, and then he commenced talking about two classes of people whom they intended to put to rights, the colored people and the loyal white men. I asked him in what respect he was going to put them to rights; said he, "That is for myself."

Q. Is he a man of standing and condition in the neighborhood? — A. He owns property there.

Q. Is he a rebel? — A. Oh, yes.

Q. Can you speak of any acts of violence committed by the whites upon the blacks? — A. Yes, sir; about three weeks ago a colored man got another one to cut some wood for him, and sent him into the woods adjoining the property of a Mr. Britner, a white man. The colored man, not knowing the line between the two farms, cut down a tree on Britner's land, when Britner went into the woods and deliberately shot him as he would shoot a bird.

Q. Was he not indicted and punished for that? — A. They had him in prison.

Q. Is he not in prison now? — A. I heard that they had let him out last Sunday morning.

Q. Do you know any other instances of cruelty? — A. I have church once a month in Matthews County, Virginia, the other side of the bay. The last time I was over there an intelligent man told me that just below his house a lady and her husband, who had been at the meeting, received thirty-nine lashes for being there, according to the old law of Virginia, as if they had been slaves. This was simply because they were told not to go to hear a Yankee darkey talk. They said he was not a Yankee but was a man born in Virginia, in Hampton.

Q. Why did they not resist being flogged? — A. They are that much down.

Q. Did they not know that they had a right to resist? — A. They dare not do it.

Q. Why? — A. I do not know. On the 1st of January we had a public meeting there, at which I spoke. The next night when I was coming from the church, which is about a mile and a half from my house, I met a colored man who told me that there was a plot laid for me; I went back to the church and got five of my church members to come with me. I afterwards learned that a fellow named Mahon, a white man, had determined, for my speech that day, to murder me the first chance.

Q. Did that come to you in so authentic a form as to leave no doubt upon your mind? — A. I believe he made the threat. The next day he said to me, "We hope the time will come that these Yankees will be away from here, and then we will settle with you preachers." That gave me to understand that the threat was made.

Q. Do you wish to state any other instances? — A. These are as many as I care to speak of.

Q. You are up here as a delegate to make representations to the President in reference to the condition of the colored people? — A. Yes, sir.

Q. Are you a regularly ordained minister of the gospel? — A. Yes, sir.

Q. In what church? — A. In the Baptist church.

Testimony of Daniel Norton

Dr. Daniel Norton was a Negro physician from New York who during the Civil War had returned to his former home in Virginia to practice medicine. His observations are especially interesting because of his education and background.

Mr. Howard: What is the feeling among the rebels in the neighborhood of Yorktown towards the government of the United States? — A. They do not manifest a very cordial feeling toward the government of the United States. There are some, of course, who do, but the majority do not seem to manifest a good spirit or feeling.

Q. How are they disposed to treat you? — A. Me, as a man, they are generally disposed to treat well, but there are others of my fellowmen whom they do not treat as well.

Q. Are you employed as a physician in white families? — A. I have not been employed in any white families, except in one case, since I have been there. I principally practice among the colored.

Q. How do the returned rebels treat the colored people? — A. They have in some cases treated them well, but in more cases they have not. A number of persons living in the country have come into Yorktown and reported to the Freedmen's Bureau that they have not been treated well; that they worked all the year and had received no pay, and were driven off on the first of January. They say that the owners with whom they had been living rented out their places, sold their crops, and told them they had no further use for them, and that they might go to the Yankees.

Q. What is the condition of the colored people in that neighborhood?

— A. They are poor, sir. There is a large settlement near Yorktown, called Slabtown, settled by the government during the war with those who came within the lines. The colored people there are doing such work as they can get to do, oystering, etc.

Q. Are not their old masters ready to employ them for wages? — A. There have been some sent for, and in several cases they received such bad treatment that they came back again. (Witness related several instances of this kind.)

Q. Are the colored people in your neighborhood willing to work for fair wages? — A. They are, sir.

Q. Do they find any difficulty in obtaining employment at fair wages? — A. They do find some difficulty. The slaveholders, who have owned them, say that they will take them back, but cannot pay them any wages. Some are willing to pay a dollar a month, and some less, and some are only willing to give them their clothing and what they eat. They are not willing to pay anything for work.

Q. Are the colored people generally provided with houses in which they can eat and sleep? — A. Yes, sir; such houses as they have built themselves, slab-houses.

Q. How do the colored people feel toward the government of the United States? — A. They feel determined to be law-abiding citizens. There is no other feeling among them.

Q. Are you a delegate sent to the city of Washington by some association? — A. I am. I was sent by three counties; I represent, perhaps, something like fifteen or twenty thousand people. The great trouble, in my opinion, is, that the colored people are not more disposed to return to their former homes on account of the treatment which those who have gone back have received.

Q. State generally whether or not the treatment which these colored people receive at the hands of their old white masters is kind or unkind. — A. It is not what I would consider kind or good treatment. Of course I do not mean to be understood that there are not some who treat them kindly, but I mean generally; they do not treat them kindly.

Q. In case of the removal of the military force from among you, and also of the Freedmen's Bureau, what would the whites do with you? — A. I do not think that the colored people would be safe. They would be in danger of being hunted and killed. The spirit of the whites against the blacks is much worse than it was before the war; a white gentleman with whom I was talking made this remark: he said he was well disposed toward the colored people, but that finding that they took up arms against him, he had come to the conclusion that he never wanted to have anything to do with them, or to show any spirit of kindness toward them. These were his sentiments.

2 TESTIMONY OF SOUTHERN WHITES

Testimony of Charles Douglas Gray

Charles Douglas Gray was a lawyer from the Valley of Virginia. Although he had voted for the ratification of the secession ordinance, his outlook was that of a conditional Virginia Unionist. At the time of his testimony, he had given up his profession and was engaged in farming.

Mr. Howard: Where do you reside? — A. In Augusta County, Virginia.

Q. Are you a native of Virginia? — A. Yes, sir. . . .

Q. You have been a loyalist during the war? — A. Yes, sir; uniformly so. I, however, voted for the ratification of the ordinance of secession. That is the only act I am ashamed of in the whole transaction; I was forced to do it, by the pressure of the moment.

Q. Have you been so situated as to be tolerably well acquainted with the state of public feeling among the white people of Virginia since the close of hostilities? — A. I have not; I have stayed very closely at home on my farm, and have mingled very little with the people.

Q. Are you well acquainted with the state of public feeling in Augusta County? — A. Yes, sir; I think I am.

Q. Have you been holding any public position there since the war? — A. No, sir.

Q. Nor during the war? — A. No, sir; none at all. . . .

Q. Among the people at large in your vicinity, what is the feeling toward the freedman? Is there a disposition to keep him under; to withhold from him the ordinary rights and privileges of a free man; to constrain him to labor for under-wages, or for no wages; to treat him with contempt and injury, or with justice? — A. I will endeavor to give you some idea of that. You must remember that the relation has been suddenly and violently changed between the white man and the black man. From a slave he has suddenly become a free man. Before the abolition of slavery, and before the war, it was the policy of the slaveholders to make a free Negro as despicable a creature and as uncomfortable as possible. They did not want a free Negro about at all. They considered it an injury to the slave, as it undoubtedly was, creating discontent among the slaves. The consequence was that there was always an intense prejudice against the free Negro. Now, very suddenly, all have become free Negroes; and that was not calculated to allay that prejudice. But that feeling is in my section of the country gradually subsiding. There is a great deal less feeling of that kind now than there was six or eight months ago. They all predict, of course, that the Negro will not work; that some means will have to be found by which he can be forced to work, or that he will not work. However, they hire them, and I hear very little complaint. There is great dissatisfaction, of course, with the abolition of slavery. We have not become reconciled to that.

Q. The coat does not fit? — A. The coat does not fit at all; but I have no doubt that in course of time they will be reconciled to it, and a better feeling will exist toward the Negro.

Q. State whether you have noticed anything like a general repugnance on the part of whites to the black man becoming the owner of lands, houses, and other property. — A. There was at the start. A great many houses were burned down in my neighborhood, which it was feared would be rented to Negroes. They do not like Negro families to settle in the neighborhood if they can prevent it; but that feeling, too, is not so strong as it was six months ago. They are beginning to see that it was a mistaken policy. They are beginning to see that they require and need the Negro labor. I do not know (to be perfectly frank and candid) but that the predominant feeling in the State is a disposition to get rid of them at present. I think, however, that that feeling will change sooner or later.

Q. Must it not necessarily change? — A. I think it must necessarily change.

Q. Must it not necessarily, in the end, change to a feeling which would retain the black laboring man in the midst of the white people as a laborer? — A. I would think so. They are making a great effort to introduce foreigners. My own opinion is that our Negroes will be a great deal better laborers, and that the people will see it. That was my view from the start.

Q. At the present time, of course, there is no great friendship for Negro schools? — A. No; there is a disposition to laugh it down, to ridicule it, and make fun of it.

Q. Have you yourself noticed the capability of the black to acquire learning in the ordinary elements of education? — A. I have not; but I have no doubt at all of it.

Q. What do you hear said of it generally by those who have given attention to that subject? — A. There has been very little attention given to that subject. There are a great many Negroes in our country who learned to read when it was against the law to teach them. The children of the families would teach them their A, B, C's, and they would go on from that to learn to read. The children would sit upon their laps and teach them to read. At present the Negro himself is in a restless, unsettled condition, which is a very natural thing; and there is a disposition on their part to congregate in the towns, which is a misfortune for them.

Q. Do they congregate there for mutual protection? — A. I do not know, sir. There is a great deal of disposition on their part to go to housekeeping. Their idea of liberty and independence is to keep house; and no matter what sort of a shanty or shelter they can get up, they prefer that. But they will soon see that that is not a wise course at all, and that they will starve if they congregate in towns where there is no employment.

Q. What is the general susceptibility of the Negro for religion? Is he more or less religious in his nature than the white man? — A. He is very susceptible to religious impressions, and prefers the more emotional forms of religion — the Methodist and the Baptist.

Q. Is he not inclined to be superstitious? — A. Yes, sir, very.

Q. More than the white man? — A. Well, I do not know that he would be. The ignorant white people are as superstitious as the Negroes.

Q. Do you think of any particular facts that you would wish to incorporate in your statement, illustrating your ideas? — A. No, sir; I think that if the right course is pursued down South, we can have the best peasantry in the world by securing the Negro in all his civil rights. I do not mean by that the right of suffrage at present; I do not think they are in a condition at present to exercise that right; I think that in the course of a generation, when they have been educated, it will be time enough to agitate that question. But let the Negro understand that he is a *bona fide* free man, and that his wages will be paid, and let him understand the worth of money (he does not understand the worth of money now, and has no idea of the expenses of housekeeping), and I think he will be industrious and frugal. I have known a great many very successful Negroes.

Q. Do you think that there is, as a general thing, a feeling of unkindness on the part of the Negroes toward the white people? — A. I do not think there is at all; in my section there is none at all.

Q. Do you think there is any danger of Negro insurrection in your neighborhood? — A. We have no apprehension whatever. There are too few there, in the first place.

Q. So far as your knowledge extends in Virginia, have you any reason to apprehend any danger from the Negroes? — A. I have none. I have heard some gentlemen express some apprehension, but they did not seem to be very serious at all.

Q. Have the Negroes arms? — A. Not that I know of.

Testimony of Dale Carter

Dale Carter was a Virginia state senator from Russell County in the extreme southwestern part of the state. A lifelong Whig, he had been opposed to secession but acquiesced during the war. Because of his political activities of many years standing — he had been a member of the constitutional convention of 1850–51 and of the legislature in 1857–58 — he had a wide acquaintance with the leaders of the state. His testimony was that of a moderate Unionist.

Mr. Howard: Do you hold any public office in Virginia? — A. I am the senator from [Russell County] in the Virginia senate.

Q. Have you a pretty general acquaintance with the people of Virginia? — A. I was in the convention assembled to frame the constitution in 1850–51, which formed the constitution of the state previous to the Alexandria constitution; then I have been in the legislature of Virginia; I was in the legislature in 1857–58; I was then in the house of delegates; I am now in the senate. I can say that I have a tolerable acquaintance with the people of Virginia. . . .

Q. How do they regard the abolition of slavery? — A. I can say in truth that they have given up slavery.

Q. And do not expect to reinstate it? — A. Never, sir; I can say most positively, so far as my acquaintance goes, that they have no hopes or desires at all ever again to make an effort of the kind in any way.

Q. How do they generally treat the emancipated blacks? — A. I was a slaveholder to the amount of about thirty-eight or thirty-nine slaves. My neighbors and myself, so far as my acquaintance went, had a sort of common understanding, perhaps owing to the proclamation issued by Governor Peirpoint, that the Negroes were free, and we kept our Negroes in this way a long while, until they became so thoroughly aware of their condition, and until everybody became so well informed of their condition that they were told, "Here you are as free as I am. I will keep you as you have been living with me, if you stay." Some would say, "If you stay with me I will pay you wages." Others would say, "If you do not stay with me as you have been staying I cannot keep you at all." A great many did leave their old homes. The Negroes seemed to get it into their heads that they would not be free unless they left where they had been living; they seemed to regard it that they were only then free. None of my acquaintances have since had any slaves. About the 1st of August my Negroes and myself had a sort of treaty on the subject, and they agreed to stay with me until the harvest was over; they told me that they would lease my lands; I did lease land to three of them; they were going on to prepare houses, and I was to aid them in preparing log-cabins to live in and in fencing some land to cultivate, which was clear, and other land which they could clear and open up; but an acquaintance of mine induced my Negroes to believe that they could do better about fifteen miles up the country, and they left and went up there; they are now leasing lands up there and intend to farm it. In fact, it was a brother-in-law of my own to whose lands they went; he had a large tract of country and owned slaves, about as many as I did; I do not know whether his own Negroes rented land from him, but mine went up there and rented land from him, and are there yet. I have one old woman and two small children (colored) who have staid at my house, and are there yet; but they are as free as I am, and are so treated.

Q. The rest will probably come back to you? — A. I believe so; I think they will come back whenever they can better their condition by doing so.

Q. How do the whites feel in that section of the country in reference to the education of freedmen — is there any repugnance to it? — A. None at all, if it could be done without expense to them. If the blacks could do it themselves, or if it could be done by any other authority, the whites have no objection to it; but at the same time the country is so ground down that they cannot educate their own children.

Q. And they would therefore feel an unwillingness to contribute out of their own funds to educate the freedmen? — A. They would, I think, because they do not consider themselves able to do it.

Q. Suppose that particular difficulty were removed, and that they were in possession of their property, as ordinarily, would they be willing then to assist in the education of the freedmen by a general tax upon property? — A. Well, now, sir, I cannot answer that question whether they would or not; perhaps if the tax were a general one — one on whites and blacks both.

Q. Suppose it were imposed on whites and blacks both? — A. I do not know; I cannot say what change that might produce, nor can I say that the whites are opposed to educating them at all, except, as I said before, they do not feel able to educate even their own children. There are no schools in the country, and there is very little personal property in the country; fences are burned a great deal and destroyed; the country is in a desolate and unproductive condition everywhere.

Q. Would a person who should come among them and undertake to become an instructor of the freedmen be treated with respect by the whites, provided his character was good? — A. Well, now, I cannot answer that either. As I said before, if a teacher was sent there to teach them in a free school, I do not think there would be any objection to it by the people.

Q. Would they receive the teacher of a colored school into society, provided he was worthy of it in other respects? — A. I cannot say about that.

Q. You think there is some doubt about it? — A. There might be. I dare say that, in some places, remarks would be made about it, particularly if the expenses of the schools had to be defrayed by the white men of the country. If it could be done by taxes levied upon property common to whites and blacks, I do not think they would make any objection. As to the fact that the man was a teacher of colored people, I do not think that would make much difference to the people. However, I live where there never have been a great many slaves, and I am speaking now of what I know about the sentiments of my own acquaintances in my own district.

Testimony of James Sinclair

The Reverend James Sinclair was a Presbyterian minister of Scottish birth who moved to North Carolina before the Civil War. Strongly Unionist although a slaveholder, he preached unpopular sermons during the conflict. Then, in order to clear himself, he enlisted in the Confederate army. His military career was cut short, however, when he was accused of sympathy with the enemy and discharged. After the war he served for a short time as an agent of the Freedmen's Bureau.

Mr. Howard: Is the Freedmen's Bureau acceptable to the great mass of the white people in North Carolina? — A. No, sir; I do not think it is; I think the most of the whites wish the bureau to be taken away.

Q. Why do they wish that? — A. They think that they can manage the Negro for themselves; that they understand him better than Northern men do. They say, "Let us understand what you want us to do with the Negro — what you desire of us; lay down your conditions for our readmission into the Union, and then we will know what we have to do, and if you will do that we will enact laws for the government of these Negroes. They have lived among us, and they are all with us, and we can manage them better than you can." They think it is interfering with the rights of the state for a bureau, the agent and representative of the federal government, to overslaugh the state entirely, and interfere with the regulations and administration of justice before their courts.

Q. Is there generally a willingness on the part of the whites to allow the freedmen to enjoy the right of acquiring land and personal property? — A. I think they are very willing to let them do that, for this reason: to get rid of some portion of the taxes imposed upon their property by the government. For instance, a white man will agree to sell a Negro some of his land on condition of his paying so much a year on it, promising to give him a deed of it when the whole payment is made, taking his note in the meantime. This relieves that much of the land from taxes to be paid by the white man. All I am afraid of is, that the Negro is too eager to go into this thing; that he will ruin himself, get himself into debt to the white man, and be forever bound to him for the debt and never get the land. I have often warned them to be careful what they did about these things.

Q. There is no repugnance on the part of the whites to the Negro owning land and personal property? — A. I think not.

Q. Have they any objection to the legal establishment of the domestic relations among the blacks, such as the relation of husband and wife, of parent and child, and the securing by law to the Negro the rights of those relations? — A. That is a matter of ridicule with the whites. They do not believe the Negroes will ever respect those relations more than the brutes. I suppose I have married more than two hundred couples of Negroes since the war, but the whites laugh at the very idea of the thing. Under the old laws a slave could not marry a free woman of color; it was made a penal offence in North Carolina for any one to perform such a marriage. But there was in my own family a slave who desired to marry a free woman of color, and I did what I conceived to be my duty, and married them, and I was presented to the grand jury for doing so, but the prosecuting attorney threw out the case and would not try it. In former times the officiating clergyman marrying slaves could not use the usual formula: "Whom God has joined together let no man put asunder"; you could not say, "According to the ordinance of God I pronounce you man and wife; you are no longer two but one." It was not legal for you to do so.

Q. What, in general, has been the treatment of the blacks by the whites since the close of hostilities? — A. It has not generally been of the kindest character; I must say that; I am compelled to say that.

Q. Have you witnessed any instances of cruelty and ill treatment of the blacks on the part of the whites? — A. I have.

Q. State one or two instances. — A. In relation to the supply of food, here is a piece of meat (the witness here produced and exhibited a piece of bacon) which was a man's allowance for an entire week. I had it weighed in my office when the skin was on it, and it weighed just four ounces. The case was brought to my notice, and I made his employer treat him better; but the better treatment was not continued. This was the case of a wealthy man who owned a hundred Negroes.

Q. Was it in consequence of his own poverty that he put his laborers on that short allowance? — A. He said that it was; but the Negroes pointed out to me that he had plenty of meat and plenty of cattle to kill for food.

Q. What, besides that meat, was allowed for a week's supply? — A. A half a peck of corn meal; that was all.

Q. Are you aware of any instance of personal ill treatment towards the blacks by the whites? — A. Yes, sir.

Q. Give some instances that have occurred since the war. — A. I knew a young woman, between nineteen and twenty years of age, a fine-looking girl, who was made by her former master to lie down flat on her face, while he beat her across her buttocks and over her private parts, he having first pulled up her clothes, leaving her person bare.

Q. What was the provocation, if any? — A. Something in regard to some work, which is generally the provocation.

Q. Was there no law in North Carolina at that time to punish such an outrage? — A. No, sir; only the regulations of the Freedmen's Bureau; we took cognizance of the case. In old times that was quite allowable; it is what was called "paddling."

Q. Did you deal with the master? — A. I immediately sent a letter to him to come to my office, but he did not come, and I have never seen him in regard to the matter since. I had no soldiers to enforce compliance, and I was obliged to let the matter drop.

Q. Have you any reason to suppose that such instances of cruelty are frequent in North Carolina at this time — instances of whipping and striking? — A. I think they are; it was only a few days before I left that a woman came there with her head all bandaged up, having been cut and bruised by her employer. They think nothing of striking them.

Q. And the Negro has practically no redress? — A. Only what he can get from the Freedmen's Bureau.

Testimony of T. J. Mackey

T. J. Mackey was a Southerner who had served in the Confederate army as chief engineer of the Trans-Mississippi Department. After the war, when he was living in Shreveport, Louisiana, he was appointed special provost marshal for Lamar County in neighboring Texas and was wounded in the performance of his duty while seeking to arrest suspected wartime murderers of local Unionists. His testimony is of interest because of his efforts to cooperate with the government he had fought.

Mr. Howard: How do the former slaveholders treat the freedmen? — A. They are the best masters now, as they are more familiar with the habits and character of the blacks. I have observed that those who were not slave-owners are now the most rigorous masters. To hire freedmen now requires a large fraction of their capital, and they are more rigorous in exacting their labor. The freedmen are more willing to work in cities, because they can there secure better protection to their persons from the better police of the cities. Negroes can be hired to work in the cities at a very considerable fraction below what they will demand to work in the country districts; not that the labor is less severe in the cities, but because they have more protection there. The official records of Shreveport, Marshall, and Jefferson, during the last eight months, will abundantly sustain the statements I have here made.

Q. In the rural districts of Texas are the lives and property of the freedmen secure as against the prejudices and feelings of the people? — A. They are not; they are very far from being secure.

Q. Have you heard of any homicides being committed upon the freedmen? — A. Yes, sir; of many.

Q. And do the state authorities interfere in those cases? — A. Wherever the case is brought to the attention of the civil authorities, action is taken so far as to issue writs of arrest; but it is almost, if not quite, impossible to secure the necessary testimony to convict parties.

Q. Is the testimony of Negroes allowed to be taken in the civil courts? — A. Under the amended constitution of Louisiana the testimony of Negroes is admitted in courts.

Q. Then why are the freedmen peculiarly exposed to injustice, if the testimony of blacks is admitted in trials before the state courts? Is it because of the prejudice of the people there against the race? — A. In cases where Negro testimony can be obtained a conviction is practicable; but it is not always practicable to secure that testimony. The men who commit these outrages are not always open in their demonstrations. The assault is made when no others are present; the body of the Negro is found; the evidence of his murder is complete; but the doer of the deed is gone; or, at least, it is impossible frequently to fix the crime. There are no doubt thousands in Louisiana who would revolt at these deeds of atrocity. But what I mean to state is, that the prevailing sentiment is so adverse to the Negro that acts of monstrous crime against him are winked at; and this sentiment will increase just in proportion as the privileges of the Negroes are extended. . . .

Q. Have you any further statements to make in regard to the treatment of freedmen in Louisiana and Texas? — A. Since the surrender freedmen have been tried under the old slave code of Texas, convicted under that code, and sentenced to the penitentiary. One case, the most prominent, was that of Orange Bray, a freedman in Lamar County, Texas. He was charged with raising an axe against his former master, who shot him. He was subsequently tried, in November 1865, by the judge of the eighth judicial district of Texas, convicted, and sentenced to several years' imprisonment in the penitentiary. I design securing his release through the intervention of the authorities here.

Q. Was the assault upon the former master a wanton and unprovoked one? — A. There was no assault upon the master. The fact was that the wife of the freedman had been very cruelly whipped for insolence. She was an insolent woman, no doubt. Her husband came in from the timber, and witnessing the cruel whipping given his wife, he protested against it, declaring that he was free. Upon that his former master, William Bray, ordered him to strip. The Negro fled, and was followed up by Bray and two others. As they were about to overtake him, he turned upon them with his axe and warned them not to approach him. He was shot by his former master and left for dead. During the night he recovered, and it was proposed to hang him; but the citizens protested against that, and he was put in jail, tried, and convicted, as I have stated. I made careful inquisition of the facts of the case, with a view to friendly intervention of the authorities here. The facts were brought before General Canby a few months after, and I presume he has taken action thereon.

Q. Was this freedman tried before a jury? — A. Yes, sir; and the jury brought in a verdict of guilty. His assailants have not been tried, or even arrested.

Testimony of Alexander H. Stephens

The testimony of Alexander H. Stephens is of special interest because of the eminent position he occupied. One of the leading Georgia Whigs before the war, he resisted secession until the end, but threw in his lot with his state after it broke with the Union. He then became Vice-President of the Confederacy and characterized slavery as the "cornerstone" of the new government. He continued his political activities after the war and returned to Congress after having been amnestied (1872). His book on the Civil War, A Constitutional View of the Late War Between the States, *was a defense of the doctrine of states rights. He testified as a representative of the old order and asserted that his constituents had seceded because they apprehended threats to their social polity, "particularly the subordination of the African race, as it existed under their laws and institutions."*

Mr. Boutwell: In what spirit is the emancipation of the slaves received by the people? — A. Generally, it is acquiesced in and accepted, I think, in perfect good faith, and with a disposition to do the best that can be done in the new order of things in this particular.

Q. What, at present, are the relations subsisting between the white people and black people, especially in the relations of employers and employed? — A. Quite as good, I think, as in any part of the world that ever I have been in between like classes of employer and employe. The condition of things in this respect on my return last fall was very different from what it was when I left home for my present visit to this city. During the fall, and up to the close of the year, there was a general opinion prevailing among the colored people that at Christmas there would be a division of the lands, and a very general indisposition on their part to make any contracts at all for the present year. Indeed, there were very few contracts, I think, made throughout the state until after Christmas, or about the first of January. General Tillson, who is at the head of the bureau in the State, and whose administration has given very general satisfaction to our people, I think, was very active in disabusing the minds of the colored people from their error in this particular. He visited quite a number of places in the state, and addressed large audiences of colored people; and when they became satisfied that they were laboring under a mistake in anticipating a division of lands after Christmas and the first of January, they made contracts very readily generally; and since that time affairs have, in the main, moved on quite smoothly and quietly.

Q. Are the Negroes, generally, at work? — A. Yes, sir; they are generally at work. There are some idlers, but this class constitute[s] but a small proportion.

Q. What, upon the whole, has been their conduct? Proper, under the circumstances in which they have been placed, or otherwise? — A. As a whole, much better than the most hopeful looked for.

Q. As far as you know, what are the leading objects and desires of the Negro population, at the present time, in reference to themselves? — A. It is to be protected in their rights of persons and property — to be dealt by fairly and justly.

Q. What, if anything, has been done by the legislature of your state for the accomplishment of these objects? — A. The legislature has passed an act, of which the following is a copy:

An act to define the term "persons of color," and to declare the rights of such persons.

Sec. 1. Be it enacted, etc., That all negroes, mulattoes, mestizoes, and their descendants having one-eighth negro or African blood in their veins, shall be known in this State as "persons of color."

Sec. 2. Be it further enacted, That persons of color shall have the right to make and enforce contracts, to sue, be sued, to be parties and give evidence, to inherit, to purchase, and to have full and equal benefit of all laws and proceedings for the security of person and estate, and shall not be subjected to any other or different punishment, pain, or penalty, for the commission of any act or offence, than such as are prescribed for white persons committing like acts or offences.

The third section of this act simply repeals all conflicting laws. It was approved by the governor on the 17th of March last.

Q. Does this act express the opinions of the people, and will it be sustained? — A. I think it will be sustained by the courts, as well as by public sentiment. It was passed by the present legislature. As an evidence of the tone of the legislature of the state, as well as that of the people of the state, upon this subject, I will refer you simply to a letter I wrote to Senator Stewart upon the same subject. I submit to you a copy of that letter. It is as follows:

WASHINGTON, D.C., April 4, 1866

Dear Sir: In answer to your inquiries touching the sentiments and feelings of the people of Georgia towards the freedmen, and the legal *status* of this class of population in the State, etc., allow me briefly to say that the address delivered by me on the 22d of February last before the legislature (a copy of which I herewith hand you) expresses very fully and clearly my own opinions and feelings upon the subjects of your inquiry. This address was written and printed as you now see it, before its delivery. It was delivered *verbatim* as you now read it, that there might be no mistake about it. It was as it now stands unanimously indorsed by the senate in a joint resolution, which was concurred in in the house without dissent, and was ordered to be spread upon the journals of both houses. This I refer you to as a better and more reliable index of the feelings and views of the people of the State on this subject than any bare individual opinion I might entertain or express. The legislature of the State, it is to be presumed, is as correct an exponent of the general feelings and views of the people of the State upon any political question as any that can be obtained from any quarter. In addition to this, the legislature subsequently evinced their principles by their works in passing an act, which I also enclose to you. This act speaks for itself. It is short, concise, pointed, as well as comprehensive. It secures to the colored race the right to contract and to enforce contracts, the right to sue and to be sued, the right to testify in the courts subject to the same rules that govern the testimony of whites, and it subjects them to the same punishments for all offences as the whites. In these respects, embracing all essential civil rights, all classes in Georgia now stand equal before the law. There is no discrimination in these particulars on account of race or color.

Please excuse this hasty note. I have no time to go more in detail.

Yours, most respectfully,

ALEXANDER H. STEPHENS

Hon. William M. Stewart, United States Senate

Q. What, if anything, is being done in Georgia with regard to the education of the Negroes, either children or adults? — A. Nothing by the public authorities, as yet. Schools are being established in many portions of the state under the auspices, I think, of the Freedmen's Bureau, and quite a number by the colored people themselves, encouraged by the whites.

Q. What disposition do the Negroes manifest in regard to education? — A. There seems to be a very great desire on the part of the children and younger ones, and with their parents, to have them educated.

Testimony of Caleb G. Forshey

Founder and superintendent of the Texas Military Institute, Caleb G. Forshey served as an engineer in the Confederate army. He was called before the Joint Committee on Reconstruction as a representative of the former Confederates in Texas.

Mr. Williams: What is your opinion as to the necessity and advantages of the Freedmen's Bureau, or an agency of that kind, in Texas? — A. My opinion is that it is not needed; my opinion is stronger than that — that the effect of it is to irritate, if nothing else. While in New York City recently I had a conversation with some friends from Texas, from five distant points in the state. We met together and compared opinions; and the opinion of each was the same, that the Negroes had generally gone to work since January; that except where the Freedmen's Bureau had interfered, or rather encouraged troubles, such as little complaints, especially between Negro and Negro, the Negro's disposition was very good, and they had generally gone to work, a vast majority of them with their former masters. I was very gratified to learn that from districts where I feared the contrary. Still this difference was made, particularly by Mr. Carpenter, from Jefferson, the editor of the *Jefferson Herald.* He said that in two or three counties where they had not been able to organize the Freedmen's Bureau, there had been no trouble at all; nearly all the Negroes had gone to work. The impression in Texas at present is that the Negroes under the influence of the Freedmen's Bureau do worse than without it.

I want to state that I believe all our former owners of Negroes are the friends of the Negroes; and that the antagonism paraded in the papers of the North does not exist at all. I know the fact is the very converse of that; and good feeling always prevails between the masters and the slaves. But the Negroes went off and left them in the lurch; my own family was an instance of it. But they came back after a time, saying they had been free enough and wanted a home.

Q. Do you think those who employ the Negroes there are willing to make contracts with them, so that they shall have fair wages for their labor? — A. I think so; I think they are paid liberally, more than the white men in this country get; the average compensation to Negroes there is greater than the average compensation of free laboring white men in this country. It seems to have regulated itself in a great measure by what each neighborhood was doing; the Negroes saying, "I can get thus and so at such a place." Men have hired from eight to fifteen dollars per month during the year, and women at about two dollars less a month; house-servants at a great deal more.

Q. Do the men who employ the Negroes claim to exercise the right to enforce their contract by physical force? — A. Not at all; that is totally abandoned; not a single instance of it has occurred. I think they still chastise children, though. The Negro parents often neglect that, and the children are still switched as we switch our own children. I know it is done in my own house; we have little house-servants that we switch just as I do our own little fellows.

Q. What is your opinion as to the respective advantages to the white and black races, of the present free system of labor and the institution of slavery? — A. I think freedom is very unfortunate for the Negro; I think it is sad; his present helpless condition touches my heart more than anything else I ever contemplated, and I think that is the common sentiment of our slaveholders. I have seen it on the largest plantations, where the Negro men had all left, and where only women and children remained, and the owners had to keep them and feed them. The beginning certainly presents a touching and sad spectacle. The poor Negro is dying at a rate fearful to relate.

I have some ethnological theories that may perhaps warp my judgment; but my judgment is that the highest condition the black race has ever reached or can reach, is one where he is provided for by a master race. That is the result of a great deal of scientific investigation and observation of the Negro character by me ever since I was a man. The labor question had become a most momentous one, and I was studying it. I undertook to investigate the condition of the Negro from statistics under various circumstances, to treat it purely as a matter of statistics from the census tables of this country of ours. I found that the free blacks of the North decreased 8 percent; the free blacks of the South increased 7 or 8 percent, while the slaves by their sides increased 34 percent. I inferred from the doctrines of political economy that the race is in the best condition when it procreates the fastest; that, other things being equal, slavery is of vast advantage to the Negro. I will mention one or two things in connection with this as explanatory of that result. The Negro will not take care of his offspring unless required to do it, as compared with the whites. The little children will die; they do die, and hence the necessity of very rigorous regulations on our plantations which we have adopted in our nursery system.

Another cause is that there is no continence among the Negroes. All the continence I have ever seen among the Negroes has been enforced upon plantations, where it is generally assumed there is none. For the sake of procreation, if nothing else, we compel men to live with their wives. The discipline of the plantation was more rigorous, perhaps, in regard to men staying with their wives, than in regard to anything else; and I think the procreative results, as shown by the census tables, is due in a great measure to that discipline.

I think they are very much better off in having homes than the free blacks are. The free blacks in Louisiana, where we had 34,000, with a great deal of blood of the whites in them, and therefore a great deal of white sense, were nothing like so happy and so well off as our slaves are. My observation for many years leads me to this conclusion.

Q. What is the prevailing inclination among the people of Texas in regard to giving the Negroes civil or political rights and privileges? — A. I think they are all opposed to it. There are some men — I am not among them — who think that the basis of intelligence might be a good basis for the elective franchise. But a much larger class, perhaps nine-tenths of our people, believe that the distinctions between the races should not be broken down by any such community of interests in the management of the affairs of the state. I think there is a very common sentiment that the Negro, even with education, has not a mind capable of appreciating the political institutions of the country to such an extent as would make him a good associate for the white man in the administration of the government. I think if the vote was taken on the question of admitting him to the right of suffrage there would be a very small vote in favor of it — scarcely respectable; that is my judgment.

Q. What civil rights are the people of Texas disposed to give to the Negro, such as the right to testify as a witness, to hold and sell real estate and property of any kind? — A. They have no objection to giving them all those rights. The elective franchise is the point of difference, and there is no other. I think they would be disposed to allow him to bear testimony in any case; not that they believe he is a good witness, for he is not a reliable witness; but they would be willing to let his testimony go for what it was worth. It has been so in Louisiana, where we have seen its influence, and it has not been very pernicious. All rights in respect to contracts, to giving full force and efficiency to them, would be granted to Negroes as to white persons. To that I have seen no objection.

Q. The right to sue in court? — A. Yes, sir.

Q. Did the Negroes generally sympathize with the Union cause during the rebellion? — A. None of them. There has been this: a disposition on their part to try something new — to be free; and when they came within reach of the federal army a great many of them ran away to it. But there was no resistance to discipline and authority at home. That was so much the case that a single woman on a plantation with a hundred slaves carried on the place as before and without trouble.

Testimony of William L. Sharkey

One of the best-known jurists in Mississippi, William L. Sharkey had been elected Chief Justice of the Court of Errors and Appeals in 1832. In 1850 he presided over the Southern Convention at Memphis and in 1857 became one of the commissioners to frame the state code. He strongly opposed secession. In June 1865, when Andrew Johnson reinaugurated the state government of Mississippi, he appointed Sharkey Governor. In October 1865, the jurist turned over the administration of the state to the elected government, which sent him to Washington as United States Senator. Because of Congressional opposition, like other Southern members-elect he did not take his seat. His testimony may be considered illustrative of that of conservative Unionists.

Mr. Boutwell: What is the general condition of the freedmen in Mississippi? Are they disposed to labor, and are they laboring and receiving fair wages? — A. I can give an accurate account of that matter, as I have had very authentic reports. They have gone to work with a great deal of good will, and in most parts of our state they are hiring freely and cheerfully. I have received a letter from a very intelligent gentleman, a friend of mine, who states that in his part of the state the freedmen are going to work, and the people are hopeful and expect a return of prosperity; that there was not a discontented man in his particular locality; that they had given up the idea of secession, buried it out of sight, and never wish to hear of it again. The freedmen, as I hear from all parts of the state, are doing remarkably well. I have heard from one of the northeastern counties of the state, in which it is said there is not an idle freedman. However, there is no disguising the fact that the Freedmen's Bureau and the colored troops there have done more mischief than anything else. General Howard is a very clever gentleman; but there are men in charge of the Freedmen's Bureau in Mississippi who are disposed to speculate on white and black; they encourage the black man and discourage the white man. And wherever there is a Negro garrison the free Negroes congregate around it, and, as a matter of course, crimes and depredations are committed. I verily believe that if at the time I was there all the troops and the Freedmen's Bureau had been withdrawn, I could have had a perfect state of order throughout the state in two weeks. The great amount of complaints originate from the localities where the Negro soldiers are. I do not say that the Negroes do not make good soldiers, but they encourage the congregation of freedmen around them, and from the freedmen come crime and depredations. As a general thing — there may be exceptions — the freedmen have gone to work; some receiving a share of the crops, and some receiving their wages. And there is a promise of prosperity there; there is a promise that the freedmen will work; how long it will last I cannot tell. They certainly have gone to work, as a general thing, in the state; and the people are buoyant and hopeful. In some parts of the state the freedmen are receiving exceedingly high wages. Mr. Alcorn, my colleague in the Senate, authorizes me to state that in the river counties — he mentioned one county in particular — if labor could be had, a thousand freedmen could be employed at $25 a month.

Q. In addition to their board? — A. Yes, sir; board them and furnish them with sugar and coffee, and give them $25 a month over and above their board. He told me that a thousand freedmen could find employment in that one county, if they could be had, and I think that on the Mississippi generally they are getting almost any wages they are pleased to ask.

Q. What amount of land do you estimate will be under cultivation in Mississippi this year as compared with the amount under cultivation in 1859 or 1860? — A. I can only speak from conjecture. I do not think there will be half the amount cultivated this year that there was just before the war, and I will give my reasons for that opinion. I believe that there are now in the state very little over half the number of freedmen that there were formerly of slaves — certainly not more than two-thirds. They have died off. There is no telling the mortality that has prevailed among them; they have died off in immense numbers. I should say that very little more than half the amount of land that was under cultivation before the war will be under cultivation this year; but that is with me a mere matter of conjecture.

Q. Does the mortality among the freedmen continue as great as ever? — A. Yes, sir; they have contracted habits and diseases which take a great many of them off. The people are laboring under a great mistake in regard to our attachment to the Negroes. We are all kindly disposed towards them; we are disposed, with few exceptions, to treat them as they should be treated. The poorer classes, who have always had an antipathy to them, still have that antipathy; but as a general thing, our people are disposed to treat the Negroes well. We were all attached to our slaves, and that attachment has not been broken off, because we think they have acted well. In a great many instances they have shown uncommon fidelity and friendship, and of course we cannot forget those things. Our feelings towards them are of a kindly character, and we want to treat them well, and educate them if we can.

Testimony of Robert E. Lee

Robert E. Lee's views serve as an important counterweight to radical testimony. At the time of his appearance before the committee, General Lee was easily the most revered figure among the former Confederates. Having risen to high rank in the Federal army, in 1861 he resigned to follow his state and then led the Confederate armies with such skill that his military reputation became legendary. After the war, he became President of Washington College (now Washington and Lee) in Lexington, Virginia.

Mr. Howard: How do the people in Virginia, the secessionists more particularly, feel toward the freedmen? — A. Everyone with whom I associate expresses kind feelings towards the freedmen. They wish to see them get on in the world, and particularly to take up some occupation for a living and to turn their hands to some work. I know that efforts have been made among the farmers, near where I live, to induce them to engage for the year at regular wages.

Q. Do you think there is a willingness on the part of their old masters to give them fair, living wages for their labor? — A. I believe it is so. The farmers generally prefer those servants who have been living with them before. I have heard them express their preference for the men whom they know, who had lived with them before, and their wish to get them to return to work.

Q. Are you aware of the existence of any combination among the whites to keep down the wages of the Negroes? — A. I am not. I have heard that, in several counties, landowners have met in order to establish a uniform rate of wages; but I never heard, nor do I know, of any combination to keep down wages, or establish any rate which they did not think fair. The means of paying wages in Virginia are very limited now, and there is a difference of opinion as to how much each person is able to pay.

Q. How do they feel in regard to the education of the blacks? Is there a general willingness or a general unwillingness to have them educated? — A. Where I am, and have been, the people have exhibited a willingness that the blacks should be educated, and they express an opinion that that would be better for the blacks and better for the whites.

Q. General, you are very competent to judge of the capacity of black men for acquiring knowledge: I want your opinion on that capacity, as compared with the capacity of white men. — A. I do not know that I am particularly qualified to speak on that subject, as you seem to intimate; but I do not think that he is as capable of acquiring knowledge as the white man is. There are some more apt than others. I have known some to acquire knowledge and skill in their trade or profession. I have had servants of my own who learned to read and write very well.

Q. Do they show a capacity to obtain knowledge of mathematics and the exact sciences? — A. I have no knowledge on that subject. I am merely acquainted with those who have learned the common rudiments of education.

Q. General, are you aware of the existence among the blacks of Virginia, anywhere within the limits of the state, of combinations having in view the disturbance of the peace, or any improper and unlawful acts? — A. I am not. I have seen no evidence of it, and have heard of none. Wherever I have been they have been quiet and orderly, not disposed to work, or rather not disposed to any continuous engagement to work, but just very short jobs, to provide them with the immediate means of subsistence.

Q. Has the colored race generally as great a love of money and property as the white race possesses? — A. I do not think it has. The blacks with whom I am acquainted look more to the present time than to the future.

Q. Does that absence of a lust of money and property arise more from the nature of the Negro than from his former servile condition? — A. Well, it may be, in some measure, attributable to his former condition.

They are an amiable, social race. They like their ease and comfort, and, I think, look more to their present than to their future condition. . . .

Mr. Blow: Has there been any considerable change in the number of the Negro population in Virginia during the last four years? — A. I suppose it has diminished, but I do not know.

Q. Diminished in consequence of more Negroes going South than was made up by the natural increase? — A. My general opinion is that the number has diminished, and for the reason you give.

Q. I suppose that the mass of the Negroes in Virginia, at the present time, are able to work; that there are not many helpless ones among them? — A. There are helpless ones, certainly, but I do not know to what extent.

Q. What is your opinion about its being an advantage to Virginia to keep them there at all. Do you not think that Virginia would be better off if the colored population were to go to Alabama, Louisiana, and the other Southern states? — A. I think it would be better for Virginia if she could get rid of them. That is no new opinion with me. I have always thought so, and have always been in favor of emancipation — gradual emancipation.

Q. As a question of labor alone, do you not think that the labor which would flow into Virginia, if the Negroes left it for the cotton states, would be far more advantageous to the state and to its future prosperity? — A. I think it would be for the benefit of Virginia, and I believe that everybody there would be willing to aid it.

Q. Do you not think that the State of Virginia is absolutely injured and its future impaired by the presence of the black population there? — A. I think it is.

Q. And do you not think it is peculiarly adapted to the quality of labor which would flow into it, from its great natural resources, in case it was made more attractive by the absence of the colored race? — A. I do.

Testimony of James D. B. DeBow

One of the best known Southern editors, James D. B. DeBow achieved nationwide recognition for his journal, DeBow's Review, *which he published for many years at New Orleans. He was a self-made man who, by dint of hard work, had raised himself from poverty. Interested in economics as well as journalism, he became Head of the Louisiana Bureau of Statistics and Superintendent of the Census under President Franklin Pierce. During the Civil War he served as Chief Confederate Agent for the Purchase and Sale of Cotton. After reviving the* Review *during the era of Reconstruction, he continued his activities in the affairs of Louisiana and the South.*

Mr. Williams: What is your opinion of the necessity or utility of the Freedmen's Bureau, or of any agency of that kind? — A. I think if the whole regulation of the Negroes, or freedmen, were left to the people of the communities in which they live, it will be administered for the best interest of the Negroes as well as of the white men. I think there is a kindly feeling on the part of the planters towards the freedmen. They are not held at all responsible for anything that has happened. They are looked upon as the innocent cause. In talking with a number of planters, I remember some of them telling me they were succeeding very well with their freedmen, having got a preacher to preach to them and a teacher to teach them, believing it was for the interest of the planter to make the Negro feel reconciled; for, to lose his services as a laborer for even a few months would be very disastrous. The sentiment prevailing is, that it is for the interest of the employer to teach the Negro, to educate his children, to provide a preacher for him, and to attend to his physical wants. And I may say I have not seen any exception to that feeling in the South. Leave the people to themselves, and they will manage very well. The Freedmen's Bureau, or any agency to interfere between the freedman and his former master, is only productive of mischief. There are constant appeals from one to the other and continual annoyances. It has a tendency to create dissatisfaction and disaffection on the part of the laborer, and is in every respect in its result most unfavorable to the system of industry that is now being organized under the new order of things in the South. I do not think there is any difference of opinion upon this subject.

Q. Do you think the white men of the South would do justice by the Negroes in making contracts and in paying them for their labor? — A. Before these Negroes were freed, there were some two or three hundred thousand free Negroes in the South, and some four or five hundred thousand of them in the country. There were a great many in Louisiana. There were in New Orleans some free Negroes among the wealthiest men we had. I made a comparison when I was superintendent of the United States census in 1850, and found that the condition of the free Negroes in the South, their education, etc., was better; that as a class they were immeasurably better off than the free people of the North. I never heard any cause of complaint of our treatment of these people in the South before the war, even from Northern sources, and I do not presume there would be more cause of complaint now. If we performed our duty to this same class of population when the great mass of Negroes were held by us as slaves, I think it should go very far to indicate that we should not be lacking in our duties to them now. There are free Negroes in Louisiana who owned fifty or a hundred slaves, and plantations on the coast, and there were hundreds of them who owned more or less property.

Q. What is your opinion as to the relative advantages to the blacks of the present system of free labor, as compared with that of slavery as it heretofore existed in this country? — A. If the Negro would work, the present system is much cheaper. If we can get the same amount of labor from the same persons, there is no doubt of the result in respect to *economy*. Whether the same amount of labor can be obtained, it is too soon yet to decide. We must allow one summer to pass first. They are working now very well on the plantations. That is the general testimony. The Negro women are not disposed to field work as they formerly were, and I think there will be less work from them in the future than there has been in the past. The men are rather inclined to get their wives into other employment, and I think that will be the constant tendency, just as it is with the whites. Therefore, the real number of agricultural laborers will be reduced. I have no idea the efficiency of those who work will be increased. If we can only keep up their efficiency to the standard before the war, it will be better for the South, without doubt, upon the mere money question, because it is cheaper to hire the Negro than to own him. Now a plantation can be worked without any outlay of capital by hiring the Negro and hiring the plantation.

Q. What, in your opinion, is to be the effect upon the blacks? — A. I think it will be disastrous to them. I judge that because of the experience of other countries, and not from any experience we have had ourselves. I judge by their shiftless character, and their disposition to crowd into the cities. It is what I see all over the South. You will find large numbers of them in every city, crowded together in miserable shanties, eking out a very uncertain subsistence; and, so far, the mortality has been very great among them. They were not disposed to enter upon any regular work before the first of January. They were confident in the expectation that the lands were to be divided among them up to that time. But after the first of January they became satisfied they were not to get the lands, and they very generally went to work.

Q. What arrangements are generally made among the landholders and the black laborers in the South? — A. I think they generally get wages. A great many persons, however, think it better to give them an interest in the crops. That is getting to be very common.

Q. What do you find the disposition of the people as to the extension of civil rights to the blacks — the right to sue and enforce their contracts and to hold property, real and personal, like white people? — A. I think there is a willingness to give them every right except the right of suffrage. It is believed they are unfit to exercise that. The idea is entertained by many that they will eventually be endowed with that right. It is only a question of time; but the universal conviction is that if it ever be conceded, it will be necessary to prepare for it by slow and regular means, as the white race was prepared. I believe everybody unites in the belief that it would be disastrous to give the right of suffrage now. Time and circumstances may alter the case. There is no difference of opinion upon this subject now.

Q. Suppose the Negroes were to vote now, what would be the influences operating upon them as to the exercise of that vote? — A. The Negro would be apt to vote with his employer if he was treated well. That is his character. They generally go with their employer; but it is probable they would be tampered with a great deal. There would be emissaries sent among them to turn their minds; so that, although I understand some prominent men think the Negro would generally vote with his master, I doubt it. I think the tendency would be in that direction; but that they would be drawn off by emissaries sent there for malicious purposes, though a great many would, no doubt, go with their former masters. You cannot make any rule. I find that Northern men who have come to the South, purchased land, and gone to cultivating cotton or anything else, talk now very much as we do on these questions. Their views upon all these questions, with the little experience they have had, are very much the same as those of Southern men. They say our experience, in regard to these questions, is worth more than their theories.

Q. What facilities are the people disposed to give the freedmen in becoming educated? — A. I think they generally laugh at the idea of the Negro learning. They have been accustomed to the idea that the Negroes are pretty stupid. I do not think there would be any opposition to their becoming educated. We have schools all about for them, but the people sometimes laugh at the idea of the Negroes learning much. Under the institution of slavery we used to teach them everything nearly except to read. On almost every plantation they were taught the Bible, the catechism, prayers, hymns, etc. But in regard to their being educated, so far as they are capable, I think the people regard it as for their best interest to afford them every facility — that is, the better informed people.

Q. Do the employers of Negroes in the South claim or exercise the right of physical compulsion to enforce their contracts? — A. No, sir. I know of no such claim — nothing of the kind.

Testimony of Bedford Brown

For many years a Democratic Senator from North Carolina, Bedford Brown strongly supported the policies of Andrew Jackson. The result was that he earned the bitter enmity of the Calhoun wing of the party. In 1861, he sought terms for the South within the Union but went with his state when it seceded. After serving in the Reconstruction convention which had been summoned in accordance with President Johnson's plan, he continued to play an active role in the affairs of the Democratic party, then committed to conservatism.

Mr. Howard: How do the mass of Carolinians feel in respect to the freedmen; especially in regard to their education? — A. Well, sir, that feeling has changed a good deal. Last year there was a great deal of feeling against the freedmen, because, in truth, they behaved rather badly after Lee's surrender. Before that they had been very quiet and orderly; but afterwards they abandoned work, most of them, and became wanderers, and dissatisfied. They would not work on the farms even for pretty fair wages; but the present year they have returned to labor, and, as far as I have any knowledge, certainly in my part of the state, they are acting very well. There is a good feeling between the blacks and whites, and I believe the general sentiment is, certainly among the farmers and planters, that it is not only proper in itself, as a matter of justice, but that it is good policy to treat them with fairness and liberality. I can say, so far as those employed by me are concerned, that is my course of treatment towards them. Very few of those I owned have left me, and some I should have been glad to have had gone have remained. For instance, I have no doubt nearly four hundred loads of wood have been used from my farm this winter, and three-fourths of it at least have been used by black people, with many of whom I have had nothing to do, being the families of laborers living on my farm. They used the wood and I charged them nothing at all for it.

Q. Is there not generally among the mass of white people there a disinclination to see schools established among the blacks, and would they not be likely to break up such schools when established, if they could? — A. I do not think they would. There is a disinclination for promiscuous schools of whites and blacks; but I do not think they would object to schools for the blacks. Indeed, all reflecting persons must know it is better for the country that they should be educated. I do not think there is any prejudice against their education. There are some schools for blacks, which have been established in my county, and I have never heard of any attempts to break them up. Negro children would not be admitted into white schools.

Q. What is the opinion of the Freedmen's Bureau in your state, as far as your observation extends? — A. So far as I have any knowledge of it, I think the gentlemen who have conducted it, as a general rule, have been liberal and just both towards the freedmen and the white people.

Q. Do you think it has been beneficial upon the whole? — A. It was, I think, for last year. I think there is scarcely a necessity for it now.

Q. I do not speak of its necessity. What I want to inquire into is, whether upon the whole it has had a beneficial effect upon the blacks and whites? — A. There was a state of things last year among the blacks and whites requiring some authority of that kind, resulting from the immediate termination of the war; but it seems to me that state of things has now passed. I think the freedmen would now be protected in their rights without the intervention of the bureau. If I mistake not, our legislature have passed laws for their protection by the civil courts.

Q. Would a black man stand an equal chance for justice in a state court of North Carolina with a white man now before a jury? — A. If he was a man of good character, with no particular prejudice against him, I think he would. For instance, there are some Negroes who are notoriously dishonest; their existence, in some numbers, may be, to some extent, accounted for by their degraded condition as slaves. I am inclined to think a black man, with a fair character, would receive justice in our courts; indeed, I am sure of it, and for this reason: it is regarded, not simply as a matter of justice, but as a matter of policy among the white people that they should be treated with fairness, in order to produce the amicable relations between the blacks and the whites necessary to carry on the labor of the country.

Q. Are black men permitted to testify in courts of justice in your state? — A. I think our legislature, at its late session, authorized it to some extent.

Q. You think there is some limitation to that extent? — A. It is limited to some extent. I have not seen the acts of the legislature. They adjourned but a short time since; and, in fact, we have not any mail facilities scarcely in our part of the country.

Q. Is the low white man esteemed as possessing more veracity than the black man of the same grade and condition, in North Carolina? — A. As a general rule, they are considered as having a higher claim to credibility.

Q. What has been your experience with the two classes in regard to veracity and truth-telling? — A. My impression is that perhaps the white class would be entitled to a higher grade of character in that respect, because the servitude of the Negro and everything has tended to degrade his moral sense. They have not the same pride of character. The poor man has frequently a great deal of pride of character and desire for the good opinion of his compeers. Those recently slaves have not risen exactly to that. It will take some time to go through that process.

Q. As to the capacity of the Negro to acquire knowledge and become educated; is he, in your judgment, much or at all inferior to the white man in that respect? — A. There is a difference in that respect; the Negro in childhood, up to twelve years of age, is very nearly or quite as capable as the white child, but after that the superiority is considered decidely with the white. The mind of the white man seems to grow and develop itself, while that of the Negro from that time does not seem to be capable of so extensive development.

Q. What would the white people of North Carolina say to a proposition to allow the Negroes or a part of them the right of suffrage? That would not be a novelty in the history of North Carolina, would it? — A. There is a sentiment somewhat against that, although I think there are a good many persons who would have no objections to seeing qualified Negro suffrage, but universal suffrage would be regarded as very objectionable and inadmissible.

Q. Does universal suffrage exist among the whites of North Carolina? — A. Yes, sir; among those who have obtained the age of twenty-one and who have been residents of the state a certain length of time.

Q. Do you suppose it would be practicable in North Carolina to restrict that universal suffrage among the whites? — A. No, sir; there is a general sentiment in favor of it.

Q. You cannot imagine any machinery by which restricted suffrage among the whites could be established? — A. No, sir; I think it is a right they would never surrender if they could avoid it. Free Negroes at one time voted in North Carolina, but they were very limited in number.

Q. What qualifications for the Negro voter were then required in North Carolina? — A. Precisely the same as for white men at that time. For the house of commons, as we call it, retaining the old British parliamentary name, they were required to have been residents of the state a certain time and to have paid a *per capita* tax. For the senate, the voter must be a landholder; they have changed that now; the white man can vote for the senator without being a landholder, and the Negro cannot vote at all. The unfortunate agitation between the North and South gave rise to that change, no doubt. I must say the free Negroes of that day, though, voted generally for what they called "gentlemen"; they did not vote for any man they did not regard as a gentleman.

Q. Would they now? — A. I am inclined to think they would vote the same way; still there are such masses of them that it would be regarded as a rather dangerous experiment.

3 TESTIMONY OF NORTHERN WHITES

Testimony of Rufus Saxton

General Rufus Saxton was a West Pointer from Massachusetts who became military governor of the Sea Islands. Raised in an abolitionist home, he was well disposed toward the experiment of settling Negroes on their own lands in his area of responsibility, where he gained the confidence of the freedmen. After the war, in which he had taken a distinguished part (he was later awarded the Medal of Honor), he became Assistant Commissioner of the Freedmen's Bureau for South Carolina. In this post, he soon ran into difficulty, and after refusing to carry out orders restoring the Negroes' lands on the Sea Islands to their former owners, was removed by President Johnson. The General gave the following testimony shortly afterwards.

Mr. Howard: How do the whites in South Carolina feel about the education of the freedmen? — A. I believe it to be the desire of a large majority of the white people that they shall not be educated. Some intelligent planters, however, have assured me that they would not oppose the education of the freedmen.

Q. Do they generally appear to want the black people to remain among them? — A. If they could manage them in their way they desire them to remain.

Q. How do you think they will manage them if the federal troops are withdrawn, and the Freedmen's Bureau is withdrawn? — A. I think it will be the purpose of their former masters to reduce them as near to a condition of slaves as it will be possible to do; that they would deprive them by severe legislation of most of the rights of freedmen. I think that the Black Codes that have passed the legislature of the state are a sufficient indication of the truth of what I say, and the most unjust contracts which they try to force upon the freedmen, and which they ask the aid of the military authorities to enforce.

Q. If the state should have its own way in regard to the freedmen, what, in your judgment, would be the result in the course of time? — A. I believe it will lead to insurrection and a war of races, in which the United

States troops will be called upon to aid in the extermination of the black race. I think it is the belief of a great majority of the former masters that the freedom of the black race is a failure, and that slavery is his best condition, and that they desire to pursue such a policy as to prove that they are correct in that belief. I can see no hope for the freedmen except through the care of the United States government.

Q. State whether that doctrine is inculcated by persons of condition in South Carolina, from the pulpit, in lectures, discourses or essays, that slavery is the best condition for the black race. — A. I believe it is; I have seen it in their papers. I think they go as far in that direction in the pulpit and press as it is possible for them to do without being subjected to the restraint of martial law.

Q. Are you aware that the blacks have arms to any considerable extent in South Carolina? — A. I believe that a great many of them have arms, and I know it to be their earnest desire to procure them.

Q. While you were in command there has any request been made to you to disarm the blacks? — A. I cannot say that any direct request has been made to me to disarm them; it would not be my duty to disarm them, as I was not the military commander, but I have had men come to my office and complain that the Negroes had arms, and I also heard that bands of men called Regulators, consisting of those who were lately in the rebel service, were going around the country disarming Negroes. I can further state that they desired me to sanction a form of contract which would deprive the colored men of their arms, which I refused to do. The subject was so important, as I thought, to the welfare of the freedmen that I issued a circular on this subject, which circular not having been approved by the military commander was not published, as I was required by my instructions to get his approval to all my circulars before I issued them. (Witness furnishes copy of circular referred to, which is annexed to his testimony.) I will further add, that I believe it to be the settled purpose of the white people of South Carolina to be armed and thoroughly organized, and to have the whole black population thoroughly disarmed and defenceless; I believe that is the settled policy.

Q. What would be the probable effect of such an effort to disarm the blacks? — A. It would subject them to the severest oppression, and leave their condition no better than before they were emancipated, and in many respects worse than it was before.

Q. Have you any reason to suppose that they would submit to be disarmed quietly? — A. I do not believe that they would, provided the United States troops were withdrawn and the state relieved entirely from the presence of martial law.

Q. Do you think they would resist by violence such an attempt to disarm them? — A. They would, provided the United States troops were not present; their respect to the United States government is very great. The whole teachings of the agents of the Freedmen's Bureau have been to them that they must never lift their hands against the United States government, and they have seen the effect of the late rebellion, so that whatever the United States government says they will observe to a very great extent. But if the government protection were withdrawn, and they were left entirely to their former owners, and this attempt to disarm them were carried out, I believe there would be an insurrection.

Q. Have you an apprehension that the state of feeling among the blacks which you have now described generally prevails throughout the cotton, sugar, and rice-growing states? — A. So far as I am informed, I believe it does; I believe there is a feeling of a mutual want of confidence between the former owner and the slave. The former owner has no knowledge of the freeman, he does not understand him; his whole teaching as a slave has been to conceal his feelings from his master, and the late master knows less of the Negro's character than any other person; he has no faith in the Negro's capacity for freedom, no faith in his capacity to take care of himself, and believes that slavery is his best condition. The Negro believes that his former master wishes to make him a slave again, and has no confidence in his promises. He desires particularly not to make any contract or to work for his old master, preferring to work for Northern men. Northern men can get all the labor they require, with capital; but not so with the former slaveholders; the only way this feeling can be broken down and a mutual confidence restored is to give the Negro all his rights, and for the old master to show him that he has given up the idea of making him a slave and is willing to recognize his rights. This, I think, will restore mutual confidence, peace, and harmony, and thus there will be a thorough reconstruction, and not before.

Q. What extent of intelligence did you discover among the freedmen of South Carolina? — A. I found many of the leading men very intelligent; I found some men as intelligent as any other men of different color. Of course the large mass of them is ignorant and degraded. They have all the vices which slavery has entailed upon them.

Testimony of John W. Alvord

One of the most dedicated of the officers of the Freedmen's Bureau, John W. Alvord was its General Superintendent of Education. He was interested in temperance as well as in the uplift of the blacks, and in carrying out his duties traveled widely throughout the South. In spite of the fact that he later became Secretary and President of the Freedmen's Bank, an ill-starred venture which finally failed amid charges of corruption, Alvord was generally considered to be both honest and altruistic.

Mr. Howard: Have you either during the war or since the close of hostilities visited portions of the rebel confederacy? — A. Yes, sir.

Q. What portions? — A. I was with the Union army in Virginia during the war.

Q. And since the close of the war you have been engaged in the Freedmen's Bureau? — A. Yes, sir.

Q. And since then you have been stationed in Washington? — A. My headquarters are here.

Q. Have you visited portions of Virginia since the close of hostilities? — A. Yes, sir. I have visited Virginia and all the states south below Tennessee and this side of the Mississippi River. I have visited Virginia, North Carolina, South Carolina, Georgia, Florida, Alabama, Mississippi, and Louisiana. I made three tours during the year; I have been during that time under the orders of General Howard as inspector of finances and schools for freedmen in all the states lately in insurrection. These tours were made in execution of his special orders; of course, I have mingled with all classes at the South, more especially with the intelligent portion. In these various journeys on railroads, in hotels, and in public meetings, I have seen every class of Southern people from the lowest Negroes to the state legislatures; on three or four of which I was in attendance during some portions of the session. These, in brief, are my opportunities. . . .

Q. Are you aware of combinations existing in those states for the purpose of subjecting the freedmen to compulsory labor, uncompensated, or not sufficiently compensated? — A. I do not know of any distinct combinations; there appears to be a universal exhibition of that purpose in all places and in all circles where I heard it talked of, privately or publicly. The idea was that the Negro was to be kept subservient to the white race and compelled to labor for low wages. Contracts, so far as I have noticed or examined them, unless regulated by the agents of the Freedmen's Bureau, have been very much on the side of the white man.

Q. How far would they carry their power if they possessed it, to declare unemployed freedmen vagrants and to treat them as such? — A. I think there was a time when they wished to declare them all vagrants and to apply vagrant laws to them. That asserted vagrancy seemed to be their vindication of their legislative action.

Q. Was that a vindication or rather a policy, on the part of the slaveholders, to re-establish a quasi-slavery among the blacks by means of vagrant acts? — A. I think that was so; it appeared to be a policy.

Q. State whether or not it appeared to be a general policy, or whether it was interrupted, existing in sections of the country and among particular classes. — A. I noticed it universally, and it led me sometimes to make the remark that it appeared to me as though such policy had been agreed upon by all the slaveholders in the Southern states.

Q. If they had the power, would they or would they not, in your judgment, reduce the black race again to slavery such as has heretofore existed? — A. I think they would, in case they thought they could hold it there.

Q. How do they feel in point of personal regard towards the freedmen generally? — A. Their feelings are, as it seems to me, very much mixed; they have a kind of affection for him as an old servant; they have ill will towards him for turning against them and going with the Union army; and they have direct hostility to him as now being in the condition of a freedman claiming the rights of a freeman.

Q. If it was for them to say, would they permit the blacks to become owners of landed property? — A. It seemed everywhere determined upon that he should not be an owner of land. I found this quite universal in all the states, in every tour I made, and I listened to debates in their legislatures on that subject.

Q. How do they feel in regard to the marital rights of the black people — the rights of husband and wife and the rights of family? — A. Well, sir, I think they care very little about that matter. Their old habits of feeling still remain; they consider the relations of husband and wife not especially sacred among the blacks. . . .

Q. In case they had the power, do you imagine they would permit the freedman to remain a resident in their communities, or would they try to expel him? — A. They seem inclined to be rid of him. They generally wish that white laborers could be procured, and they are, here and there, making experiments with that view. . . .

Q. How do they regard the truthfulness of the Negro generally? — A. They say he is very untruthful.

Q. Have you found the Negro untruthful in your intercourse with him? — A. I have not. I think he is as truthful as any other class of men of the same intelligence. I know he has been remarkably truthful to our Northern people and to the army in all matters of information.

Q. What feeling has been created on the part of the Southern whites toward the blacks in consequence of the part which the blacks have taken in the war? — A. They do not like them for having sided with the North.

Q. Has that become a ground of hatred, dislike, or increased distrust? — A. I do not think that is the sole ground. I think that that enters into their dislike as *one* of its elements. They look upon the Negro as having been seduced by the Northern people and as having been comparatively innocent in the course he took.

Q. What do they say generally about the emancipation of their slaves, either by President Lincoln's proclamation, by the amendment to the Constitution, or any other means? — A. They never have liked it. They hoped that great trouble would arise from it. They delight in all the obstacles we find to the improvement of the freedman. So it seems to me. I say this of the majority. There are very many exceptions. There are a class of men at the South, in very small numbers, who have, at heart, probably always been with us, and who are now favorable to the improvement of the Negro.

Q. In reference to these obstacles to the improvement of the Negro, do you think from your observation that the Southern people generally are endeavoring to increase those obstacles rather than to diminish them? — A. I think that is a very general disposition. They oppose Negro schools generally. There is a great hate apparently towards Northern teachers. Whatever we do for colored schools has to be done without any consultation with the Southerners.

Q. What is the great ground of objection on their part toward the education of the blacks; why do they wish to see them remain in ignorance? — A. From their old habits they seem to feel that the Negro must not become an equal. They understand that education and property and political privileges will make the Negro so, and hence they oppose everything of the kind.

Q. You think this feeling arises rather from their old prejudices to the race? — A. Very much so. I heard gentlemen say in the legislature at Montgomery that they were determined that the blacks should not rise to be equals with white men, and that all their legislation would be based on that determination; that they must not have titles to land; that if they obtained possession of property, the next thing would be to claim the right of suffrage and all other political privileges. They perceive that these things come along logically from each other.

Q. Did that declaration on the part of members seem to find favor with the other members of the legislature or with the audience? — A. A member expressed this opinion to me privately in the lobby, but it was the same in substance as I had listened to in the debate in the house, the debate being on the constitutional amendment.

Q. Did you ever find a disloyal Negro in the course of your travels? — A. I saw one during the war, who came into our army lines and said he was with the rebels; that is the only instance that I remember. It may be said that they are universally loyal.

Q. State what is the degree of attachment which they exhibit towards the government of the United States. — A. Well, sir, it is unbounded. It was in Mr. Lincoln; it is now in the government, and in what they expect the government will do for them.

Q. You mean to say that universally they are the strong friends of the government? — A. I do. When, on the Sea Islands, a proposition was made to restore the lands to their original owners, there was a most distressing breaking in upon that confidence in the government which they had been cherishing. It would be impossible for anyone to describe the feeling they manifested on that occasion.

Q. Have you been aware of the existence of combinations among the

Negroes to rise in insurrection against the white men — the proprietors of lands? — A. I do not think that there has ever been any such combinations. They have often told me, when I questioned them, that there was nothing of the kind. I came through a number of the states just before the holidays, and of course my curiosity, at least, was excited to know how they felt.

Q. And you conversed with them on that subject? — A. Yes, sir.

Q. You conversed with the intelligent portion of the Negroes? — A. Yes, sir; with the most intelligent.

Q. Had they confidence in you as a friend? — A. I think they had. My work of getting up schools among them and looking after their financial concerns brought the most intelligent of them around me in every place, sometimes in large crowds. I was in Richmond on Christmas Eve when there was a great deal of excitement among the white people, but I saw not the least among the blacks.

Q. What was the reason of the excitement? — A. The white people were in expectation of disturbances. The blacks were in their churches engaged in their usual religious services.

Q. Suppose all protection on part of the United States towards the freedmen should be withdrawn, including the Freedmen's Bureau and the presence of the military forces, thus leaving the freedmen to be dealt with by the authorities of the states solely, what would be the result? — A. They would suffer in all their interests as laborers; and as to attempting any education or improvement, the whole would be arrested and, I think, turned backward.

Q. Would the blacks endure it without resistance? — A. I should fear that there might be resistance. The soldiers of the disbanded colored regiments talk as though there would be, and yet I think, from the general quiet nature of the colored people, that they would bear long and patiently before such a thing took place. It would be only an extremity that would force them to such an insurrection.

Q. In such a case would the whites of the states, through their governments, or by popular movements, be likely to attempt the expulsion of the blacks from their limits? — A. I think they would attempt to destroy them, or to expel them, if they could not destroy them.

Q. In such an event would the colored men fight? — A. I think they would.

Q. Regarding the rebel states as they are now conditioned, and as they probably would be conditioned in the case of the removal of the Freedmen's Bureau and the withdrawal of the military forces of the United States, could you look upon these political communities as supports of the government of the United States, or as elements of weakness? — A. As elements of weakness, most decidedly, unless there should come a very great change over them.

Q. Looking upon them in their present condition? — A. Decidedly, elements of weakness. I everywhere listened to conversations which were seditious in their character, planning for the future, not for the government but for themselves, cursing the Northern people and cursing the dominant party of the country.

Testimony of Charles H. Howard

Brigadier General Charles H. Howard was the brother of General O. O. Howard, the Head of the Freedmen's Bureau. Having accompanied his brother on various Civil War campaigns, after Appomattox he became an inspector of the Freedmen's Bureau with headquarters at Charleston, South Carolina. His testimony is significant because of his manifold opportunities to observe conditions in his district, especially in the Sea Islands, where lands transferred to the freedmen during the war were afterwards restored to their former owners.

Mr. Howard: Have you any knowledge respecting the state of things on the Sea Islands, as they are called? — A. Yes, sir; I have visited the Sea Islands recently.

Q. How many of these islands are there? — A. There are some eight or ten or more of the larger islands.

Q. Famous for their production of cotton? — A. Yes, sir; Sea Island cotton.

Q. Can you state how these islands are now principally occupied? — A. A number of plantations on each, and sometimes entire islands, have been formally restored to their former owners. They were all abandoned during the war. On several of the islands Negroes have been located and have been engaged in cultivating the land. Some, and a considerable number, previously to General Sherman's celebrated order [setting aside a strip along the coast for the use of black farmers], issued last winter at Savannah, and a large number under the provisions of that order, have been located on the different islands. A considerable number have received formal titles to forty acres each on these islands. Where there were large numbers of them on any given plantation they still remain in possession; but where there were very few on a plantation, the plantation has been, in some cases, restored. The understanding was that the orders were that where there were very few Negroes on a plantation the plantation should be restored if the Negroes were properly provided with homes.

Q. How long is it since they were restored? — A. They have been in process of restoration since the latter part of October, more or less, all along. It was by direction of the President.

Q. What has become of the blacks who were formerly located on them; are they chiefly there? — A. As I stated, the limitation has been to where there were only a few Negroes on a plantation, and these few sometimes have made contracts to work for the former owners at fair rates, while some of them have preferred to leave altogether. The general disposition is, when they cannot get titles themselves, that they would rather leave altogether than make contracts with their former owners.

Q. They would prefer to be owners themselves? — A. Yes, sir; and I may add that there is a strong desire, amounting almost to a passion, on the part of a large number of the more enterprising of the blacks, to obtain land by lease, or to own land, and that there is a corresponding repugnance on the part of the citizens of South Carolina to allow them either to obtain land by lease or purchase. That is the case in Georgia also. In fact, I may say that there is a determination on the part of the old white residents, so far as I could see, not to allow them either to own or to rent land.

Q. Is that feeling very general? — A. That feeling is universal among the white residents; so much so, that, meeting the other strong desire on the part of the blacks, it produces a great deal of distrust and ill feeling which would not otherwise exist.

Q. Judging from what you know of the popular feeling in South Carolina on the subject of Negroes owning real estate, would not the legislature of that state, if left unrestrained by act of Congress, prohibit the black race entirely from owning land within the state? — A. I think they would.

Q. Have you any doubt about it in your own mind, judging from what you know about the popular feeling there? — A. I have no doubt that the majority of the people of South Carolina would insist on such a thing.

Q. In such a case as that, what is the idea of the South Carolinians as to the disposition to be made of the black race — what would they do with them? — A. They would put them in a condition of compulsory labor. Those who have the kindest disposition, apparently, toward the Negro, seem to consider it as inevitable that he shall be under some compulsory system of labor. They do not seem to have a proper understanding of what free labor is, or else their feelings towards the blacks are such as to prevent them considering the question fairly.

Q. In such a case as that, would they allow the Negro to stand as a free contracting party in regard to his own labor without restraint or compulsion of law? — A. Judging from what I know of the public sentiment, and from the laws passed already, I should say not.

Q. They would not allow him to be a free contractor? — A. No, sir. They did give him a certain appearance of fairness in contracting, but they threw about him so many compulsory regulations in the matter of making contracts, and in the fulfilment of contracts, and in all the business of the plantation, that it virtually amounted to the same thing as depriving him of the power of making free contracts, as you understand it.

Q. What is the general feeling among the whites there in regard to the domestic relations of the freedmen? —

The Witness: Do you mean in the direction of bringing about any reformation?

Mr. Howard: Yes. — A. I have found a lamentable absence of interest in the moral well-being of the Negroes.

Q. Is there a willingness on the part of the whites to concede to the black race the rights of husband and wife, and parent and child, as regarded and guarded by law? — A. Yes, sir; I think that the legislature made moves to that end; but there is such a total indifference to the matter on the part of the people that very little would be accomplished, although the laws were correct in that respect. Very little would be accomplished in bringing about a reform; and a reform is needed, because of the condition to which the blacks have been reduced by the former system of slavery. That is something which I consider to be important — to be taken hold of by some exterior agency; and if the Freedmen's Bureau continues, that would become a legitimate subject for it to take up and regulate, as I have recommended in my written reports.

Q. As to the domestic virtues among the black people in South Carolina, what can you say as to the chastity of their women and the chastity of their men as the matter at present exists? — A. I have to say that I have not observed so great a lack of chastity on the part of the women as I had been previously led to suppose existed; and I have been somewhat surprised at this fact as I found it. But I found numerous evidences (although it does not come within the scope of your question) that their chastity had been disregarded by the whites in times past. I could name a great many instances of that kind.

Q. Suppose the shield of legal protection should be thrown around their domestic relations, would that protection be respected by the whites in South Carolina practically? — A. If it was mere law, I should apprehend that it would be entirely inadequate in the present state of public sentiment. In fact, I may say generally that laws may be made impartially in South Carolina, but with the existing public sentiment they would not be sufficient for the protection of the Negroes in their rights.

Q. Suppose a white man should dishonor a black husband, by having illicit intercourse with his wife, obtained either by violence or seduction, would the black husband, in a South Carolina court, have much prospect of obtaining redress? — A. I think not.

Q. Would a white jury give him damages? — A. I think not, sir.

Q. How strong is your conviction on that subject? — A. I feel certain that he would not get adequate redress. They might award him something as a cover, for the appearance of the thing; but the great difficulty would be that in the existing state of sentiment the Negro would not dare to bring any prosecution whatever. He would not dream of such a thing.

Q. Why not? — A. The fear of personal violence to himself, and because he would think it would be utterly futile to attempt to seek any redress.

Q. Suppose a black man should bring a suit in a state court there for the redress of any other wrong to his person or property, would he be likely to obtain adequate redress? — A. I believe not; I cannot say how it would be under a new law.

Q. A black man there is not allowed to testify as a witness in the state courts, I believe? — A. Except under the new regulations, which have not gone into force.

Q. The new regulations only include cases where a Negro is a party to the suit — either a party plaintiff or defendant? — A. Yes, sir.

Q. But he is not allowed to testify in a case where the parties are both white? — A. No, sir.

Q. What is your idea as to the ground of such exclusion of blacks as witnesses in cases where the parties are whites? — A. They assert that the colored man would favor his own race, and that he cannot be trusted when one of his own race is involved. Why he should not be employed as a witness when none of his own race are involved, the only reason anyone would attempt to give is his unreliability as a witness; but they would be unable to sustain that position, because they rely upon him as a truthful man in other respects.

Q. Is not the Negro of South Carolina as much a truth-teller as a white of South Carolina, both being in the same condition as to education and position? — A. Yes, sir, I think so. Where I find an intelligent Negro, I find that he tells me the truth, and the whole truth, the same as an intelligent white man.

Q. You know of no difference between the two races in that respect? — A. No, sir. I have found it so as a soldier at all times when I wanted to get information of roads or anything that was of importance.

Q. How do the whites there feel towards the Negro race for the part which they took in the war? — A. I have not often heard any antipathy expressed against them on that ground. The whites do not often accord to them importance enough to acknowledge any antipathy on that ground.

Q. Do they not regard the Negro as the great occasion of the war? — A. Yes, sir; but the innocent and unconscious occasion of it.

Q. If the whites there had the power would they not again reduce the black race to complete slavery? — A. Yes, sir, unquestionably.

Q. Would they be likely to wait a long time before accomplishing that object? — A. I think not.

Q. Do you think of any other fact that is of interest in regard to South Carolina? — A. The matter of violent treatment to Negroes, and in some cases to soldiers, has not been brought out. In my tour of inspection in the western and interior portion of South Carolina I found a great many complaints of ill treatment towards the Negroes that had to be adjudicated by our military authorities and by the agencies of the bureau, which were identical in South Carolina. We had military agencies in every county throughout the state. I found in some sections of South Carolina the utmost bitterness towards the United States soldiers, towards the flag, towards the uniform, manifested in their faces and in their talk, and in violence even towards our soldiers. Three soldiers were killed in Anderson County while I was there. I helped to investigate the case — it is now on trial. There were some respectable citizens committed for trial on the examination at which I was present.

Q. So far as you have been informed, did these soldiers give provocation for the violence? — A. No provocation. I am positive that they had given no provocation; it was not claimed that they had given provocation.

Q. Were they under your orders? — A. No, sir. They had no connection with the Freedmen's Bureau, which is more obnoxious than any other form of United States agency. But they had no connection with it. In some sections the returned rebel officers were wearing their uniforms, and seemed rather disposed to make a display of them than otherwise. In some sections they had been required to take off their buttons and insignia of rank. In other sections they were not required and did not do it. Some of the railroad cars that were made during the war still bear the rebel flags as decorations painted upon them, with pictures of battles in which confederate soldiers dressed in gray are seen pursuing Yankee soldiers. These things were somewhat interesting, and, I must confess, a little annoying to me. I think it worthwhile perhaps to mention them as exhibiting the state of things there. Every section of South Carolina is not equally embittered in this respect. Still my feelings were very much worked up by these causes while travelling as a United States official, although generally going *incognito*. For instance, in the cars sometimes little children would be set to sing the rebel songs — songs that would be very obnoxious to United States soldiers — songs containing reproaches upon the flag and upon everything that we hold sacred. To see little innocent children, now that the war is over, taught to sing these songs and imbibe these sentiments, seemed to me one of the very worst features of the country. The feeling is very intense among the female portion of the community, without exception, against the United States government and all Northern men.

Q. The women appeared to be more bitter and proscriptive than the men? — A. Yes; especially more so than the men who expect to have any business contact with the people of the North.

Testimony of Alfred H. Terry

Alfred H. Terry was one of the few Civil War volunteers to become a permanent major general in the regular army. Connecticut-born Terry distinguished himself at Hilton Head, Battery Wagner, and especially Fort Fisher; for the capture of the Fort, he received the thanks of Congress. At the time of the testimony, he was the Commanding General of the Department of Virginia. (Later in 1866 he took charge of the Department of Dakota.) His testimony is important because of his position and his reputation for an ability to get along with people.

Mr. Howard: What do the secessionists appear to desire? What great object have they in view? — A. In the first place, having failed to maintain the separate nationality which they asserted, they desire to keep themselves a separate people, and to prevent, by any means in their power, our becoming a homogeneous nation; secondly, they desire to make treason honorable and loyalty infamous, and to secure, as far as they may be able, political power. . . .

Q. What is their treatment generally towards the freedmen? — A. It is very various. Many persons are treating the freedmen kindly and justly, endeavoring to accommodate themselves to the changed circumstances of the times, and to enter into the proper relations with them as between employers and employed. Many others, on the contrary, treat them with great harshness and injustice, and seek to obtain their services without just compensation, and to reduce them to a condition which will give to the former masters all the benefits of slavery, and throw upon them none of its responsibilities.

Q. So far as you can judge, which class is the more numerous, those who treat the freedmen kindly, or those who treat them with injustice and severity? — A. The latter.

Q. Do you think they greatly predominate in numbers? — A. I can hardly estimate the relative proportions; I think that they predominate.

Q. Do you suppose, from what you have seen and heard, and from what you know, that it would be safe to entrust the great body of freedmen in Virginia, or elsewhere in the South, to the care of the local authorities or the local legislatures? — A. I do not.

Q. Suppose this were done, what consequences, in your judgment, would be likely to follow? Would they not maltreat the black race, deprive them of their rights, embarrass them in the enjoyment of their property, if they should have any, provoke them, goad them, if necessary, to acts of violence, which the blacks might suppose they were performing in their own defence, and in their own interests, and in this way, within some short time, bring about an open bloody resistance on the part of the black population? — A. I should say there would be danger that the blacks would commit those acts which an oppressed people sooner or later commit against their oppressors.

Q. Have you reason to believe that the blacks possess arms to any extent at the present time? — A. I have been told that they do. I have received that information from citizens of Virginia, including state officials, who have entreated me to take the arms of the blacks away from them.

Q. Who were those officials? — A. Some were members of the present legislature. I have been also asked to do so by a public meeting held in one of the counties.

Q. Have you, in any case, issued orders for disarming blacks? — A. I have not.

Q. The blacks, I suppose, are almost universally loyal? — A. I think there is no question about that.

Q. How do the Virginians feel in regard to the education of the blacks? — A. There is great difference of opinion in that respect in different communities. In some places the people approve of it cordially, and many have taken part in it. In other places the reverse is the case. Cases have come to my knowledge where persons coming to teach blacks were not permitted to rent a place either for a school or for their own personal occupation; and it has been reported to me that teachers sent to teach the blacks have been treated with great contempt, and in some places threatened. Then, again, in the city of Lynchburg, for instance, the city authorities cordially entered into the arrangements for teaching the blacks in connection with the military authorities. There is this variation of feeling, and what is the prevailing feeling I cannot tell.

Testimony of Orlando Brown

As Assistant Commissioner of the Freedmen's Bureau in Richmond, Colonel Orlando Brown had an excellent opportunity to observe conditions of the freedmen in Virginia. A New Englander, he had come to Virginia with the army and gained considerable experience as a commander of a black regiment.

Mr. Howard: Are the freedmen willing to work generally for fair wages? — A. Yes, sir; for what any Northern man would consider fair wages.

Q. Is there a disposition on the part of their white employers to allow them fair living wages? — A. That disposition might exist if they had the means. They have not the means to allow them what would be considered living wages — wages to support a man and his family. It is unnecessary to say that they are wholly exhausted. A great deal of the land in Virginia is very poor, and on that poor land the farmer cannot afford to pay more than ten dollars per month to a laborer, even with the disposition to pay more. There is little other business in the state than agriculture. . . .

Q. Suppose the Freedmen's Bureau were discontinued and the troops withdrawn, what would be the treatment of the secessionists towards the black people? — A. By vagrant laws, and by availing themselves of the ignorance of the Negroes in the making of contracts, by getting them in debt, and otherwise, they would place them, I think, in a worse condition than they were in when slaves. I speak of the majority. The sentiment towards the freedmen in Virginia is changing, I think, and becoming more favorable to them; I hear the expression frequently that they would prefer, now that the blacks are free, that they should remain so; there may be something that smacks of dollars and cents in that. The slave system in Virginia has been such as to exhaust very largely the able-bodied laborers; I have been informed that twenty thousand of that class were annually sold from Virginia; consequently, a very large proportion of the colored population there is composed of the aged, infirm, women and children, and the being freed from the necessity of supporting them is really a great relief in the present poverty of the people — a relief to their former owners.

Q. Do they appear to be willing that the Negro should acquire property, and have houses and homes, and school-houses? — A. I think they are coming to feel that the Negro will make a better citizen educated; that is not generally the sentiment, but it is improving in that direction. We have now some fifteen thousand children in school, and there is very little hostility evinced to the teachers; occasionally there are unpleasant remarks made about them, but still there is comparatively little hostility. We have schools now in localities remote from troops which are not broken up. They recognize the freedom of the Negro as a fixed fact.

Q. If they had an opportunity, would they reduce the Negro again to slavery? — A. If I can believe their assertions, I should hardly think they would; I think they would prefer to hold him, by their laws, etc., in a situation which would be slavery in effect but not in name, so as to have the benefit of his labor without the responsibility of supporting him.

Q. That smacks of a piece of Yankee ingenuity? — A. Why, sir, in that respect, they out-Herod Herod. . . .

Q. How are they pleased with the Freedmen's Bureau? — A. I think they are anxious to have it out of the way.

Q. Would they be likely to oppress the freedmen if that bureau were removed and the troops were removed? — A. I think they would.

Q. Would the Negro stand any chance of obtaining justice in the courts? — A. I have the assurance of one of the first lawyers in the city of Richmond that his opinion is that the Negroes could not obtain justice before a Virginia jury.

Q. Justice to the Negro and justice to the white man are different articles, I suppose; it changes with the complexion? — A. Yes, sir.

Q. Your bureau exercises jurisdiction over cases in which freedmen are parties? — A. Yes, sir; in all cases where his rights are involved.

Q. Is much of the time of the bureau at Richmond occupied in settling these controversies? — A. Yes, sir; it is occupied most of the time in every county in the state in settling controversies and aiding the Negroes to make contracts; but it is very largely occupied in settling controversies.

Q. Have you heard of any cases of violence between whites and blacks down there? — A. Yes, sir, I have.

Q. Are they of frequent occurrence? — A. Of nearly every day occurrence in the state.

Q. Can you relate some instances of violence on the part of whites towards the blacks? — A. A case came before me yesterday. A Negro was shot through the head and killed while sitting by his fire in his cabin, near Suffolk; circumstantial evidence points very strongly toward a white man with whom he had had an altercation, and who had shot at him before.

Q. Was the white man arrested? — A. I sent officers for him at once. A few weeks ago, near Fredericksburg, a Negro, who had been a soldier, was making some remarks in a boasting manner of his having served in the Federal army; he was overheard by a citizen, who said he would not allow him to boast of having served in the Federal army — that he considered it an insult. The Negro said he had served, and was not ashamed to say so; that he felt it something to be proud of. The man drew a revolver and fired at him, the ball going through the Negro's clothing; then he overtook him and struck him over the head with the butt end of the revolver, laying the skull bare. A physician who was sent for said, in the preliminary examination before the Freedmen's Bureau, that he considered the insult strong enough to justify the outrage; we have arrested the physician, but have not been able to catch the other yet.

Q. Was the physician a secessionist? — A. Oh! Of course, yes. I might multiply instances of the kind to any extent. Outrages have increased very much since the diminution of our troops in the state; perhaps there is a little holding up now as they find that, even with few troops, we are determined to reach them; the bureau has not the power to reach all cases that occur; it wants more men; it wants the opportunity of selecting its officers, which it now has not; it has to take such as it can get.

Q. In case of the removal of that bureau, would you apprehend a great increase of those scenes of violence towards the blacks? — A. I should.

Q. What would it result in? — A. I think it would eventually result in an insurrection on the part of the blacks; the black troops that are about being mustered out, and those that have been mustered out, will all provide themselves with arms; probably most of them will purchase their arms; and they will not endure those outrages, without any protection except that which they obtain from Virginia; they have not confidence in their old masters, notwithstanding their great love for them, in which they have tried to make us believe.

Q. Are there many arms among the blacks? — A. Yes, sir; attempts have been made, in many instances, to disarm them.

Q. Who have made the attempts? — A. The citizens, by organizing what they call "patrols" — combinations of citizens.

Q. Has that arrangement pervaded the state generally? — A. No, sir; it has not been allowed; they would disarm the Negroes at once if they could.

Q. Is that feeling extensive? — A. I may say it is universal; they have no confidence in the Negroes, and they have every reason for not having it. They apprehended very much an insurrection during the holidays; I was called on by gentlemen from every section of the state about it, but there was at that time no disposition at all on the part of the Negroes to make any difficulty.

Q. Have you reason to believe that there have been combinations among the Negroes with a view to insurrection? — A. No, sir, I am satisfied there were no such combinations; there have been combinations to secure their suffrage, and other things of that kind, but nothing further. They have a great disposition to form secret combinations for very trivial objects; for instance, I recollect one charitable association called "The Holy Sons of God"; they get up such names. Their object was simply to take care of the sick and helpless, bury the dead, etc.; their meetings were all secret.

Q. Have you ever seen Negro troops under fire? — A. No, sir, I have not.

Q. What is your idea about their courage in active operations in the field? — A. I can only base my opinion on what I have heard and read; I think they make good soldiers; I think that in case of insurrection, they would fight desperately.

Q. How would they fight the Union troops, in case Union troops were brought against them to put down an insurrection? — A. They were examined on that subject by my officers when there was talk of an insurrection at the holidays, fearing that they might have such ideas, although we had no confidence in the report; but there was so much alarm expressed that we took occasion to talk to them on that subject, and told them that federal troops would be brought against them if any such attempt were made. I think that a regiment of federal troops would create more demoralization among them than a brigade of confederates would — far more.

Q. Do you hear anything said among the whites in Virginia about expelling the blacks from their midst? — A. No, sir; I think, though, they would prefer to have them away; they would not expel them, but it would be their fancy to have them away.

Q. With what kind of people would they supply their places? — A. An attempt was made a few months ago to introduce foreign labor, but, from the best evidence I can get, it proved a failure; those who employed foreigners were perfectly willing to go back to the Negroes; still the feeling was very general when they were first freed, and is not done away with yet, that "if we cannot have them as slaves, take them away; we don't want them."

Q. Is not that rather the result of a feeling of mortification that the Negroes are made free — mere spite? — A. I do not know how to analyze the feeling they seem to have; they have been always in the habit of having this control over them, and now the Negro comes and asserts his rights and says, "I am free as well as you"; that creates an irritation, a dislike; I hardly know what it is.

Q. And they think they would be glad to get rid of the Negro? — A. Yes, sir.

Q. And when they think of the labor which they find it necessary to have performed, they want the Negro to stay with them? — A. Yes, sir; that is it.

Q. So that really, between the two motives — the motive of spite, ill-will, and disappointment, and the other, a sort of respect for him because he is a good laborer — they are divided? — A. That is it, sir.

Q. They do not propose to do the labor themselves? — A. No, sir; and they do not propose to break up their large estates if they can help it. That is one thing which keeps them back; they seem indisposed to sell their real estate; they do not like to part with it. I remember seeing an editorial article in one of the Richmond papers containing such an expression as this: "If the estates were to be broken up so as to destroy the old Virginia gentleman, Virginia would cease to be Virginia."

Q. "One of the olden time?" — A. "One of the olden time."

Q. Do you think of anything else that you wish to state? — A. No, sir.

Part Two

CONDITIONS OF WHITES IN THE SOUTH

4 TESTIMONY OF FORMER CONFEDERATES

Testimony of Robert E. Lee *

Mr. Howard: Where is your present residence? — A. Lexington, Virginia.

Q. How long have you resided at Lexington? — A. Since the first of October last; nearly five months.

Q. Are you acquainted with the state of feeling among what we call secessionists in Virginia, at present, toward the government of the United States? — A. I do not know that I am. I have been living very retired, and have had but little communication with politicians. I know nothing more than from my observation, and from such facts as have come to my knowledge.

Q. From your observation, what is your opinion as to the feeling of loyalty towards the government of the United States among the secession portion of the people of that state at this time? — A. So far as has come to my knowledge, I do not know of a single person who either feels or contemplates any resistance to the government of the United States, or, indeed, any opposition to it. No word has reached me to either purpose.

Q. From what you have observed among them, is it your opinion that they are friendly toward the government of the United States, and that they will cooperate to sustain and uphold the government for the future? — A. I believe that they entirely acquiesce in the government of the United States, and, so far as I have heard anyone express an opinion, they are for cooperating with President Johnson in his policy.

Q. In his policy in regard to what? — A. His policy in regard to the restoration of the whole country. I have heard persons with whom I have conversed express great confidence in the wisdom of his policy of restoration, and they seem to look forward to it as a hope of restoration.

Q. How do they feel in regard to that portion of the people of the United States who have been forward and zealous in the prosecution of the war against the rebellion? — A. Well, I do not know. I have heard nobody express any opinion in regard to it. As I said before, I have not had much communication with politicians in the country, if there are

* See above, page 29.

any. Everyone seems to be engaged in his own affairs, and endeavoring to restore the civil government of the state. I have heard no expression of a sentiment toward any particular portion of the country.

Q. How do the secessionists feel in regard to the payment of the debt of the United States contracted in the prosecution of the war? — A. I have never heard anyone speak on the subject. I suppose they must expect to pay the taxes levied by the government. I have heard them speak in reference to the payment of taxes, and of their efforts to raise money to pay the taxes, which I suppose are for their share of the debt. I have never heard anyone speak in opposition to the payment of taxes, or of resistance to their payment. Their whole effort has been to try and raise the money for the payment of the taxes.

Q. From your knowledge of the state of public feeling in Virginia, is it your opinion that the people would, if the question were left to them, repudiate and reject that debt? — A. I never heard anyone speak on that subject, but from my knowledge of the people I believe that they would be in favor of the payment of all just debts.

Q. Do they, in your opinion, regard that as a just debt? — A. I do not know what their opinion is on the subject of the particular debt. I have never heard any opinion expressed, but I have never heard any expressed contrary to it. Indeed, as I said in the beginning, I have had very little discussion or intercourse with the people. I believe that the people would pay the debts they are called upon to pay. I say that from my knowledge of the people generally.

Q. Would they pay that debt, or their portion of it, with as much alacrity as people ordinarily pay their taxes to their government? — A. I do not know that they would make any distinction between the two. The taxes laid by the government, so far as I know, they are prepared to pay to the best of their ability. I never heard them make any distinction.

Q. What is the feeling of that portion of the people of Virginia in regard to the payment of the so-called Confederate debt? — A. I believe, so far as my opinion goes (I have no facts to go upon, but merely base my opinion on the knowledge I have of the people), they would be willing to pay the Confederate debt too.

Q. You think they would? — A. I think they would if they had the power and ability to do it. I have never heard anyone in the state with whom I have conversed speak of repudiating any debt.

Q. I suppose the Confederate debt is almost entirely valueless, even in the market of Virginia? — A. Entirely, as far as I know. I believe the people generally look upon it as lost entirely. I never heard any question on the subject.

Q. Do you recollect the terms of the Confederate bonds — when they were made payable? — A. I think I have a general recollection that they were made payable six months after a declaration of peace.

Q. Six months after the ratification of a treaty of peace between the

United States and the Confederate government? — A. I think they ran in that way.

Q. So that the bonds are not due yet by their terms? — A. I suppose, unless it is considered that there is peace now, they are not due. . . .

Mr. Blow: What is your opinion in regard to the material interests of Virginia? Do you think they will be equal to what they were before the rebellion under the changed aspect of affairs? — A. It will take a long time for them to reach their former standard. I think that after some years they will reach it, and I hope exceed it; but it cannot be immediately, in my opinion.

Q. It will take a number of years? — A. It will take a number of years, I think.

Q. On the whole, the condition of things in Virginia is hopeful, both in regard to its material interests and the future peace of the country? — A. I have heard great hope expressed, and there is great cheerfulness and willingness to labor.

Q. Suppose that this policy of President Johnson should be all that you anticipate, and that you should also realize all that you expect in the improvement of your material interests, do you think that the result of that would be the gradual restoration of the old feeling? — A. That would be the natural result, I think, and I see no other way in which that result can be brought about.

Q. There is a fear in the public mind that the friends of the policy in the South adopt it because they see in it the means of regaining the political position which they lost in the recent contest: do you think that that is the main idea with them, or that they really look to it, as you say, as the best means of restoring civil government and the peace and prosperity of their respective states? — A. As to the first point you make, I do not know that I ever heard any person speak upon it. I never heard the points separated. I have heard them speak generally as to the effect of the policy of President Johnson. The feeling, so far as I know, now is that there is not that equality extended to the Southern states as is enjoyed by the North.

Q. You do not feel down there that while you accept the result, that we are as generous as we ought to be under the circumstances? — A. They think that the North can afford to be generous.

Q. That is the feeling down there? — A. Yes, and they think it is the best policy — those who reflect upon the subject and are able to judge.

Q. I understand it to be your opinion that generosity and liberality towards the entire south would be the surest means of regaining their good opinion? — A. Yes, and the speediest.

Mr. Howard: I understood you to say, generally, that you had no apprehension of any combination among the leading secessionists to renew the war, or anything of the kind? — A. I have no reason in the world to think so.

Q. Have you heard that subject talked over among any of the politicians? — A. No, sir; I have not. I have not heard that matter even suggested.

Q. Let me put another hypothetical state of things: Suppose the executive government of the United States should be held by a President who, like Mr. Buchanan, rejected the right of coercion, so-called, and suppose a Congress should exist here entertaining the same political opinions, thus presenting to the once rebel states the opportunity again to secede from the Union, would they or not, in your opinion, avail themselves of that opportunity, or some of them? — A. I suppose it would depend upon the circumstances existing at the time. If their feelings should remain embittered, and their affections alienated from the rest of the states, I think it very probable they might do so, provided they thought it was to their interest.

Q. Do you not think that at the present time there is a deep-seated feeling of dislike towards the government of the United States on the part of the masses of the secessionists? — A. I do not know that there is any deep-seated dislike. I think it is probable there may be some animosity still existing among some of the people at the South.

Q. Is there not a deep-seated feeling of disappointment and chagrin at the result of the war? — A. I think that, at the time, they were disappointed at the result of the war.

Q. Do you mean to be understood as saying that there is not a condition of discontent against the government of the United States among the secessionists generally? — A. I know of none.

Q. Are you prepared to say that they respect the government of the United States and the loyal people of the United States so much, at the present time, as to perform their duties as citizens of the United States and of the states faithfully and well? — A. I believe that they will perform all the duties that they are required to perform. I think that is the general feeling, so far as I know.

Q. Do you think that it would be practicable to convict a man in Virginia of treason for having taken part in this rebellion against the government, by a Virginia jury, without packing it with direct reference to a verdict of guilty? — A. On that point I have no knowledge, and I do not know what they would consider treason against the United States. If you mean past acts ——

Mr. Howard: Yes, sir.

The Witness: I have no knowledge as to what their views on that subject in the past are.

Q. You understand my question: Suppose a jury was impanelled in your own neighborhood, taken up by lot; would it be practicable to convict, for instance, Jefferson Davis for having levied war upon the United States, and thus having committed the crime of treason? — A. I think it is very probable that they would not consider he had committed treason.

Q. Suppose the jury should be clearly and plainly instructed by the court that such an act of war upon the United States, on the part of Mr. Davis, or any other leading man, constituted in itself the crime of treason under the Constitution of the United States; would the jury be likely to heed that instruction, and if the facts were plainly in proof before them, convict the offender? — A. I do not know, sir, what they would do on that question.

Q. They do not generally suppose that it was treason against the United States, do they? — A. I do not think that they so consider it.

Q. In what light would they view it? What would be their excuse or justification? How would they escape in their own mind? I refer to the past. — A. I am referring to the past and as to the feelings they would have. So far as I know, they look upon the action of the state, in withdrawing itself from the government of the United States, as carrying the individuals of the state along with it; that the state was responsible for the act, not the individual.

Q. And that the ordinance of secession, so-called, or those acts of the state which recognized a condition of war between the state and the general government, stood as their justification for their bearing arms against the government of the United States? — A. Yes, sir. I think they considered the act of the state as legitimate; that they were merely using the reserved right which they had a right to do.

Q. State, if you please (and if you are disinclined to answer the question you need not do so), what your own personal views on that question were? — A. That was my view; that the act of Virginia, in withdrawing herself from the United States, carried me along as a citizen of Virginia, and that her laws and her acts were binding on me.

Q. And that you felt to be your justification in taking the course you did? — A. Yes, sir.

Q. I have been told, General, that you have remarked to some of your friends in conversation that you were rather wheedled or cheated into that course by politicians? — A. I do not recollect making any such remark. I do not think I ever made it.

Q. If there be any other matter about which you wish to speak on this occasion, do so freely. — A. Only in reference to that last question you put to me. I may have said, and I may have believed, that the position of the two sections which they held to each other was brought about by the politicians of the country; that the great masses of the people, if they understood the real question, would have avoided it; but not that I had been individually wheedled by the politicians.

Testimony of Alexander H. Stephens *

Mr. Boutwell: What means have you had since Lee's surrender to ascertain the sentiments of the people of Georgia with regard to the Union? — A. I was at home in Georgia at the time of the surrender of General Lee, and remained there until the 11th of May, and during that time conversed very freely with the people in my immediate neighborhood, with the governor of the state, and with one or two other leading or prominent men in the state. From the 11th of May until my return to Georgia, which was the 25th of October, I had no means of knowing anything of the public sentiment there, except through the public press and such letters as I received. From the time of my return until I left the state on my visit here, I had very extensive intercourse with the people, visiting Augusta, visiting Milledgeville during the session of the legislature, first on their assembling, again in January upon their reassembling, and again in the latter part of February. While there I conversed very freely and fully with all the prominent leading men, or most of them, in the legislature, and met a great many of the prominent influential men of the state not connected with the legislature. And by letters from and correspondence with men in the state whom I have not met. I believe that embraces a full answer to the question as to my means of ascertaining the sentiments of the people of that state upon the subject stated in the question.

Q. As the result of your observations, what is your opinion of the purposes of the people with reference to the reconstruction of the government, and what are their desires and purposes concerning the maintenance of the government? — A. My opinion, and decided opinion, is that an overwhelming majority of the people of Georgia are exceedingly anxious for the restoration of the government, and for the state to take her former position in the Union, to have her senators and representatives admitted into Congress, and to enjoy all her rights as a state under the Constitution of the United States as it stands amended.

Q. What are their present views concerning the justice of the rebellion? Do they, at present, believe that it was a reasonable and proper undertaking, or otherwise? — A. My opinion of the sentiment of the people of Georgia upon that subject is that the exercise of the right of secession was resorted to by them from a desire to render their liberties and institutions more secure, and a belief on their part that this was absolutely necessary for that object. They were divided upon the question of the policy of the measure. There was, however, but very little division

* See above, page 22.

among them upon the question of the right of it. It is now their belief, in my opinion — and I give it merely as an opinion — that the surest, if not only hope for their liberties is the restoration of the Constitution of the United States and of the government of the United States under the Constitution.

Q. Has there been any change of opinion as to the right of secession as a right in the people or in the states? — A. I think there has been a very decided change of opinion as to the policy by those who favored it. I think the people generally are satisfied sufficiently with the experiment never to make a resort to that measure of redress again by force, whatever may be their own abstract ideas upon that subject. They have given up all idea of the maintenance of those opinions by a resort to force. They have come to the conclusion that it is better to appeal to the forums of reason and justice, to the halls of legislation and the courts, for the preservation of the principles of constitutional liberty, than to the arena of arms. It is my settled conviction that there is not any idea cherished at all in the public mind of Georgia of ever resorting again to secession or to the exercise of the right of secession, by force. That whole policy of the maintenance of their rights, in my opinion, is at this time totally abandoned.

Q. But the opinion as to the right, as I understand, remains substantially the same? — A. I cannot answer as to that. Some may have changed their opinions in this respect. It would be an unusual thing, as well as a difficult matter, for a whole people to change their convictions upon abstract truths or principles. I have not heard this view of the subject debated or discussed recently, and I wish to be understood as giving my opinion only on that branch of the subject which is of practical character and importance.

Q. To what do you attribute the change of opinion as to the propriety of attempting to maintain their views by force? — A. Well, sir, my opinion about that — my individual opinion, derived from observation — is that this change of opinion arose mainly from the operation of the war among themselves, and the results of the conflict from their own authorities on their individual rights of person and property, the general breaking down of constitutional barriers which usually attend all protracted wars. . . .

Q. State whether, from your observation, the events of the war have produced any change in the public mind of the South upon the question of the reserved rights of the states under the Constitution of the United States. — A. That question I answered in part yesterday. While I cannot state from personal knowledge to what extent the opinions of the Southern states upon the abstract question of the reserved rights of the states may have changed, my decided opinion is that a very thorough change has taken place upon the practical policy of resorting to any such right.

Q. What events or experience of the war have contributed to this change? — A. First, the people are satisfied that a resort to the exercise of this right, while it is denied by the federal government, will lead to war, which many thought before the late attempted secession would not be the case; and civil wars, they are also now very well satisfied, are dangerous to liberty; moreover, their experience in the late war, I think, satisfied them that it greatly endangered their own. I allude, specially, to the suspension of the writ of habeas corpus, the military conscriptions, the declaration of martial law in various places, general impressments, and the levying of forced contributions, as well as the very demoralizing effects of war, generally.

Q. When were you last a member of the Congress of the United States? — A. I went out on the 4th of March, 1859.

Q. Will you state, if not indisposed to do so, the considerations or opinions which led you to identify yourself with the rebellion so far as to accept the office of Vice-President of the Confederate States of America, so-called? — A. I believed thoroughly in the reserved sovereignty of the several states of the Union under the compact or Constitution of 1787. I opposed secession therefore as a question of policy, and not one of right, on the part of Georgia. When the state seceded against my judgment and vote I thought my ultimate allegiance was due to her, and I preferred to cast my fortunes and destiny with hers and her people rather than take any other course, even though it might lead to my sacrifice and her ruin. In accepting position under the new order of things my sole object was to do all the good I could in preserving and perpetuating the principles of liberty as established under the Constitution of the United States. If the Union was to be abandoned either with or without force — which I thought a very impolitic measure — I wished, if possible, to rescue, preserve, and perpetuate the principles of the Constitution. This I was not without hope might be done in the new Confederacy of states formed. When the conflict arose my efforts were directed to as speedy and peaceful an adjustment of the questions as possible. This adjustment I always thought, to be lasting, would have ultimately to be settled upon a continental basis founded upon the principles of mutual convenience and reciprocal advantage on the part of the states on which the Constitution of the United States was originally formed. I was wedded to no particular plan of adjustment except the recognition as a basis of the separate sovereignty of the several states. With this recognized as a principle I thought all other questions of difference would soon adjust themselves according to the best interests, peace, welfare, and prosperity of the whole country, as enlightened reason, calm judgment, and a sense of justice might direct. This doctrine I regarded as a self-regulating principle of American state institutions extending possibly over the continent.

Q. Have your opinions undergone any change since the opening of the rebellion in reference to the reserved rights of the states under the Constitution of the United States? — A. My convictions on the original abstract question have undergone no change, but I accept the issues of the war and the result as a practical settlement of that question. The sword was appealed to, to decide the question, and by the decision of the sword I am willing to abide.

Testimony of James D. B. DeBow *

Mr. Williams: State if you have been, at any time since the cessation of hostilities, in the State of Louisiana and if so, how long, and what opportunities you have had to ascertain the temper and disposition of the people towards the general government. — A. I spent five or six weeks of the present year in Louisiana, and was in intimate association with the citizens there of all classes. I am a resident of that state, and of course largely acquainted, and having been absent during the war, after the surrender of the city, I met a great many of the people on my return. I have also just returned from a general tour at the South.

Q. What are the views and feelings of the people there as to the late war and its results, and as to the future condition of that state in its relations to the federal government? — A. There seems to be a general — you may say universal — acquiescence in the results. There is a great deal of dissatisfaction as to the course in reference to their condition pursued by the federal government. I think the people having fairly tried the experiment of secession are perfectly satisfied with the result, and that there is no disposition in any quarter, in any shape or form, to embarrass the United States government, or to refrain from the most complete performance of all the duties of citizenship. I saw nothing of that sort. All parties, those who were opposed to the war and those who were in favor of the war, are now agreed that it is for the best interest of the state to perform all the duties of citizenship, and to accept whatever the government has effected in reference to the Negro, as well as in reference to other questions.

Q. What are the alleged grounds of dissatisfaction among the people as to the action of the federal government? — A. The Freedmen's Bureau is very largely complained of, and the delay in admitting their representatives. They confidently expected a very early restoration of their civil condition and political rights from the promises which were made. I think that feeling of hostility has grown up since the surrender. I think at the period of the surrender the feeling was very much more kindly, and the attitude and condition of the country more favorable than it is now. This constant irritation has produced the feeling. I do not think it is very serious, but still it exists; it would be dissipated immediately on

* See above, page 31.

the passage of liberal measures, such as, for instance, an order restoring the states to their status under the Constitution, restoring their political rights, the removal of the Freedmen's Bureau, or some such regulation which would be fair to both parties. . . .

Q. Is there or not a bitter feeling between those who supported the rebellion and those who supported the general government during the war in Louisiana? — A. I think those parties who have remained in the state and who were assuming they were good Union men during the war, perhaps making more claims in that regard than they are entitled to, are received with hostility. I think those who went away honestly for those reasons, and have returned, are respected, and receive very much consideration. I know of many cases of this kind, of men who went away, did not take any part in the war, and have since returned. But there is a feeling in my state against those who remained there during the war and profess now that they were Union men all the time, but that their rights were taken away. There is a feeling against them, though not of any such hostile character as to endanger their personal safety or condition in any way.

Q. Are there any considerable number of the citizens of Louisiana who went into the Union army and fought against the rebellion? — A. I do not think there are. There were some few from New Orleans who have returned since. I do not think there were many outside New Orleans from the state. There were some few companies of whites raised in New Orleans by the federal authorities. I do not think they got many from the city, and those were generally not citizens of the state, but persons who were temporarily residing there. I do not think many creoles went in. The population of French descent were generally almost entirely on the Confederate side.

Q. Do you think those who have been, or profess to have been, Union men in Louisiana would be perfectly safe there with the military protection of the government withdrawn? — A. Perfectly safe. I have no idea anybody would be disturbed at all. There might be some little unkindness of look or expression towards them. They would not be received, of course, on the same terms with those who have been in sympathy with the great body of the people there. They would respect those who were with them much more than they would that class of persons; but there would be no physical hostility, or any attempt to interfere with their rights — none whatever.

Q. Do not those who were in the rebel army, or supported the rebel cause, make distinctions in social intercourse and business transactions between those who cooperated with them and those who favored the cause of the Union, as well as men who came there from the North? — A. The secession men, the men who were in the war, are generally ruined, their families are destitute, and there is a great disposition to sustain them, if they undertake any business at all. I think a great deal grows out of that, and a great deal grows, of course, out of actual sympathy with these men. Although, on the other hand, I can point in New Orleans to men who were not in sympathy with the South during the war, but the very opposite, who are doing a large and successful business. I could give you a house, of my own name, though in no way related to me, unless very remotely — a Mr. Samuel De Bow, who came there during the war from Illinois, or somewhere in the northwest — who has, perhaps, the largest wholesale grocery in the city. I do not think the discrimination made is anything more than a social discrimination. I think that is well marked at present. There is a disposition on the part of those who have been with the South during the war not to mix a great deal with those who have remained in the South (as they say) as Union men; and the feeling extends, more or less, to Northern men, though very little towards the great majority of Northern people. Some who come there a little disposed to talk, etc., receive the cold shoulder; that is about all. I have known of balls and parties, where there was a mixture of all classes, and where certain ladies would say they would not associate with federal officers; but the party would go on all the same, all in the same room. That feeling is now stronger than it was. It is the result of political causes. I think it will wear away. . . .

Q. What have been your views on the subject of secession? — A. I was raised to believe in the doctrine of the State-rights party, and therefore believed in the right of secession. I was anxious to perpetuate the United States government, with full respect to the rights of all sections, believing in the doctrines of Calhoun on that subject. Having failed in securing that, I believed that secession was right, proper, and just, and did all I could in aiding the exercise of it. I am now satisfied with the results of the war, and regard it as utterly hopeless and useless to assert any such right again; that the event of the war was a distinct pronunciation against the exercise of the right and a final settlement of the whole question. I think that is the general sentiment of the people. The people are much better satisfied with the result than if they had not made the experiment. They think they have nothing to regret upon that question, and that although everything else be lost, honor is saved. This is the sentiment from the Potomac to the Rio Grande.

Q. Are you satisfied that the people of the South have given up all ideas of secession under any circumstances? — A. *I am perfectly satisfied of that. The leaders, and the people of all classes of opinion, agree upon that subject.* [Italics in original.]

5 TESTIMONY OF NORTHERNERS

Testimony of Rufus Saxton *

Mr. Howard: Describe the kind of loyalty of which that average of South Carolinians, in your opinion, is possessed. — A. I believe that Governor Orr belongs to the best class of so-called loyal men in South Carolina. I believe there is a small portion of people in South Carolina who desire earnestly to fulfil their obligations to the United States government. I believe that a large majority, probably nine-tenths, of the people of South Carolina are opposed to the government, and look to their connection with it as the greatest calamity which could befall South Carolina, and desire a separate organization. I believe that a Union man holding and advocating Union sentiments cannot be elected to any office in the gift of the whites of South Carolina. It is my belief that Governor Orr's great popularity in the state in former days influenced a large vote in his favor; and it is my further conviction that his popularity was weakened by the less prominent part he seemed to have taken during the rebellion. Had he been as active as Wade Hampton, his popularity would have been increased in proportion. I mention this as the indication that there is no real reformation; that, in their own words, they are overpowered, not conquered, and that they regard their treason as a virtue, and loyalty as dishonorable. General Wade Hampton positively declined to be a candidate for the office of governor. Had the white people of South Carolina thought that he would accept, in my opinion his majority would have been far greater than it was.

Q. How are secessionists there in the habit of speaking of the government of the United States; what is their tone and style in speaking of it? — A. They speak of it as "your government," or as the "United States government"; I have yet to hear a single one, even though he had taken the oath of allegiance, call it "our" government. They speak of it as the government of a foreign nation. I think their hatred of the Yankee, as they call him, is thoroughly intense.

Q. Have your opportunities been good to learn the state of popular feeling in South Carolina towards the government of the United States? — A. They have been peculiarly favorable; I have travelled over portions

* See above, page 38.

of the state and have conversed with large numbers of people in my office; I have talked with the freedmen, and I have studied the reports of my agents throughout the state. I think I have had better opportunities of discovering the real state of feeling there than any other person, from my position.

Q. Suppose the United States should be engaged in a war with any other powerful nation, such as England or France, and suppose in the progress of the strife it should become apparent to the South Carolinians that they had a reasonable chance, by connecting themselves with the common enemy, to achieve their independence and shake off the government of the United States; would they or not, in your opinion, do so? — A. I believe the feeling would be as unanimous to join that other government against the United States as it was when that state seceded from the Union at first — that is, among the white people.

Q. Does this feeling, in your judgment, more particularly pervade the higher classes, or the middle classes, or the lower classes of the whites, or does it pervade them all? — A. I think it pervades throughout. I think there are exceptions to it among the educated, but they are few, and I think that the vast number of ignorant are still guided by the same counsels which guided them in seceding.

Q. How do the leading politicians in South Carolina feel in regard to a republican government, as you and I understand it; I do not speak of universal suffrage or Negro suffrage, but of a democratic republican government, such as is guaranteed by the Constitution of the United States, and such as exists in other states of the Union? — A. I think they are opposed to it.

Q. State whether you have heard expressions on the part of persons of standing and consideration in South Carolina, or whether you know from any reliable sources, that such is the feeling. — A. That such is their feeling is so apparent to me from all my intercourse with them and from my conversations with them, that I cannot, at present, specify any individual case in which this subject has come up; but it is my belief that it is the burden of nearly all their discussions on government. If I had supposed that my attention would have been called to that subject on this examination, I would have been more particular on this point, and would have been able to furnish many instances corroborative of this view.

Q. Do you think that, to use a common, plain expression, the great masses of the people of South Carolina hate the government of the United States? — A. I do, sir.

Testimony of John W. Turner

General John W. Turner, a West Pointer from Illinois, served with credit during the Civil War, especially in South Carolina and Virginia. Chief of Staff of the Department of the South, he succeeded to the command of the artillery in time to participate during the siege of Forts Wagner and Sumter. Later on, he served as Chief of Staff during the siege of Petersburg. At the end of the war, he became commander of the District of Henrico, which included Richmond.

Mr. Howard: State, generally, the nature of your duties at Richmond at the present time. — A. Perhaps I had better go back a little and state what my duties have been, as they have been circumscribed somewhat lately.

Q. Please do so. — A. On assuming command there I took the entire control and charge of the city of Richmond, exercising all the power and authority ordinarily vested in the municipal authorities of a city. The civil courts were suspended — all the ordinary tribunals before which the citizens of a community resort for the redress of their grievances.

Q. Was the district under martial law? — A. Yes, sir.

Q. Has it been ever since? — A. Yes, sir.

Q. And is now? — A. Yes, sir. From time to time I have turned over to the regularly constituted civil authorities which have been established all actions in civil cases. During the summer, and until October, I took cognizance, as a sort of equity court, of all civil cases that I could adjudicate upon. I was consequently brought in contact with a great many citizens, who necessarily came to me for relief of their wants of various kinds.

At present my duties are confined almost exclusively to affairs in which freedmen are involved. The state civil courts all having been established, a mayor having been elected and his police court established, they have taken from me all jurisdiction over matters tending to the peace and quiet of the community. At present, therefore, I take cognizance only of those matters in which freedmen are involved; and of those I take action only in criminal cases; all civil cases go to the Freedmen's Bureau. But Richmond being a large city, and there being a large congregation of Negroes there, there is required a court constantly in session to dispose of criminal cases of daily occurrence. I have from ten to twenty cases every day to dispose of, mostly for petty misdemeanors.

Q. Is there in your district any interruption of the courts of justice by mobs or violence? — A. No, sir.

Q. Are juries regularly assembled in the state courts for the trial of causes? — A. The courts were established only late in the fall, and the only court that has been going on is what is called the hustings court. Of that court there are two branches — the one composed of a judge, the other of fifteen magistrates. That court does not have a jury. I think that in the circuit court and in Judge Meredith's court there is a jury.

Q. How are the sheriffs of those courts appointed? — A. They are all elected.

Q. Have you been present in Richmond or in any other place in Virginia on any day of election? — A. Yes, sir.

Q. What do you know in regard to ex-rebels voting? — A. The first election in Richmond was for mayor, aldermen, members of the council, sheriff, high constable, commonwealth's attorney, etc. So far as tumultuous proceedings were concerned, that election was conducted very quietly; there was no disturbance. I took every precaution that the soldiers should not interfere with the voting; that they should keep away from the polls. The people had free scope to do and say just what they pleased. I only took the precaution, in case of a riot or disturbance, to have the means at hand to suppress it. I know that at that election the people of Richmond electioneered on the streets and made harangues and speeches in favor of ex-rebel officers.

Q. Was this done within your own hearing? — A. I cannot say I heard it; it was so reported to me.

Q. Was the information you received so direct and authentic as to leave no doubt upon your mind as to its correctness? — A. Yes, sir.

Q. Did you, at that election, hear any outcries or shouts, indicating that the people were generally more in favor of those candidates who had been rebels than of those who had not been? — A. I did not, personally, for I took the precaution to keep out of sight of anything of the kind that day; but my officers, whom I had on duty, reported to me that such things did occur, and I am fully confident they did.

Q. Have you mingled freely with the people of Richmond and of other portions of your district since you have been in command there, so as to be able to ascertain the state of their feelings towards the government of the United States? — A. I have been thrown in contact with a great many of them; but when you ask me if I have mingled with them — gone into their society — I must say that I have not, because they will not permit me to do it.

Q. Why not? — A. Because I am a "Yankee," and they will not permit me to go inside their houses.

Q. Can you give an instance of any exclusion of that sort? — A. No, sir; not of any direct exclusion; only that none of them have ever invited me to visit their houses. I know of only one instance where I was invited to the house of a citizen of Richmond who was, and has been during the war, a secessionist. I judge from the manner in which they avoid me; the nature of their conversation when they are in my presence, when they are obliged to approach me on matters of business; their deportment and their acts on the streets indicating — all these things satisfy me that I am not welcome among them. On the contrary, that they have towards me, and I am constantly reminded of it, a deep-abiding hate. I am filled with the consciousness of it every day. I have not been on the streets of Richmond scarcely a day for the last four months that I have not seen some indication from man or woman marking his or her contempt for me because I am a "Yankee"; by a shrug of the shoulders, by walking across the street to avoid meeting me, by their turning their backs on me, or leaving a store when I enter it, turning their noses up at me. I do not suppose a day has passed in any week for the last four months that that has not been done.

Q. Are you aware that any of those citizens have any cause of personal dislike towards you? — A. They have not.

Q. Have you had any personal altercation with any of them? — A. Not with a single person in the city of Richmond. When I have been brought in contact with them, in the exercise of my official duties, I have always treated them kindly; I have spoken pleasantly to them; I have avoided in every way the giving any offence by word or act.

Q. Have you received any instructions from your superiors in relation to your demeanor towards them? — A. No, sir; I have never received any instruction on that point.

Q. I do not mean any official instructions; but have you not been informed of the desire of the President of the United States on that point? — A. I conceived it to be my duty, when I was assigned to the command there, to do all in my power to conciliate and harmonize the people, and I did it conscientiously. I have forced down many a time against my inclination the indignation that arose in me, feeling that it was my duty to do so; that perhaps I ought to forbear showing my feelings. I think it probable that if you should ask the citizens of Richmond, they would speak of my course there as having been charitable and kind. At any rate, such are the reports that are brought to me; that they have nothing to gainsay of what I have done. Of course, in the proper discharge of my official duties there, I have been obliged to take some measures that were not very pleasant to some of them.

Q. It was your uniform and firm intention and inclination to treat them fairly and kindly? — A. Yes, sir; as much so as I ever attempted to perform any duty in my life.

Q. And you are not conscious of ever having acted differently? — A. No, sir.

Q. What is your conviction of the general sentiment of the people in your district, or in Virginia generally, so far as you know, towards the government of the United States; as a general thing, as a prevalent feeling, do they like it or do they hate it? — A. It is my conviction that they hate it.

Q. And you derive this conviction from what? — A. From a long intercourse with them; from watching them as carefully as I could and judging them as dispassionately as I could; and I think I am able to judge them dispassionately. I do not think they love the country or the government. It is their belief, or their expression of belief, that they cannot live with the North; that they are a different people. I do not think that their oath of allegiance conveys to them any binding force or obligation whatever to support and defend the government. I do not believe that they, for an instant, think it does.

Q. As a general thing? — A. As a general thing.

Q. Why not; in what sort of casuistry do they indulge in that regard; in other words, how does it happen that a man, honorable and honest in his private relations, can reconcile it to his conscience to violate and disregard his oath? — A. That is a matter entirely beyond my comprehension. I can only attribute it to the fact that they are an impulsive people, and speak and act from their impulses more than from their reason and judgment. I have had related to me scores, and I may say hundreds of times, instances of men who have taken the oath of allegiance, asserting that they would never fight for the old flag.

Q. Does this information came to you from authentic sources? — A. Yes, sir. I call to mind distinctly now one instance where a man told me that he was sitting at the breakfast table in a private boardinghouse, when the conversation turned upon the probability of a war with France or England. One man present at the table remarked, "Well, if we get into a war with England, I am going on that side."

Q. On the side of England? — A. Yes, sir. "I am going to fight for England; I will not fight for this country."

Q. Was that man one of position in society there? — A. That I cannot say. He was certainly living at a genteel boardinghouse.

Q. Was he an educated and well-bred man? — A. He was boarding with the gentleman who related the circumstance to me, and who goes in the first society there. I have heard these things so often that I have ceased to pay attention to them; they pass in one ear and out of the other. It is from hearing these remarks, and from their deportment towards me, that I have been brought to the conviction that their oath of allegiance does not bear with any force or obligation upon them.

Testimony of Sidney Andrews

Sidney Andrews was a Northern newspaperman who during the years 1864 and 1865 traveled in the South. After reporting his experiences in Georgia and the Carolinas through a series of letters in the Boston Advertiser *and the* Chicago Tribune, *he finally published his impressions in a full-length book. He was considered a skilled observer of men and events.*

Mr. Boutwell: State your residence and occupation.—A. I reside in Washington. My occupation is that of correspondent.

Q. Have you travelled in the South since the surrender of Lee? If so, through what portions and during what period of time?—A. I spent the months of September, October, November, and the first week in December in the states of North Carolina, South Carolina, and Georgia. I reached Georgia on the 24th of October, I think, and left Savannah about the 3d of December, spending some six weeks in Georgia, writing letters during that time for the *Boston Advertiser* and *Chicago Tribune*, travelling considerably through the central, western, and northern parts of the state and down its eastern line, attending the session of the state convention, conversing with numbers of all classes of people, from rice-plantation Negroes to provisional governors.

Q. What was the principal object of your visit?—A. I went out as correspondent of the two papers named mainly to study the political situation—partly because I wanted to look into it on my own account, and partly because the proprietors of those papers were exceedingly anxious to lay before their readers information on that subject.

Q. Were the letters written by you on this occasion published?—A. They were mostly published in the *Advertiser* and *Tribune*. I wrote a few for one or two other papers, but these were the two to which I mainly contributed.

Q. Did you write over your own name?—A. I did not. I wrote to the *Advertiser* over the signature of "Dixon," by which name I am well known to the readers of that paper, and to the *Tribune* over the signature of "Israel," by which I am known to the readers of that paper, and, to some extent, in Illinois generally, having, during the last half dozen years, corresponded for two or three papers of that state over that signature.

Q. As the result of your observations, what is your opinion of the people of Georgia as to their loyalty or disloyalty to the government?—A. I think they are satisfied they cannot accomplish anything through war on the government, but I did not, at the time I was there, find a spirit of sympathy with the Union as such, or with the administration as representing the will and sovereignty of the Union. I found hostility manifested, not only in conversation with the people, but, it seemed to me, in the result of the elections held while I was in the state. The men who were elected to Congress were, without an exception, men who heartily sympathized with the course pursued by the state during the war. I do not now recollect that more than one or two of them were what were called original secessionists, but four of the seven had been in the rebel army. One of them, elected by a district generally spoken of as the most loyal in the state, with one exception, was the worst malcontent I found in the whole state convention. I allude to Colonel Matthews, who was elected from the Augusta district. He made a great many speeches in the convention, and each of them was, with, perhaps, one exception, more bitter in language and hostile in spirit, I think, than any single speech made by any other man in that body. It seemed to me that the result of the elections, quite as much as the conversation of the people, indicated, at that time, a very determined spirit of hostility toward, and a very significant lack of sympathy with, the Union. The gentleman elected from the district usually known as the Columbus district, Mr. Buchanan, is a man who served in the rebel army, and who announced himself in a card, which he published during the canvass, to the people of the district, as a radical secessionist. I learned that he entered the rebel army in April 1861, as a lieutenant, and passed subsequently through the intermediate grades to a lieutenant colonelcy. He was wounded in the battle of Pavilion Station, in June 1864, and did not recover from his wounds in time to go into active service again before the breaking up of the Confederacy. His card contained this paragraph:

> It may not be amiss or improper to state, for the information of those not acquainted with me, that at the commencement of the late war I volunteered my services, and, through the executive of the State of Georgia, entered into the army of the Confederate States, served in the army of Virginia, and did all in my power to sustain the cause of the South and secure the independence of the Confederate States. No law was ever passed by the congress of the Confederate States by which I could be required to take up arms during the whole struggle. I was exempt by the laws of the Confederate States. I refused to avail myself of the exemption, and continued in the service to the last. The cause failed, the Confederacy fell, and our expectations of a separate and distinct nationality passed away. I feel that I am not responsible for that failure in any way. As a citizen, a soldier, and a man, I did all I could to insure success.

Mr. Cook, from the Albany district, and Mr. Walford, from the Atlanta district, were both generals in the rebel army, though I understood that neither was an original secessionist. Mr. Cabonnis, from the Macon district, and Mr. Cohen, from the Savannah district, were both civil officers of the rebel government. The fact that a candidate had been in some way connected with the rebel service seemed to be his best indorsement in the eyes of the people.

Q. Were you present during the entire session of the convention? — A. I was.

Q. How were such views as those presented by Mr. Matthews received by the convention — favorably or otherwise? — A. Quite generally favorably. During the session of the convention — in fact, on the second day of its session, a resolution was moved for the appointment of a committee to memorialize the President in behalf of Jeff Davis and others. There was some debate upon it. The only man in the convention who objected to it was Joshua Hill. It was endorsed by two or three gentlemen quite strongly. Finally it came to Colonel Matthews to make a speech. He said — and I read now from proof-slips of a book which I am having published, *The South Since the War*, and the matter for which, in this regard, was written the very evening after the speech was made:

> Why should we not ask this favor? We have been pardoned by the national Executive, and by our pardon we become free and sovereign citizens, clothed with all the rights and privileges pertaining to Americans. Among the most sacred of these rights is that of petition, and we mean, in the passage and carrying out of this resolution, to exercise that sacred right. I understand that the President of the United States is inclined to mercy, that his policy is one of leniency, and I believe that the presentation of the petition proposed by this resolution will rather strengthen his hands than weaken and embarrass him. These men, as I have said, are no more representative men of the Confederacy, but they represent the cause for which we battled. We have been pardoned, and have resumed all our rights as citizens of the United States, and I declare that I will not be deterred from asking pardon for these unfortunate gentlemen now languishing in military prisons. (Hearty applause throughout the house.) Mr. Davis is no more a traitor than the rest of us. Nor need he, nor any of us, be ashamed of our records. We have illustrated Southern manhood on a hundred battlefields, and we have shown that we can honorably submit to the decrees of God. Now let us come up as men—not as criminals for a favor, but as men for our rights, and ask the pardon of our late and beloved leaders. (Further applause.)

On another occasion, while the question of repudiating the rebel war debt was under discussion, the proposition being to pass a resolution asking the provisional governor if the President had signified what the convention must or ought to do, Colonel Matthews made another speech, which was received with much favor. After saying that neither Congress nor the President had a right to interfere in the matter, he continued:

> We shall not be back in the Union till our representatives are admitted to their seats, and if Congress requires us to repudiate, it will be time then to act. Don't let us do more than is required of us. True, we have no rights but such as the conqueror chooses to give us, but I will not yield one inch more than military force requires me to yield. The convention is the representative of what is left of the sovereignty of Georgia; let us do what in us lies to assert that sovereignty. I shall never give my vote to add the damning disgrace of repudiation to the humiliation of subjugation. Let our members go to Congress and be refused before we even take it into consideration. I will never consent to do so sooner.

Colonel Matthews made several speeches, during the debate, on the ordinance repudiating the rebel war debt, from one of which I make a further brief quotation — the proposition at the time being to make the ordinance a part of the new constitution:

> I see no necessity for putting this thing into the constitution, for an ordinance of this body is just as much a part of the fundamental law as that document itself. I ask gentlemen to be satisfied with a simple repudiation. Let the damning instrument which records our everlasting shame and disgrace be kept as inconspicuous as possible; let it go into darkness among the musty archives of the state, so that our children need not be called upon to blush at its sight, so that future

generations must seek long to find it, and, haply, not discovering it, may cherish the hope that we were found to be not slaves, but men of honor, even in our hour of sorest distress! I do not wish to be represented here as charging the President with being a tyrant, but it is little less than tyranny to make this demand upon us. I will not crawl in the dust to lick the hand of power. We are not yet slaves; we are the same men we were four years ago; and I bid my associates stand as we stood when we flung the flag of rebellion to the breeze, as we stood through the long and bloody years in which we upheld that flag! (Hearty applause.)

Q. Did you form any opinion from your observations while in Georgia as to whether the people would prefer the reestablishment of the Confederacy, if that were possible, or to remain in the United States? — A. I concluded that they would have preferred the establishment of the Confederacy, had it been possible, and that they very generally regretted the failure of the effort to establish it.

Testimony of Alexander P. Ketchum

A New York officer who was a graduate of the Free Academy (later City College), Alexander P. Ketchum in 1862 became Civil Aide to General Rufus Saxton, one of the first officers to raise a regiment of Negro soldiers. Entering the army in 1864, Ketchum served with black troops and became a member of Saxton's staff at Port Royal, South Carolina. After the war, he joined the staff of General O. O. Howard, the Head of the Freedmen's Bureau, as Assistant Adjutant General at Charleston. His connection with efforts to uplift the freedmen makes his testimony especially significant.

Mr. Howard: How have you been treated socially by the secessionists? — A. I have had scarcely anything to do with them socially.

Q. Have you ever been invited to their houses? — A. Never but once, since I have been at Charleston; the invitation came from a party quite humble in place and position. Their social hostility to us I think is complete. At Savannah I boarded with pleasant people, secessionists; but through the city the same social distinction was observed. These distinctions are so marked in Southern cities that Northern people who board and lodge with, and so support Southern families, are sometimes denied a participation in the social receptions of these very families they support, although persons of refinement and good social position. The Southerners socially ostracize even those upon whom they are dependent. This practice is very general. I think there is a disposition to permit pleasant relations between themselves and our officers in some cases, but it is for personal reasons. A few days since a lady of Charleston spoke to one of our officers of the bitterness that exists between the North and the South, and said she hoped that bitterness would continue; she wished to see it continue to her dying day, and never wanted it obliterated or modified.

Q. Does it appear to be a dislike, a cultivated habitual dislike to the Northern people, because they are such, or what is the foundation of it? — A. Not because they are Northern people, but because they acknowledge in their hearts the superiority of the North, the superiority of Northern enterprise and the Northern mind; I believe this firmly. They think their power as a community is departing; that their immense estates are eventually to be divided up, and bought by Northern men and Negroes; that before the law, at least, the Negro will be equal with the white man. A theory which may seem strange is more or less current. There are thousands of mulattoes at the South whose fathers are white gentlemen of high standing in the community. I believe there is an intense and peculiar feeling of hate existing on the part of the whites towards colored persons of this class, the fear being that the latter will have an equal civil standing with the whites — will acquire riches, perhaps, and influence, and that the baseness and wickedness of slavery will then be made to appear before the world in a light which will be agonizing to the Southern people; the advent among them of Northerners who have caused the destruction of slavery, bringing poverty to the inhabitants and liberty to the Negro, with possible future advancement. These facts, combined with a dislike of the North, to which they have been educated, cause them to hate Northern men with a malignant hate.

Q. Will it not take a long time to allay this hatred? — A. The inner feeling, perhaps, will never be allayed, but the outward manifestation of it, I firmly believe, can be prevented by a rigid course upon the part of the government. I remarked to a gentleman of Charleston that I could tell what was going on at Washington by the bearing of the Southern people without seeing the newspapers. When a lenient policy prevailed, I observed in the people an autocratic reserve, and an exacting manner towards United States officers. If the other policy, which obtains more generally in Congress, was in the ascendant, their bearing was totally different; a gentle spirit was manifest, they would be well behaved, submissive, and resigned. He greeted the remark with a smile, and although a Southern man himself, and a Charlestonian, did not deny the truth of what I said.

6 TESTIMONY OF SOUTHERN UNIONISTS

Testimony of Josiah Millard

Born in Massachusetts, Josiah Millard had resided in Virginia before the war. When the conflict began, he was taken prisoner by the Confederates, and after its close, he was appointed assessor of internal revenue for the third district of Virginia, which comprised the northern part of the state. His testimony shows him to have been a radical.

Mr. Howard: What is your occupation? — A. I am now assessor of internal revenue for the third district of Virginia.

Q. What counties does your district include? — A. Alexandria, Fairfax, Prince William, Loudon, Clark, Shenandoah, Frederick, Warren, and other counties.

Q. You must be quite well acquainted with the state of public feeling in your collection district? — A. Tolerably well.

Q. Is it loyal or friendly to the government of the United States? — A. No, sir, except a very small proportion compared with the population.

Q. About what proportion? — A. The original Union men, who were favorable to the government from the commencement, are about one out of twenty — perhaps hardly that.

Q. Were you residing in Alexandria during the war? — A. No, sir; I was residing in Loudon County. I was taken prisoner by the rebels on the 28th of May, 1861. I was the first prisoner taken in Virginia.

Q. What effect had the Emancipation Proclamation upon the rebels? — A. They did not think it had any effect at all. They did not think it would ever be executed.

Q. Did they look upon it as a pleasant proceeding on the part of Mr. Lincoln? — A. They looked upon it as something that could not be maintained.

Q. As if it was the "Pope's bull against the comet"? — A. Yes, sir.

Q. How did they like the fact that their slaves were all emancipated? — A. They did not like it at all. They protested against it to the very last, and some of them in the country now are trying their very best to make the colored men believe that they are still theirs; that they are not free.

Q. Have you ever occupied any other public station than you now hold? — A. No, not in Virginia.

Q. How do the rebel people feel in regard to the preservation of the government of the United States? Are they willing to pay the taxes necessary to preserve it and carry it on? — A. It is with great reluctance that they pay their taxes.

Q. Suppose they had it in their power, would they abolish all taxes to pay the national debt? — A. Yes, sir, unanimously so. I do not think there would be one dissenting voice among them. I have heard it repeatedly.

Q. Would they consent to contribute their proper share to the payment of the rebel debt if they had the opportunity? — A. I think they would. They simply claim that they are loyal now from necessity.

Q. Suppose that necessity was taken off? — A. To illustrate what I believe to be the general feeling among the rebels, I will state a conversation I had with one of the leading ones the other day. He said to me, "Sir, I entered into this thing in good faith. I honestly believed it to be right. I now propose to be a loyal man, to accept the laws of the United States, and to carry out all proclamations and requirements of the President of the United States in good faith." I said, "Suppose we examine the record and see. There is one thing you have not done; you did not open your church on Thanksgiving day." He seemed to be very much agitated when I spoke about that, and said, "Why, sir, do you think I could get upon my knees and ask God to forgive me for something which I believed to be right?" Said I, "That is the point. You are as big a rebel today as you ever were. You are simply loyal because the strong arm of the government makes you so." And that is the general feeling with all the leading men I have conversed with, and I have conversed with a great many.

Q. Has there been great destruction of property in your district during the war? — A. Yes, sir, very great.

Q. What kind of property has suffered principally? — A. Agricultural property, livestock, and mill property.

Q. Have you ever heard anything said by leading men in your neighborhood about a foreign war with the United States? — A. Not directly. I have heard it intimated that if such a thing should come up, and if there was a possible chance of their gaining their independence, they would join any power to accomplish that object.

Q. Have you heard that intimated very frequently in conversation? — A. Not very frequently. They do not intimate it unless you get them rather excited and warmed up in conversation. They do not like to be heard saying that, particularly persons who have taken the oath, because they think there might be some advantage taken of it.

Q. Could a jury be called in your collection district which would convict a rebel of treason for making war against the government of the United States? — A. No, sir, it could not, nor could there be one selected in the ordinary way to give a Union man any justice.

Q. What is that owing to? — A. To their violent prejudices against Union men.

Q. Would they treat men from the free states in the same way in your courts? — A. Yes, sir; I think they would.

Testimony of John B. Baldwin

*John B. Baldwin was a Virginia Whig who had long been active in the political life of the Old Dominion. A decided opponent of secession, he was elected as a Unionist to the 1861 Virginia convention called to decide the state's fate, and shortly before the firing upon Fort Sumter had an interview with Abraham Lincoln. According to John Minor Botts (**see below, page 111**), the President offered Baldwin the evacuation of Fort Sumter in return for the adjournment of the state convention* sine die. *In his testimony before the committee, however, Baldwin denied the story; he had evidently misunderstood the President. Typical of the conditional Unionists of his state, after the war he became a member of the new House of Delegates and remained active in public life as a conservative.*

Mr. Howard: What is the state of feeling on the part of the secessionists of Virginia towards the government of the United States? — A. Well, sir, I believe the feeling that it is and is to be our government is universal. If there is any feeling of dissatisfaction (and there is a feeling of dissatisfaction in reference to the delay and the refusal of representation), it is more like the feeling which a political party out of power has toward the political party in power, in a government recognized by both and intended to be recognized by both, than anything else. It has no kinship whatever with the idea of resisting or overthrowing the government.

Q. You have no ground to suspect any combination as still existing in Virginia, having in view the overthrow of the government? — A. Not only have I no ground to suspect it, but I think I can say I know it is not so, because I have been in intercourse with the most bitter, determined, obstinate, and violent of all the men in Virginia who were concerned in the whole affair, and I not only do not know of such a thing, and do not suspect it, but anybody who would tell me that he did know it I would suspect of being a liar.

Q. You understand the contemplated amendment of the Constitution relating to the basis of representation now pending in the United States Senate? — A. Yes, sir; I think I do.

Q. If that amendment should be ratified, and become a part of the Constitution of the United States, would the people of Virginia, in your apprehension, ever be willing to grant the blacks the right of voting? — A. Of course no man can tell what would be the wearing effect of generation, or agitation of a subject of that sort; but I think it is clear as any proposition in the world, that if you place the people of Virginia in the attitude that they are to be diminished in consideration and in influence, and in their due power in the government, because of their unwillingness to place the Negro on the ground of political equality, it will plant a root of bitterness such as has not been known even in the bitterness of the war. That is my judgment and belief. It would lead to political combinations of every sort. We would have advocates of suffrage of women, of minors, and foreigners, and Negroes, in every shade of combination and confusion. I would regard it as being the entering wedge of more mischief, more trouble, more ill will, more dissatisfaction and disloyalty to the government of the United States, than all other causes that have ever combined together.

Q. So that you are fully of opinion that, instead of being a measure of peace, conciliation, and tranquillity, it would be a renewal of the agitation in another form still more bitter than that which existed before the war? — A. So thorough is my conviction on that subject that, while I believe I have local attachment and state attachment as strong as any man living, the moment that amendment was adopted I should feel bound, as a matter of ordinary self-protection, to quit Virginia, to avoid every Southern state as I would a pest house, and to seek to make my living somewhere else.

Testimony of Bedford Brown *

Mr. Howard: How extensive is your acquaintance with the state of public feeling among the people of North Carolina in reference to the war, its causes, and its results? — A. It is pretty general. I was a member of the state senate when the subject was first brought under consideration in 1860.

Q. Have you taken any personal part in the war against the United States? — A. None, voluntarily. I was a member of the state senate for some years. After the war commenced I declined being a candidate; I

* See above, page 34.

desired to take no part in it; but my constituents insisted on my going back, although I positively declined. I was a member of the convention of 1861 which passed the ordinance of secession, but was sent there contrary to my will. I was a candidate in my county in the election ordered after South Carolina had seceded. I took most decided ground against secession and carried my county. I carried my county by a vote of three to one and was elected a member of the convention, but the people of the state decided, by a majority, that there should be no convention. When the second convention was ordered I declined being a candidate; I wished to have no part in it; but my constituents again sent me against my will.

Q. You have then been all along a non-secessionist in principle? — A. Always. There has not been an hour in my life that I did not regard it as the greatest political calamity that could befall the people of any country.

Q. How do the masses of the people of North Carolina now feel in regard to the government of the United States — friendly, unfriendly, or indifferent? — A. There was a most overwhelming majority of the people of North Carolina loyal to the United States government before secession took place. I would say that from two-thirds to three-fourths of the people of North Carolina were utterly opposed to secession.

Q. Can you give the result of the first vote upon that subject? — A. I think there were sixty-odd thousand cast for Union delegates in the respective counties for the first convention, and perhaps thirty thousand for secession delegates.

Q. Can you give the vote on the second occasion? — A. I know of no direct popular vote on the subject after the first; but the election of Governor Vance indicated that there was still a Union majority in the state even after the war commenced. He was run as a Union candidate, and was elected by a decided majority over his secession opponent.

Q. In what year was that? — A. I think in 1862 or 1863; probably in 1862. I think he was elected by between thirty and forty thousand majority. It is due to truth to say that Governor Vance afterwards became a war man, but he was voted for at the first election as one who was in favor of pacification and Union.

Q. Was he, when first voted for, understood to be a Union man; that is, a man supporting the government of the United States and opposed to secession and rebellion? — A. He was originally very much opposed to secession, though he went into the army as most men did, under the peculiar circumstances. When he was first voted for as governor it was supposed his proclivities were still for the Union, running as he did against and beating a secession opponent by thirty-odd thousand majority.

Q. Can you state any reasons why Governor Vance afterwards became a supporter of the rebellion against the United States? — A. If I did it would be mere conjecture, and perhaps it would not be proper to indulge in that. I have every confidence that Governor Vance accepts in good faith the situation and will prove a loyal citizen to the government of the United States.

Q. I ask you again to state how the mass of the people of North Carolina feel towards the government of the United States? — A. The masses of the people, I believe, at the time of General Lee's surrender, were more gratified than otherwise because they saw that the result was inevitable, and a great many of them were for peace and attached sincerely to the federal Union, and believed there was no safety out of the Union. They were gratified that the thing had been settled. They wanted it settled in some way, for they had been exceedingly harassed during the war, which was commenced against their consent in the first instance. Of late, however, it is due to truth to state that, from various circumstances, they have come almost to despair. Perhaps it is in part from the loss of their slave property, though I think they were prepared to acquiesce in that. I think it is chiefly from their long delay in being admitted to an equal participation in the Union. It has produced a feeling of discontent even among Union men. My belief is that if they could be perfectly sure that with these constitutional amendments which have been adopted, accepting the condition of things as they are now, within a reasonable time they would be admitted to political equality and to equal privileges with the other states, there would be a general feeling favorable to the federal Union. The great mass of them are exceedingly anxious to have their relations between the state and the federal government restored.

Q. Is there not a large proportion of these people who dislike and contemn the government of the United States? — A. There are a certain number of reckless unscrupulous men there, as everywhere in the country, who, I believe, would be willing for anything almost. For instance, some few persons would perhaps be gratified by a foreign war, but the great mass of the people of North Carolina, even including the secessionists, although they have been utterly opposed to me, and I opposed to them, yet I think a majority of the secessionists are exceedingly anxious for peace and quiet, perfectly willing to live under the laws of the United States, provided they can have political equality with the other states accorded to them. I think an overwhelming majority of the mass of the people of the State of North Carolina are perfectly willing to acquiesce in the laws of the United States on these conditions. I will go further and say, that I think the longer it is procrastinated the worse that feeling of discontent will become. I may remark that I have heard many persons say that if there was any attempt at an outbreak against the government of the United States, they would not do as they did at first — allow them to get complete military control — but would seize the opportunity to vindicate themselves against these men immediately.

Q. In case of a foreign war with any powerful European nation, such as Great Britain or France, and in case the war should take on such an attitude as apparently to present a fair chance for success in another attempt at secession and the establishment of Southern independence, would there not be in North Carolina a pretty large number of men who would engage in such a movement if they had the opportunity? — A. There might be some portion of the people; but if a reasonable expectation was indulged that they could be admitted to equal political rights, I believe there would be an overwhelming majority to suppress such an attempt. There is no question about it. I will further express the opinion that the better way to remove this discontent among the people, would be to declare these states members of the federal Union — for Congress, of course, to judge of the members presenting themselves separately. If a disloyal man should present himself, claiming a seat as a member, he should be excluded, but I would admit such as came here properly qualified.

Q. Would you recommend the admission, for instance, of a representative, the great majority of whose constituents were actually disloyalists against the government? — A. I would if Congress should be convinced that he was loyal. I would have it depend very much upon the member himself.

Q. Should it not depend rather upon the character of the constituency he represents? — A. It would be very difficult to ascertain the loyalty or disloyalty of a body of men in that way.

Q. Suppose that fact was ascertained upon proof, would you recommend the admission of a member from a disloyal district? — A. If the district was manifestly disloyal beyond all question, it would be a justification perhaps for the exclusion of its members.

Q. Is there any considerable portion of the intelligent citizens of North Carolina who entertain the idea that there is a purpose to exclude the state permanently from the Union? — A. The people there have become somewhat in a state of despair. To speak with candor, a vast number of them despair of ever enjoying the equality in the federal government they once did. I do not speak in reference to slavery, because every sensible man regards that as irrevocably gone, and a vast number of those who have been slaveholders express the wish that it may never be restored again.

Testimony of William J. Dews

William J. Dews was a music teacher in Staunton, Virginia. A firm Unionist throughout the war, in 1864 he escaped from Richmond by making his way across the mountains into West Virginia, then held by federal forces. After the war, he took up residence in the Valley of Virginia.

Mr. Howard: How do the ex-rebels treat Union men? — A. As a general thing, they look upon them with contempt.

Q. Do they exhibit in their intercourse bitterness and hostility towards the Union men? — A. They do.

Q. Are you aware of any scenes of violence recently growing out of feelings of Unionism and rebelism? — A. I am; of attempted violence and of direct violence.

Q. Narrate such circumstances as occur to you as illustrations of the state of feeling. — A. A gentleman named Davis, a returned refugee and well-known Union man, was insulted on the cars about three weeks ago, near the village of Mount Sydney, and a fight got up. Two Union men were attacked at Mount Sydney (quite a strong Union place too) on the day of an election for magistrates, and an attempt was made to put them out of the hotel. They had been both in the Federal army and had been discharged. But they drew their revolvers and held their assailants at bay. Some government officers who were passing at the time (the assistant superintendent of the Freedmen's Bureau among them) were insulted. Some of them were for stopping and settling it then, but better counsels prevailed. Several other cases have been reported to me, but the names have escaped my memory. I have not heard a complaint against a Union man for having attempted reviling against secessionists, or anything of that sort.

Q. How is it in regard to social intercourse between ex-rebels and Unionists? — A. There is not much. There is some. Where ex-rebels regard a Union man as having simply exercised his judgment and acted conscientiously, they look at the matter fairly.

Q. State whether the ex-rebels in your vicinity outnumber the Unionists? — A. Yes, sir; probably eight or ten to one in the county.

Q. The Unionists are in a very small minority? — A. Yes, sir.

Q. Can Unionists be elected to any office in that county? — A. Oh no, sir; on the occasion when the difficulty occured at Mount Sydney the magistrates who were elected were, as I was informed, ex-rebels.

Q. How are Northern men treated in that vicinity by ex-rebels? — A. They are regarded pretty much in the same light as Union men of the county; perhaps the latter are thought even less of.

Q. Are Northern men welcome as settlers down there, when they go to transact business or to purchase property? — A. They are, to a certain extent, as a matter of business.

Q. What chance does a Unionist stand to get justice in the state courts? — A. I should not suppose, with perhaps a few exceptions, that he would have any chance; that is the impression of all the Union men. Union men are preparing a petition to Congress to have all their lawsuits, of every description, referred to a military court or some other tribunal, because they are convinced that they cannot have justice done them on account of the prejudice against them; probably two hundred and fifty persons in the county have already signed the petition.

Q. Is that feeling very extensive among the Union people there? — A. Yes, sir; it is universal. I learn that there are only two Union men in the county who refuse to sign the petition, and they decline from a fear of being interfered with. . . .

Q. How do they feel toward the freedmen? — A. Very bitter; but, to use their own terms, they regard the Union man about as they do the nigger. Since I went back to Staunton I have been invited to act as a commissioner in the bureau of refugees, in my leisure time. Some five days since, Mr. Tukey, assistant superintendent, was absent in Richmond on business, and the business of the office was left in my charge. I had some difficulty with a magistrate there, an ex-rebel, who interfered with me; I threatened him with the military if he did not desist; he refused to desist, and I went to the mayor and requested him to do what I wanted, and he instantly did so; it was to take a man out of jail who had been put in without a hearing; there was nothing at all against the man, and he was simply held in a small amount to keep the peace; the same corporation council appeared there, and argued that they should arrest me for interfering; the town sergeant, who is a loyal man, spoke up and said that I had done nothing in the world but my duty; the corporation attorney suggested that I should be arrested first and examined afterwards; the magistrate, after hearing the town sergeant, said there was nothing against me; the attorney seemed very much chopfallen, and used some insolent language towards me, which stirred up my anger; he offered to make a test case of it in some other manner, and I told him just walk out of the office and make a test case of it in any way he chose, which settled the matter.

Q. Whereupon he did not walk out? — A. He did not. Another man, named Bunch, a well-known rebel, also appealed to the crowd to excite it against me; I was alone, but armed; some few Union men gathered around, and some loyal blacks also; I told them to be quiet, and under no circumstances to disturb the peace. The affair produced so much excitement that I dropped a line to the commander of the troops at Charlottesville, asking him whether, if it became necessary, he would be prepared to start some troops up to Staunton by the train. He immediately answered that he was prepared.

Part Three

EFFECTS OF JOHNSON'S PLAN OF RECONSTRUCTION

7 TESTIMONY OF SOUTHERN GOVERNORS

Testimony of James Johnson

James Johnson, one of the provisional governors appointed in 1865 by Andrew Johnson, had been a well-known Georgia Unionist before the war. After graduating from Georgia State University as a classmate of Alexander H. Stephens, he became a lawyer and practiced his profession in Columbus. In 1851 he was elected to Congress on the Union ticket but lost two years later to A. H. Colquitt. After opposing secession, he remained inactive during the war. From June to December 1865, he served his state conscientiously as Provisional Governor. Afterward, he became Collector of Customs of Savannah and Judge of the Superior Court of Georgia. In 1872, he ran as an elector on the Grant ticket, but was generally considered a moderate.

Mr. Boutwell: The object of the committee is to ascertain the condition of Georgia, and the sentiments of the people with reference to this government; how far they are loyal, and how far they are disloyal; and we would be glad to have you give your opinions upon that subject, and any facts you may have. — A. The condition of public affairs in Georgia, in my estimation, is improving now, and has been improving for some time past. Our people are becoming better and better satisfied, with the lapse of time, and their passions are gradually abating. As an evidence of this fact, I could point to the legislation of the state on particular subjects; the provisions which are being made by law for the protection of freedmen, and securing them in their rights. While I say that our people are gradually improving, it is due to truth that I should say there are individual exceptions. We have some bad men among us, whose passions have not yet abated; but there are not a great many of them.

Immediately after emancipation went into actual effect there was some hostility manifested towards the Negroes, by some classes of persons. But that hostility is abating, particularly on the part of those who formerly owned slaves. I would qualify this general remark, by saying that, whilst it is true of the most, there are individual exceptions; there are individual cases of outrage and wrong perpetrated upon the freedmen. But such acts do not meet the approval of the great mass of our people. This being true, that there are violent men, evil-disposed men, as a matter of course they easily associate themselves together; and a few men can do a great deal of harm and make a great deal of noise. For this reason, in my judgment a few troops of the United States should still be kept in Georgia for the present, for the purpose of keeping in restraint these evil-disposed men to whom I have referred. These troops are further necessary to aid and assist the Freedmen's Bureau, whilst it remains, in my judgment. And, in my opinion, it is proper, at present, that that bureau, or something akin to it, should be continued in the state for a time. In my judgment, when the district and circuit courts of the United States are properly organized in the state, and when our own legislature shall have perfected their system of laws in reference to Negroes, then the bill which has already passed one branch of Congress, which proposes to declare and secure the civil rights of persons, if passed by the other branch, will dispense with the necessity of the presence of the Freedmen's Bureau, or of the troops of the United States. But until that is done, I think it is proper that both should be continued.

I think, and I have so stated to General Grant and the Secretary of War, that, judging from the feelings of our people and the relations which they have sustained to the freedmen, it would be good policy to withdraw the black troops from among them. Their presence is irritating and tends to bring about collisions. Our people having made the experiment which they did, the trial of arms, and having been overcome, whatever they might feel under other circumstances, or desire in a different condition of affairs, a majority of them are now willing to submit to the Constitution of the United States, and desire that peace should be restored throughout the country. While they are thus anxious on that subject, and willing to obey the laws, still, as is very natural, in all their political arrangements for office, etc., they prefer men who have cooperated with them in the prosecution of the war to those who were opposed to them. My own judgment is that the people are progressing towards a state of peace and harmony and reconciliation as rapidly as could be expected after such a conflict of passions and of arms, and I have no doubt that peace will be fully restored before any great length of time; but animosities have been generated and passions have been inflamed to such an extent that in certain localities we shall still see manifestations of them for some time to come. I think that is about a fair statement of the general condition of affairs in Georgia.

Q. Do you know the persons who are claiming seats in Congress in Georgia? If so, will you state, if you have no objection, what you know of their course during the rebellion, and their conduct with reference to this government since Lee's surrender? — A. I know both of the gentlemen elected to the United States Senate, and have known them for many years. Mr. Stephens and myself were classmates and graduated together. I think I am pretty well acquainted with the course that each of them pursued. It is known generally to the country that Mr. Stephens was opposed to secession; but after the ordinance of secession was passed, under the pressure of circumstances, I suppose, and I believe because he thought it would bring about a conflict at home if he did not do so, he fell in with the current after the commencement of hostilities. Mr. Johnson, his colleague in the United States Senate, was also opposed to secession. He was a Douglas man, as was Mr. Stephens, but, like him, he fell in with the current to a certain extent after the commencement of hostilities. Mr. Johnson accepted the place of Confederate States senator under the Confederate government, being elected while the war was in progress. But notwithstanding that, I have reason to believe that for some time before the termination of the Confederacy, he insisted that negotiations should be had, so that an end might be put to the strife; but his representations were unheeded. I am certain of that, from such information as I have received. I think that this is his present status: that while he may object to certain Congressional and administrative measures, he would submit to them, and is well affected towards the government. He must be satisfied, as a man of judgment, that an effort to separate this Union will not succeed; that our destinies are to be those of one nation. He was the president of the state convention that recently assembled and adopted a new state constitution. He cooperated in the line of policy suggested by the administration for the purpose of restoring the state. Mr. Stephens was the Vice-President of the Confederate States, and he acted some time in that capacity, and I believe he continued to hold the office until the downfall of the Confederacy. But while that is true of him, I think he became satisfied during the war that the effort to establish the Confederacy would be a failure, and he would gladly have terminated the strife long before it was terminated, and in a different manner in which it was terminated. He has been using his efforts to get our people to lay aside their prejudices and passions and accept the results of the war, and I have no doubt he will do everything in his power to restore harmony throughout the whole length and breadth of the land. In fact, I feel sure that he is extremely anxious that such a state of things should be brought about at as early a day as possible. He has been an open advocate of giving the freedmen their civil rights and maintaining them in those rights, and I have no doubt he will continue to advocate those measures. I cannot answer so positively about the members-elect to the House of Representatives. I can answer about some of them. Mr. Wofford was a brigadier general in the Confederate service. He was a Union man before the war, and a Union man during the war, and is a Union man still; but the current of public feeling was so strong that he went into the war. I suppose he would have been conscripted if he had not done so. In my judgment, he is as well affected towards this government as any man, North or South. He is a well-behaved man, not at all violent. General Philip Cook was another confederate general who was elected to the House of Representatives. He was opposed to the war, and was termed a cooperationist. He was violently opposed to the war. After the war was commenced, he likewise fell in with the current and cast his lot with the war. During the progress of the war he was severely wounded several times, and was finally captured. He stated his position and feelings to the federal officers who had charge of him, and I believe they made representations to the proper department here, asking for his pardon, and he was released. He came to visit me at Milledgeville after his release, and told me that he was willing to cooperate with me to carry out the wishes of the administration as far as he could do so. I think he is a proper man, notwithstanding he has committed errors. He is a man of good feelings and of liberal sentiments. Mr. Christy was a cooperationist. I cannot speak positively about him; I can only speak of him from reputation. I think he is well disposed towards the government now. I do not know what part he took after the commencement of hostilities. Mr. Buchanan was in favor of secession. He says that he accepts the results of the war and submits to them. I will not say further in regard to him, because I do not know. As to Mr. Cohen, of Savannah, my impressions about him are these: he is rather refractory, or was the last time I heard him talk, refractory in spirit. There is another member elected to the House of Representatives; I do not recollect his name at this time. I cannot tell his present status, but he was opposed to the war at its commencement.

Testimony of William L. Sharkey *

Mr. Boutwell: The object of the committee is to ascertain the condition of civil affairs in Mississippi, and also the sentiments of the people with reference to the government of the United States; how far they are loyal and how far they are disloyal. We shall be glad to hear your views generally upon that subject, and any facts within your knowledge that may bear upon it. — A. I will state, in general terms, that when I went out there as provisional governor a very large majority of the people, I do not know but fifty to one, were perfectly reconciled to the condition of things, and very anxious to be restored to their former position in the Union. I think they were sincerely and honestly so; that was the current sentiment beyond all doubt at that time. Even the secession party admitted that they had made a miserable failure; many of them felt very sore over it, to think that they had involved the country in terrible calamities, and they were as anxious to get back into the Union as any portion of the community. I was provisional governor there, and I think

* See above, page 27.

I had an opportunity of knowing. Of course there will be exceptional cases in all communities, but those exceptions were confined mostly to men who had taken no part in the war. The military men were perfectly satisfied, and I do not know but as a general rule they were the most loyal part of the community. They gave up honorably, and all said they were disposed to accept things as they found them. But there were a few men within my own knowledge, men who had done but little during the war, who were dissatisfied. But a very large majority of our people were as loyal, to use the term in its proper sense, as any people in the United States. That is to say, they were willing to obey the government and its laws and to support and to sustain it; and I think they are so yet. I should make this remark, however: the people came up freely and voluntarily, and did, as they supposed, all that was required of them; they met all the demands of the President, and with great cheerfulness. What changes may have occurred since I left there I cannot tell, but I do not think any material changes have taken place. Still, you know, when men do all that is required of them, and all that they think is right, pressure does not in any degree contribute to their loyalty. And I have been very much afraid that the condition of things here would shake their confidence in the government. I know, however, their condition was a good one when I was in charge of the government there. The condition of things in Mississippi was not generally understood throughout this country. In the first place, a very large portion of our people were opposed to secession, and I believe if the question had been submitted to the people they never would have adopted it. But the politicians got us in hand and forced us out of the Union; and, as a general rule, those who were opposed to going out in the first place were in favor of coming back again; and to them is to be added the number who became satisfied of the folly of their course; and the two classes constitute a very large proportion of the citizens. . . .

Q. If you have no objection, please state what you know in regard to the persons now here claiming seats in Congress from Mississippi. — A. I have no objection to stating what I know. Mr. Alcorn, my colleague in the United States Senate, was an old Whig, and was very much opposed to rebellion and secession, and to the party that brought it about. The representatives-elect to the House of Representatives, without exception, were opposed to secession; they all belonged to the anti-secession party. Our people were particularly admonished by me that they ought not to send men here who were tinctured or stained with secession. And not one of our delegation, I think, had any connection with secession; they were all opposed to it. They were all Whigs except one, who was a Union Democrat. The Whig party, as a general thing, were clear of the odium of secession.

I will state this, however: several of these gentlemen engaged in the rebellion after it came on. Colonel Reynolds and Colonel Pierson had command of regiments in the Confederate service. When the state went out, I suppose they felt they should go with their state. I do not remember that any other of them was in the rebellion. Mr. Alcorn, my colleague, was in the militia; but I do not know that he ever held a commission in the Confederate service.

Q. What are the facts in regard to Governor Humphreys, and the present state government generally? Is it composed of men who were opposed to secession, or of men who favored it? — A. In regard to Governor Humphreys, there was no man in the State of Mississippi more opposed to secession than he was; and I will tell you more: he did not believe the Confederates could establish a government, even if they were free and independent. He told me that himself some months before the rebellion closed. I know his antecedents well; there was no man more opposed to secession than Governor Humphreys was. He ultimately got into the rebellion by accident, you might say; he went out with a company as its captain, and was promoted to be a general. Being a very popular man in the army, he was elected governor by the military vote, contrary to my wish. He is a good man, an excellent man, and I believe he ardently desires to see harmony restored between the North and the South. The state government, with one exception, I regret to say, is in the hands of the conservative men. The judiciary department has fallen into bad hands; but that was accidental, somewhat. The judges of the high court of errors were all secessionists. There was but a weak opposition to them, or they would not have been elected; they would have been beaten. We really had no material of respectability to run against them, and they ran in almost without opposition. The attorney general is in the same category. Three judges and the attorney general were secessionists. As to the minor officers, I do not know so much about them. But the election of these judges to the highest tribunal in the state was a very sore thing to many of us. But I will say this of them: they have given manifestations of an ardent desire to return to the Union, and to act in good faith. They admit their error frankly and freely; one or two of them have been pardoned by the President, and I think they are as loyal as any one now.

The fact is, there is very little disloyal sentiment in our country now. It is a mistake to suppose that our people are disloyal. Many of our people may be a little restless; but they do not think of such a thing as a rebellion.

Testimony of William Marvin

William Marvin was a jurist born in Herkimer County in upstate New York. Appointed District Attorney for the Southern District of Florida during Andrew Jackson's administration, he settled in Key West. Elevated to the bench by Martin Van Buren and again by James K. Polk, he served until 1863, when ill health forced him to resign. He remained loyal throughout the war — Key West always remained within Union lines — and at the conclusion of the conflict, was appointed Provisional Governor of Florida by Andrew Johnson. The new legislature sent him to Washington as a Democratic Senator, but, like other Southern members-elect, he was unable to take his seat.

Mr. Williams: Subsequent to the ordinance of secession in the State of Florida, did you discharge your duties as United States judge in that state? — A. I did. Key West is an island at the extreme southern point of the state, distant from the mainland some seventy or eighty miles; is among a cluster of islands, and, fortunately for me, there was a military support there of, I believe, one company of troops, and a naval force there to enable the government to retain possession of the island. I remained and discharged my duties until my health broke down.

Q. When you were appointed Provisional Governor of that state, what sort of a government, if any, was there in the State of Florida? — A. When I was appointed Provisional Governor of the state, the actual government was purely military. Martial law prevailed throughout the state. The civil authorities were not recognized as having any existence by the military, and I did not recognize them as having any existence for some months afterwards.

Q. Were there any persons holding office, or attempting to discharge the duties of any civil office, under the Confederate authorities in that state? — A. Not at that time. Of course there were men claiming to be in office, but they were not in the discharge of any of the functions of their offices.

Q. Can you state how long it was, after the Confederate authorities had ceased to exercise their functions in that state, to the time you became Provisional Governor? In other words, how long was the state under, exclusively, military rule? — A. I cannot state positively. I believe the State of Florida was occupied by the military forces in the first days of May; and from the time of their occupation, the civil authorities were considered as in abeyance, and overthrown.

Q. State what your first steps were, after your appointment as Provisional Governor, towards the reorganization of that state under the federal government. — A. I have not the documents here with me, or I might shorten the answer. Perhaps the first step I took towards the reorganization of a state government in Florida was to issue an address, published in all the newspapers, in which was portrayed a plan whereby the people would be enabled to meet in convention for the purpose of amending or altering their constitution and reestablish a new government.

This address was generally circulated. As soon as I got time to mature a plan whereby the people of the state could meet at the different precincts in their several counties and hold an election, I issued a proclamation appointing an election to be held in the several precincts of the different counties of the state for delegates to a convention. This proclamation recognized all persons as entitled to vote for delegates to this convention who were entitled under the constitution of the state established and existing prior to the passage of the ordinance of secession, and who should also have taken the amnesty oath at the time of voting. It was arranged by the government itself that this amnesty oath might be taken before any military officer, or any civil officer who was loyal to the government. The larger number of amnesty oaths in that state were taken before the mustering officers of the army. In some of the counties there was an inability to supply these officers, so as to enable the people to take the oaths. In a few weeks before the election I authorized the judges of election to administer these oaths at the polls. They were to allow no person to vote who did not present a certificate that he had taken the oath previously, or who did not take it at the time of voting at the polls. The oaths taken at the polls were forwarded to me with the election returns, and oaths taken before military officers were also reported to me by such military officers. The number of oaths taken exceeded seven thousand. I do not remember the precise number. The number of votes at the election for delegates in the whole state was six thousand seven hundred and odd, which is more than half of all the votes of the state given at elections when party contests were rife. I think that considerably more than half the people voted at this election. There was an election held in every county in the state. Every county in the state but two were fully represented in the convention. One county was unrepresented in consequence of the delegates having been lost at sea; and, for the other, delegates could not get there. So far as I was able to judge, I think the election itself was as full and fair an election, and as full and fair an expression of the wishes of the people as could possibly be had.

Q. State, if you please, whether or not at that election there were tickets in the field opposed to each other — one designated as the Union ticket, and the other as the opposition ticket — in any or many of the places of that state. — A. I do not think it could properly be said that there were any tickets run in any of the counties, as far as I am informed, which could be called in opposition to the reconstruction of the Union. There were in some of the counties candidates running who claimed to be old Union men, and claim to be at present the *Simon Pure* Union men all through, who were opposed by men who went into the war and were in the Confederate army. That was the case, I think, in three counties. I am not aware that it was any more than that.

Q. Who were elected in these counties? — A. In one of them the Union candidates, or men who were the old Union men (for all claimed to be

Union men at this time), were elected, and beat the secesh. In the other two, I think, according to my recollection, the secesh were elected. There were, so far as I understood, individual persons opposed to it, but there was nothing like an organization at all to defeat the plan of reconstruction; that was acceptable to almost everybody.

Q. State what, in your judgment, was the proportion of delegates elected to that convention who belonged to the Confederate army during the rebellion. — A. If I had a list of the delegates before me I could state with considerable accuracy. I can now only give an approximate answer. According to my present recollection I should say about a fourth, perhaps half, certainly fully a quarter of them; and, on further consideration, I would give one-half as an approximate estimate.

Q. State what the position of the other half was during the rebellion. — A. I should say one-quarter, or nearly a quarter, claimed to have been Union men all the time, and to have avoided being dragged into the rebel service, or any participation in the movement. The other quarter I should say rather sympathized with the secession movement; that would be my judgment of their position.

8 TESTIMONY OF SOUTHERN UNIONISTS

Testimony of James W. Hunnicutt

The Reverend James W. Hunnicutt was one of the most radical Southerners of the Reconstruction Era. A Baptist minister from South Carolina, before the war he edited a newspaper in Fredericksburg, Virginia. He voted for secession, presented a plan for the capture of federally held Fort Monroe, but eventually changed sides and in 1865 moved to Richmond to publish a newspaper catering to the freedmen. Well known for his radical ideas of racial equality, he was hated by the conservative element.

Mr. Howard: What is the effect of President Johnson's policy of reconstruction there? — A. . . . They are all in favor of President Johnson's policy of reconstruction. As soon as they get their ends served by him they would not touch him, but he is their man now. They say that in 1868 the South will be a unit, and that with the help of the copperhead party of the North they will elect a President. They do not care to have slavery back, but they will try and make the federal government pay them for their slaves. A man from Virginia told me today that they would be paid for their Negroes. This gentleman lost forty Negroes. This is their idea; they do not want slavery back, but they want to be paid for their slaves. They say that unless you accept their debt they will repudiate yours. They say they are not interested in this government.

Q. They would be glad to have Uncle Sam assume the payment of the Confederate debt? — A. Yes, sir, and to pay them for their Negroes and to indemnify them for their loss of property in the war. It is an impression of most of them, men, women, and children, that they are going to be paid for every rail burned, for every stick of timber destroyed, and for every Negro lost. One man told me in my house that as soon as they could get the reins of government in their hands they would undo everything that this administration has done, with an awful adjective prefixed to the word "administration." He said, "We have as much right to undo what the administration has done as they have to destroy the government of the Constitution" — as they claim the administration has done.

Q. They propose to get back into the Union for the purpose of restoring the Constitution? — A. Yes, sir; and the testimony of the Negroes will not be worth a snap of your finger, and all this is done for policy. A Negro can come and give his testimony, and it passes for what it is worth with the courts. They can do what they please with it; there are the judges, the lawyers, and the jury against the Negro, and perhaps every one of them is sniggering and laughing while the Negro is giving his testimony.

Q. Has not the liberal policy of President Johnson in granting pardons and amnesties rather tended to soothe and allay their feelings towards the government of the United States? — A. No, sir, not towards the government of the United States nor towards the Union men.

Q. What effect has it had in that respect? — A. It has made them more impudent. They were once humble and felt that they had done wrong, but this policy has emboldened them, and they are more impudent today, more intolerant, and more proscriptive than they were in 1864. They say that we are the traitors and went over to the damned Yankees. Our present mayor, Slaughter, had sixty men of Grant's army, who were wounded in the wilderness and sent to Fredericksburg, forwarded to General Lee as prisoners-of-war. When Fredericksburg fell into our hands Slaughter made his escape. The federals arrested sixty citizens of Fredericksburg to be held as hostages for these sixty soldiers whom Slaughter had sent to the enemy, and among them was my wife's brother, who was living in Fredericksburg, and yet that same Slaughter was reelected mayor of Fredericksburg last summer after the collapse of the rebellion. Old Tom Barton, the commonwealth's attorney, said in 1861 (and I suppose his feelings are the same still) that all these Union shriekers ought to be hung as high as Haman, and this old man was reelected commonwealth attorney by the people of the county. Every member of the rebel common council was reelected. One of the men who were elected members of the common council from that district stated that none of the Union men who went over to the Yankees during the war should be allowed to return to Fredericksburg; he was also appointed director of a bank there. These are the men we have got over us, and what kind of justice can we expect in the courts?

Q. You will probably get pretty summary justice? — A. I think so; these are facts.

Q. Where is Slaughter now? — A. He is now mayor of Fredericksburg and will be reelected next month; we need not run a Union man there; we are disfranchised.

Q. Is not Slaughter a good Union man? — A. Oh! He has been notoriously Union all the time, as the papers say — notoriously Union! I saw that stated in a Fredericksburg paper; it stated that they had been persecuting Mayor Slaughter, who had been notoriously Union all the time.

Q. You have not a great deal of confidence in the truthfulness of secession? — A. No, sir; I have not.

Q. Where their political standing is concerned? — A. I used to have some confidence, not in secession, but in the people; but it seems to me that their whole nature and character has been changed, and that when treason enters a man's heart, every virtue he has departs.

Q. Could Jefferson Davis be convicted of treason in that part of Virginia? — A. As I went home last Sunday week in the boat, I was in company with a delegation from the Virginia legislature which waited upon President Johnson, and I heard one of them say that there could not be a jury obtained south of the Potomac who would convict Jeff Davis, and that the man who would write down there that Jeff Davis should be punished would be in danger. Jeff Davis cannot be punished down there, and they would elect Lee tomorrow, if there were no difficulty in the way, governor of Virginia. There is no question about that in my mind.

Q. Do you think of anything that you wish to relate? — A. No, sir; I simply wish to state that I make these remarks conscientiously. I was born and raised in the South; my interests of every kind, social, financial, religious and political, are in the South; my church is in the South, and I am going soon to Richmond to edit a paper. Nothing but the good of the country, my own safety, and the safety of my children, and of Union men and of freedmen, could have induced me to come before you and make this statement. I am a friend of the South. I have written for the South, and I shall write in behalf of the South, but the South is one thing, and traitors and treason in the South are different things.

Testimony of John T. Allen

John T. Allen was a Texas Unionist who in 1863 left Austin to escape the Confederate draft. After moving to Louisiana, he took part in the Bayou Teche campaign, when he served on Union General Edmund O. C. Ord's staff. In 1864, he was appointed district attorney for the fourth judicial district of Louisiana, but after the war returned to Texas.

Mr. Williams: In your opinion what is the better course to pursue in regard to the recognition of that state [Texas] by Congress? Is it better at once to receive her representatives in Congress and recognize her as a state, entitled to all the rights and privileges of a state in the Union; or is it better, in view of the condition of the loyal white people there, and the condition of the blacks, to wait awhile and keep a military force there, and in that way maintain the authority of the federal government? — A. The truly loyal people are mostly ignored both by the federal government and by the state government. If these men who come here claiming seats in Congress represent truly the feelings of the state, represent the disloyal element I speak of, I see no difference in receiving them now and receiving them the day they laid down their arms, because their opinions have not had time to change. The changing of one's opinions is not within a man's powers. It takes time and circumstances to alter and modify them. They cannot change and throw off their opinions as they would a garment.

Q. What do you mean by saying that the government ignores loyal men? Do you mean that appointments are given to men who are not loyal? — A. The loyal men feel that they are ignored. Yet it is difficult to answer the question so as to be understood by one not acquainted with all the circumstances of their situation, which I will endeavor to explain.

A minority of the people of Texas voted against secession. Shortly after this fact was made known by the rebel convention, one-half or perhaps two-thirds of that minority went over to the majority, leaving comparatively very few loyal men, whose numbers by subsequent causes became still further reduced. The few that are left alive are called the loyal men of Texas.

When Governor Hamilton arrived in Texas he proceeded at once to organize the state by appointing state, district, and county officers out of the best material he had, some of it not of the choicest quality. Yet all acknowledged that it was as well as could be done under the circumstances, and were satisfied. But soon a feeling of uneasiness began to pervade the minds of loyal men; they perceived that Mr. Johnson was the real governor of Texas, Mr. Hamilton the nominal governor, but in reality only the agent of President Johnson, who caused voters to be registered, whereby every rebel soldier and secessionist, not exempted by the amnesty proclamation, had but to take the oath, have his name registered, wait until the election, then immediately proceed to govern and control the state. They perceived that the power of the rebels was being daily strengthened by the granting of pardons to great numbers of the wealthy and influential rebels, who were returning with all their former influence undiminished, and a kind of political importance added to it. A proclamation was issued for a convention, and an election ordered to be held, whereby those who had been registered could vote for its members. The loyal people were ignored by these proceedings, their feelings or wishes never consulted on those all-important matters, whereby they were completely divested of all political power in the state. In the convention they can have no influence; any state government established under it will speedily remove every loyal man from office. The few loyal men feel that had they been traitors or rebels, their condition would have been much more desirable than it now is in some respects. Yet they know and feel and say that loyalty is the highest public virtue, and that treason is the greatest political crime; that it is the duty of the President to protect, honor, and render virtue powerful, to make crime odious, despicable, and powerless. Therefore the loyal men say that Mr. Johnson has not kept his faith with his country; that he has violated the pledges he made to them, and betrayed the trust they reposed in him; that by his conduct and management of affairs in Texas he has made treason not odious, but reputable, influential, and powerful, and by the same means he has rendered loyalty odious, despicable, and powerless; consequently loyalty in that state now lies prostrate and bleeding under the heel of subjugated rebels.

The untold sufferings that these men have endured, the sleepless nights they have spent in brooding over their wrongs and contemplating their dismal future, the uncertainty, the wretchedness, cannot be explained. Most of them desire to leave the state, and many are making preparations for that purpose. Many believe that they will not be allowed to live in the state, or, if they are permitted to stay, it will be in ignominy and bondage.

This explanation of the circumstances in which the loyal men are placed may account for the feeling that they are ignored; they also feel that they are the victims of the federal and state governments. I have ever had an entire reliance in the worth and ability of the present Congress to help the loyal men in the State of Texas, but, generally speaking, they are very hopeless — almost despairing.

In regard to appointments by the President, much interest was manifested in this matter at first, and names of good men were selected for some of them; but delays occurred, and appointments were few. In the meantime incidents and events which I have just related were transpiring, and overshadowed all interests of that kind. Men who are about to be driven out of the state think nothing of these things; nay, some of the best officers themselves think of leaving.

Q. It has been pretended here, by those who control the appointments, that there are not loyal men in the South for all the offices. I desire to have your opinion upon that point in regard to Texas. Are there loyal men enough in Texas to fill the offices? — A. Your question would require some thought and reflection. It is said that there are not loyal men enough to fill the post offices.

Q. You can state, as far as you know, whether or not the offices of the general government can be filled with loyal men, should the government be disposed to select them for that purpose. — A. There are loyal men to fill all the offices, and fill them well, too, if they were selected for that purpose; but in some districts there are no loyal men — in others they are comparatively numerous; they are not equally distributed all over the state. So far as numbers go, there are loyal men enough who are capable of filling twice the number of offices. It is impossible to find loyal men in every county to fill county offices. I believe that one-half of the counties of Texas are in this situation. The old officers of these counties were mostly rebels, many of them forming vigilance committees for the destruction and murder of Union men, and were the means of driving off from the country those Union men who could escape their vigilance, many of whom will never return. I will state that there are officers of the general government who employ clerks who have been deeply identified with the rebellion, who say they cannot get Union clerks. My impression is that they cannot obtain them unless they use the proper means. Let them advertise for such, and they would have crowds of applicants to choose from. I have said this, as I repeatedly said and insisted upon in Louisiana, that the first and indispensable requisite for office was loyalty, and that they ought to send off for loyal men if they could not get enough there who were loyal.

Q. Have you been in the State of Louisiana? If so, state what position, if any, you held there, and what opportunities you have had for ascertaining the condition of affairs in that state. — A. I was in the Teche campaign, on Major General Ord's staff. I returned to New Orleans in January 1864, and then studied the laws of Louisiana. In August 1864, I was appointed district attorney for the fourth judicial district of that state.

Q. Will you state whether the offices of the different parishes in that state are in the hands of loyal or disloyal men; and what you know about any change, if any, that has taken place in those offices? — A. My district was composed of five parishes, though I attended courts in seven parishes, and was familiar with that number. I knew nearly every officer in each of those seven parishes; that is, the sheriffs, clerks, recorders, justices of the peace, and most of the police jurors. The police jury is a very important matter there — an influential body, and a kind of local legislature there, controlling the parish. During the administration of Governor Hahn great care was taken to fill those offices with loyal men, and he succeeded almost entirely in doing so. Shortly after Mr. Wells became governor, one after another of the officers appointed by Governor Hahn was removed, until very few loyal officers were left in those seven parishes with which I was acquainted. Sheriffs, clerks, recorders, justices of the peace, and police jurors, were all successively removed, and in their places were appointed disloyal men, all of them identified with secession and rebellion, having been engaged in various ways for years inflicting injuries and wrongs upon the government and her citizens — returned rebels and paroled prisoners from Johnston's army; but not one Union loyal citizen was appointed by Governor Wells in either of those parishes. I will add that those few officers that have not been removed by Governor Wells were always reputed to be of equivocal loyalty. I can think of but two or three original Union men that held office in August last; perhaps they are now removed. The number of officers in those parishes must amount to about one hundred or more. It is impossible for a stranger, or one who has not mixed familiarly among those Union men at their homes, to estimate the amount of virtue they possess, the trials they have endured, and the courage with which they have so sternly kept their faith with their country and their government. Nor is it possible to convey in language to be understood by a stranger, the sufferings, the wrongs, the despair of those men, when they saw what Governor Wells was preparing for them — rebels in their uniforms, returned from the army to their old homes, the former persecutors and personal enemies of the loyal men, whose very names were associated with "wounds inflicted not to heal," and recollections of burning wrongs — these, and such as these, were the men appointed by Governor Wells to wield the authority of office over the loyal men of those parishes. I believe the parishes of Terre Bonne and Ascension were supplied with full sets of officers — say, from fifteen to twenty each — at one swoop, the loyal incumbents having no notice of their removal until commissions were presented to them, and their books, papers, etc., demanded by the new appointees. They refused to comply with the demands. They considered the conduct of Governor Wells unjust, base, and atrocious — unjust, because he removed all the officers at once without giving notice to either, and without any reason assigned; base, because in the place of loyal, true men, he appointed those who had been false to their country — traitors and rebels; atrocious, because they were the personal enemies and persecutors of the loyal men. All the loyal men believed that the incumbents were removed because they were loyal. These loyal men still refusing to comply with the demands, and being determined to maintain themselves at the risk of their lives, prepared themselves accordingly. But the men who had persecuted and driven them from their homes before, by the aid of armed confederates, now applied for military aid from the United States for the purpose of again crushing the same men: not without trouble was it at last accomplished. Some of the loyal officers had to flee from their homes after the change was complete; and I saw the recorder of Terre Bonne parish a refugee in New Orleans a few weeks ago, when I was informed that many others were leaving the parish. I could say a great deal more in giving details that accompanied these proceedings. I have stated facts, which, if they be true, are of the most important character. It is my opinion that there is no state in which loyalty has been so deliberately, thoroughly, and, by the government, systematically crushed as in Louisiana. Texas is going the same course, unless it be arrested. The last and only hope of loyal men is in the Republican party in Congress.

Testimony of Mailton J. Safford

Mailton J. Safford was a lawyer from Montgomery, Alabama. Although he had served in the Confederate state legislature during the war, he was one of those who, during the last months of the conflict, sought to organize a Reconstruction or Union party. His testimony was that of a Southern Unionist who was shortly to participate in the anti-Johnson Southern Loyalists' Convention at Philadelphia.

Mr. Boutwell: What means, if any, have you had since Lee's surrender of ascertaining the sentiments of the people of Alabama, or any portion of them? — A. I have been a practicing lawyer in Montgomery, connected in a good degree with politics, reading the public papers, and communicating with prominent men in various parts of the state, personally and by letter.

Q. Does the legislature of the state sit at Montgomery? — A. Yes, sir.

Q. Has it been in session since Lee's surrender? — A. It has been in session since the first of December, I believe, or since sometime in November. The precise time I do not remember. It is now in session.

Q. Have you any means of knowing the opinions of its members? — A. I have this means: I have mixed with them, conversed with them, observed their proceedings, their votes, etc.

Q. What conclusions have you reached as to the loyalty or disloyalty of the people of Alabama? — A. My opinion is that the political control of the state is now in the hands of men who have heretofore been prominently disloyal to the United States government, and who now propose to keep the power of the state in their hands. The purpose for which this is done is, of course, to protect themselves against the opprobrium which might attach to their condition of treason and disloyalty. I sent to Mr. Sumner some two months ago a long, elaborate exposition of my views, which I suppose he has laid before this committee. That would give a more extended and thorough exposition of the whole subject than I shall be able to give in this short verbal examination.

It will be necessary for me to say, before coming to the precise condition of the people of that state at the present time, that at the time of Lee's surrender there was organized in the State of Alabama what was understood to be a Reconstruction or Union party. That party had a controlling majority in the lower house of the legislature. The old senate, under the constitution adopted about the date of secession, held over, so that the senate remained pretty much as it was at the time the state seceded. The house could accomplish nothing without the cooperation of the senate, and no progress was made. During the year 1865 the Union or Reconstruction party, of which I was a member, had a very confident hope of obtaining the governorship and the senate, which was for the first time to be elected under the new constitution, and so obtain control of the state. But the invasion of the state by General Wilson and by the 16th United States Army Corps happened about the time the election was to take place, and a new phase altogether was presented.

Immediately after the surrender of the Confederate forces, the rebel influence was very much appalled, overthrown, and destroyed there. The rebels were very much subjugated, to tell you the truth, and made strong professions of submission to the government. For a time, the Union men of the state, those of us who had antagonized the rebels for four years, thought their power was entirely broken and gone. But soon afterwards they began very industriously to propagate the idea (and the policy adopted by President Johnson seemed to favor the idea) that they might have great hope of regaining their ascendancy to some extent in that state. I say they entertained that hope from facts which came into my possession. They represented, for instance, that President Johnson thought more highly of rebel influence than he did of that of Union men. They would cite such instances as this: that a prominent Union man would go to see the President to get his pardon, and state to him that he had been as much of a Union man as a man could be in his circumstances for the last four years. President Johnson would say, "I am delighted to hear that." But, in the course of the conversation, the Union man would tell the President that at one time it became necessary for him to become somewhat complicated with the rebellion; that he was compelled to sell some cotton to the Southern Confederacy to raise means, and, being worth $20,000, he therefore came within the exceptions of the President's proclamation. The President would reply, "Well, sir, it seems you were a Union man who was willing to let the Union slide, and now I will let you slide." Another man from the other side would come in, as they tell it of Judge Cochran, of Alabama, representing to the President that he had been a very prominent rebel; that he had done all he could to bring about secession; that when his state seceded he took his gun and fought in the ranks as a private; that he regretted very much the war had resulted as it had; that he was very sorry the rebels had not been able to sustain themselves longer. In all respects he represented himself as a very rabid, bitter, unrepenting rebel. The President asked him, "Upon what ground do you base your application for pardon? I do not see anything in your statement to justify you in making such an application." Judge Cochrane replied, "Mr. President, I read that where sin abounds, mercy and grace doth much more abound, and it is upon that principle that I ask for a pardon." The President immediately directed the pardon to be given. In that way they have represented that the President is with them. Others have represented that the President is proposing to build up a party, composed of a united South, the Northern democracy, and such influence as he can bring to bear, by virtue of his patronage, upon the Republican party, to control the government and reelect him President in 1868. That seems to be their policy, as far as I could learn. So great was their confidence that they immediately set to work to obtain the control of the convention called to take the state back again into the Union. They succeeded in obtaining a large majority of that convention and in controlling the election of members of Congress and of members of the legislature. They have succeeded in manufacturing a public opinion which makes treason creditable and loyalty to the government discreditable. They have ostracised, so far as they conveniently or prudently could, all Union men from the political power of the state. They denounce men who have adhered to the United States government as traitors, and charge them with being the cause of the failure of the Confederacy, by creating a division of their councils. That is the present condition of Alabama. There is really a strong Union element there, which, if it could be organized, would be very valuable to the United States government.

Testimony of John Minor Botts

John Minor Botts was one of the best-known Virginia Unionists. A bitter foe of secession and the Democratic party, for many years before the Civil War he had served repeatedly in Congress, where he opposed President John Tyler, the annexation of Texas, and the Mexican War. After playing a prominent role in securing the compromise of 1850, he sought to avoid secession in 1860–61. When he failed, he was imprisoned by Confederate authorities. After the war, he became active in the moderate wing of the Virginia Republican party, which cooperated with President Johnson in the Union Convention at Philadelphia. Although he finally joined the radicals, at the time of his testimony he was a moderate Southern Unionist.

Mr. Howard: What is the present feeling of the ex-rebels in Virginia generally towards the government of the United States? — A. At the time of the surrender of General Lee's army and the restoration of peace I think there was not only a general, but an almost universal, acquiescence and congratulation among the people that the war had terminated, and a large majority of them were at least contented, if not gratified, that it had terminated by a restoration of the state to the Union. At that time the *leaders*, too, seemed to have been entirely subdued. They had become satisfied that Mr. Lincoln was a noble, kind-hearted, generous man, from whom they had little to fear; but when he was assassinated, and Mr. Johnson took his place, they remembered Mr. Johnson's declarations in the Senate of the United States before the war, his own treatment during the war by the secession party, and his declarations after he came to Washington as the Vice-President of the United States, in one or more speeches, but especially in a speech in which he declared that treason was a crime which must be punished. They felt exceedingly apprehensive for the security of their property, as well as for the security of their lives; and a more humble, unpretending set of gentlemen I never saw than they were at that time. But from the time that Mr. Johnson commenced his indiscriminate system of pardoning all who made application, and from impositions which, I have no doubt, were practiced upon Mr. Johnson in pardoning the worst class of secessionists among the first, they became bold, insolent, and defiant; and this was increased to a very large extent by the permission which was, immediately after the evacuation of Richmond, given by General Patrick, the democratic copperhead provost marshal of the army of the Potomac, to the original conductors of the public press before the rebellion to reestablish their papers, I believe, without restriction or limitation, upon any of the proprietors; since which time, I think, the spirit of disloyalty and disaffection has gone on increasing day by day, and hour by hour, until among the leaders generally there is as much disaffection and disloyalty as there was at any time during the war, and a hundredfold more than there was immediately after the evacuation and the surrender of the army. This is the conclusion to which my mind has been brought by the licentiousness of the press, and by communications which are made to me from all parts of the state, either verbally or by letter, from the most prominent and reliable Union sources. If I were to judge from anything I have ever heard personally from these gentlemen, I should not think there was any very great difference between their loyalty and yours or mine; but I hear of it elsewhere, and I see evidence of it daily, not only in the public press, but in the proceedings of the so-called legislature of the state. It is no more a body of legislature than we compose one here now. I believe if the leaders and the public press could be restrained in their expressions and inculcations of disloyalty, with the masses of the people we should have no trouble whatever. As indicative of the character of the letters I often receive, I give you the following extract of a letter from a prominent Union man of the state, received last night:

> As an individual, and I think not a very timid one, I have no hopes of future loyalty unless the President and Congress can relieve the masses of the political incubus now weighing them to the ground. Hour after hour the democracy here are becoming more bold, more intolerant, more proscriptive. Was the war in all its horrid consequences designed to establish a democratic oligarchy here in the South and eventually turn over the general government with all its patronage and power to this pack of bloodhounds? Or was it designed to preserve the Union, maintain liberty, and wipe out forever all sectional parties? If for the former, then the prevailing policy will soon effect it; and when it does, I pray that God will cause a universal earthquake and blot out that portion of his footstool comprised within the United States. Under democratic rule again, hell would be a Garden of Eden compared to the Southern states, and I should assuredly select it as a permanent place of abode if forced to choose between the two.

In this latter conclusion I think I should rather dissent from my friend. Bad as democratic rule is, I would rather bear the ills we have than fly to others that we know not of. But it is bad enough in all conscience;

and from the tone of that and other letters, of a similar character to a great extent, received from different parts of the state, and conversations which I have had with gentlemen from every portion of the state, whose opinions are reliable and trustworthy, there must be, I conclude, a very intolerable state of things existing.

Testimony of Charles H. Lewis

Charles H. Lewis was the Secretary of the Restored Government of Virginia under Governor Francis H. Pierpont, with whom he moved from Alexandria to Richmond after his appointment in May 1865. A firm Unionist, he held office until January 1866. He lived in Rockingham County in the Valley of Virginia.

Mr. Howard: What is the feeling among the secessionists in Virginia toward the government of the United States? — A. My decided impression in regard to that matter is, that the masses of the people (and by that term I do not mean only the laboring classes, but I mean all those persons who are not politicians) were very favorably disposed toward the government of the United States at the time of Lee's surrender. I believe that very decided efforts have been made by the politicians to change that feeling since that time, and I am afraid that they have had a great deal of success. I believe that the majority of the people of Virginia would still be loyal to the government of the United States if it were not for the pressure of the press and the politicians, who, to a great extent, control public opinion. I believe that many of the old secession politicians are actively engaged in promoting dissatisfaction with the government of the United States.

Q. How do these politicians feel toward President Johnson's policy in regard to the reconstruction of the states? — A. They all profess to be decidedly in favor of President Johnson's policy of reconstruction, which, they either believe or profess to believe, means the restoration to power of the men who have been disloyal at the North and at the South.

Q. Do you think that President Johnson's liberal policy in granting pardons and amnesties has made the masses of the people more or less respectful to the government of the United States than they were before? — A. When the restored government first went back to Richmond, the politicians professed great anxiety to be pardoned in order that they might get their property back, resume their avocations, and be released from the penalties of treason; and they made very loud professions of accepting the condition of things, and of being anxious to become true and loyal subjects of the United States government. After most of them got pardons, I found among the politicians a very decided change for the worse.

Testimony of F. J. Mollere

F. J. Mollere was a New Orleans sailor who had served the United States as a detective after the capture of his city in 1862. His testimony before the committee investigating the New Orleans riots was that of a Southern radical.

Mr. Eliot: Have you occupied any official position here? — A. Only as United States detective, as I stated.

Q. Are you a United States detective now? — A. No, sir; I was employed by the military commission, and am employed in special cases where the commanding general requires my services. I have been off and on pretty constantly employed by the government.

Q. Have you taken any particular pains to conceal your opinions? — A. Previous to the massacre of the 30th of July I used not to, in conversation with my friends who had returned from the Confederate army; but since the 30th of July I have taken the background. I have found myself obliged to say I was an Andy Johnson man; that was my policy. At the time it would not have been safe for me to have said otherwise.

Q. Do the majority of the people here approve of the restoration policy of President Johnson? — A. The majority of the people of New Orleans disapprove of it.

Q. Then why do you strive to make yourself popular by avowing yourself in favor of it? — A. The majority of the people of New Orleans do not favor the policy of Mr. Johnson.

Q. Do a majority of the white people of Louisiana, in your opinion, favor the policy of Mr. Johnson? — A. Yes, sir.

Q. If the restoration policy of Mr. Johnson were to prevail, would it not allay the bitterness which you seem to think exists in this community? — A. It would allay it in this way, that every man who had aided and abetted the United States government would have to go to some Northern city to live; then they would have it entirely in their own hands here, and probably things would go on smoothly. There are thirteen thousand or fourteen thousand who are registered enemies of the United States, and there are, perhaps, five thousand who would have to leave if the policy of Mr. Johnson was to prevail in the city of New Orleans.

Q. That is your opinion? — A. Yes, sir; I have known it and felt it since the riot.

Q. From what you last stated, I infer that that is your opinion, based upon what you saw that day? — A. Based, sir, upon what I saw on the 30th of July, and on what I have since heard and seen; based upon what I have heard and seen in the courts, where a counsel, pleading for his client, could not find any stronger recommendation to present to the jury than that he was a "hero of Sumter"; that he had "fought four years for the noble cause"; and where a man who had been guilty of murder would be honorably acquitted.

9 TESTIMONY OF NORTHERNERS

Testimony of George E. Spencer

General George E. Spencer was born in New York State and had lived in Iowa before coming to Alabama with the Federal army. He raised a loyal regiment in the state and remained in the South after the war. In 1868, he was elected United States Senator from Alabama, a position he filled until 1879.

Mr. Boutwell: Have you observed any change in public sentiment, either for or against the government, since Lee's surrender? — A. The greatest change. It is almost impossible to describe the change. Immediately after the surrender of the armies of the Confederacy the people were willing to accept the condition of things as they were. They only asked to be allowed to live there. But now they are haughty and overbearing and insolent, and they do not propose, if they can help it, to allow any one to associate with them politically, socially, or commercially, unless he has been a rebel, or has given the rebellion his support, or comes up to their standard. They never speak of a federal in any other way than as a "Yankee."

Q. Are there any indications as to whether they mean to support the government in good faith? — A. I do not think they do. They say that when they get power they will repudiate the national debt. That is common street talk.

Q. Do you know whether or not they intend to make any claims on the government for losses that they have sustained? — A. They do.

Q. Is it a matter of common conversation among them? — A. It is a matter of general conversation everywhere. I have had claims offered to me to the amount of several millions of dollars to take to Washington, but I have invariably told them that I did not consider that the claims were good for anything, and I have endeavored as far as I could to discourage them. I have no belief that they would be paid.

Q. If the people were left entirely free from military restraint or control to elect members of Congress, and were assured that the men they elected would be received here, what class of men would they elect? — A. The elections this year show that. No man unless he comes up to the full standard of a secessionist can be elected to any office outside of five counties in Alabama.

Q. Which five counties are those? — A. Marion, Winston, Walker, Fayette, and Randolph. They could poll a very good Union vote in some other counties. But in the counties I have named, which were non-slaveholding counties, the Union men have a very large majority. It is respectable to be a Union man there, but in the other counties it is not.

Q. To what do you attribute the change of sentiment against the government since Lee's surrender? — A. To the policy of the administration.

Q. In what particular? — A. In appointing secessionists and rebels to office, and in pardoning them. One gentleman returned from Washington with his pardon, and in conversation with me about a week after he said that a republican form of government was a failure; that he was firm in the belief that the United States government could not exist ten years.

Q. What was his name? — A. William H. Jemison, of Tuscaloosa.

Q. How would Northern settlers be received in Alabama as landholders and farmers or planters? — A. That would depend entirely upon the locality.

Q. I mean outside of the five counties you have mentioned. — A. They would be received very coldly. The general wish of the people is that they shall not come. The election in the fourth congressional district — and that has been my observation everywhere — was upon the test-oath issue; that it should not be taken. The candidates made the issue that they could not take it. It is considered disgraceful for a man to be able to take the test-oath.

Q. Do you mean that a man who cannot take the test-oath would be supported? — A. Yes, sir. And in that district the man who could not take the oath was elected by five thousand majority. He said that he thanked God that he was not able to take it, and he insisted upon the stump that President Johnson did not want anybody elected who could take it. It was insisted that that was the President's policy.

Testimony of Alexander P. Ketchum *

Mr. Howard: How do you find the condition of the secessionists of South Carolina, so far as your observation extends; are they friendly to the United States, or are they hostile? — A. To answer the question in one word, I should say they are not friendly to the United States. There are reasoning men among them who are friendly to certain policies, and

* See above, page 79.

who profess friendship to the government, but I think this is more for personal reasons than because they have any real friendship for the United States.

Q. Can you give any reason why you have drawn this inference; whether it is from expressions you have heard used, or from the acts which they commit? — A. I was stationed at Savannah in February 1865, on General Saxton's staff, charged with carrying out the order of General Sherman in Georgia. I resided then with a Southern family and came in contact with Southern gentlemen. As a general rule, even the most intelligent among them looked upon the United States as an aggressive power and complained bitterly and in unequivocal terms of the position of subjugation to which they said they were reduced. I saw no spirit of friendship manifested towards the government, although there was an expressed willingness to submit to the necessities of the situation. They complained in many cases of the officers charged with carrying out the orders of government, were quite frequent in their expressions of dissatisfaction with the Negroes, and were bitterly hostile to the order of General Sherman relative to Sea-Island lands. Officers of the late rebel army expressed themselves in strong phrases against Union officers, and in some instances insulted them openly. I do not recollect that they used violence in the first instance, but at the hotels they would abuse them, calling them d——d Yankee officers, wearing the d——d uniform of the United States. These results were on one or two occasions resented, and violence was the result.

Q. Who got the best of it? — A. The Union officers.

Q. You considered that right, didn't you? — A. Most assuredly I did. They said they had nothing to expect from the United States government. The rebellion was crushed. They at first anticipated the entire confiscation of their lands — expressed that expectation often, in my presence — and it was remarkable that notwithstanding these expectations the people were, comparatively speaking, submissive and prepared to abide the issue. They would sometimes lose control of themselves, and speak in severe language, but in general were quietly submissive to the authority of the government. Afterwards, when a different policy from the one they expected began to appear, on the part of the government — when the amnesty proclamation was published and the lenient or liberal policy of President Johnson announced, I thought I saw a marked change in their demeanor; they were more aristocratic and less inclined to submit to the authority of the government of the United States. On the 4th of July the Negro firemen of Savannah desired to parade with their engines, but were forbidden. I was then in charge of Freedmen's Bureau affairs at that city, and asked the superintendent of the fire department why he had forbidden the Negroes to parade. He said they wished to practice with their engines, which could not be permitted that day. I assembled some of the firemen and in presence of the superintendent asked them whether that was their purpose. They said it was not, and that they would be satisfied to parade with their engines on the streets. The superintendent then answered that it was too late to make the request; that if it had been presented in due form in time, it might have been granted. I told him there was no reason why it should not be granted now; that this was the first Independence Day they had had the opportunity of celebrating since their emancipation, and I thought they should be allowed to parade; that if he refused I should carry the matter before higher authority; I could see no good reason for making an invidious distinction between the black firemen and the white firemen, who had been permitted to parade. I then presented the request officially, and he yielded. The firemen paraded, but a mob of secessionists attacked them, dispersed them, and seized their engine, which they with difficulty obtained again. One of the colored firemen brought action the next day in the provost court, presided over by a United States officer, against a person he named, one of the mob, as he alleged, for assault and battery. He had four witnesses. The judge decided they had no cause of action, and the case was dismissed; but the plaintiff and his four colored witnesses were not allowed to return home, but remanded to jail.

Q. How did that happen? — A. It was for a reason unexplained at that time. I was informed that no order was issued, and that the officer directed to keep them in jail did not at first know why they were sent there. I was then out of town. When I returned these men had been tried, convicted of perjury, and sentenced to pay a fine of $500 and to serve six months in prison, this being the severest sentence the court could inflict.

Q. Who was the judge? — A. A captain of a Connecticut regiment; he is now out of the service.

Testimony of Homer A. Cooke

A newspaper editor from Massachusetts, Homer A. Cooke served as assistant quartermaster in eastern North Carolina. Because he remained in the South until December 1865, he had a good opportunity to observe conditions.

Mr. Howard: What effect has President Johnson's liberal policy in granting pardons and amnesties to rebels had upon the minds of the secessionists there; has it made them more or less favorable to the government of the United States? — A. I can, perhaps, better answer that question by saying that every unconditional Union man of my acquaintance in that state is opposed to that policy.

Q. How do the secessionists feel about it? — A. They claim the President as their friend in that matter.

Q. Has this liberal policy made them more or less friendly in their feelings towards the government of the United States; has it made them more respectful to the government, or more contemptuous towards it? — A. The fact is certain that the feeling of hostility against the government of the United States is much more intense there than it was six months ago. I do not know that I could state precisely what the cause was. My own opinion would be that at the time of Lee's surrender they were ready to accept of any terms that might have been offered; but that, no rigorous condition having been imposed, they have been led to think that they have a friend in high station.

Q. And they rely on President Johnson more than they do upon Congress; is that the fact? — A. Certainly, sir. They are very hostile in their manifestations as regards the majority in Congress.

Q. How do they speak of the majority in the two houses of Congress? — A. In terms of deep and malignant hatred.

Q. What are some of the epithets they apply to them, if they apply any? — A. They are spoken of as radicals, who would ruin their country if they cannot rule it.

Q. Is that the tone of secession newspapers published in North Carolina? — A. I do not know of a newspaper in North Carolina that comes up to the standard of what I should call loyalty to the government.

10 TESTIMONY OF SOUTHERN CONSERVATIVES

Testimony of Caleb G. Forshey *

Mr. Williams: What opportunities have you had for ascertaining the temper and disposition of the people of Texas towards the government and authority of the United States? — A. For ten years I have been superintendent of the Texas Military Institute, as its founder and conductor. I have been in the Confederate service in various parts of the Confederacy; but chiefly in the trans-Mississippi department, in Louisiana and Texas, as an officer of engineers. I have had occasion to see and know very extensively the condition of affairs in Texas, and also to a considerable extent in Louisiana. I think I am pretty well informed, as well as anybody, perhaps of the present state of affairs in Texas.

Q. What are the feelings and views of the people of Texas as to the late rebellion, and the future condition and circumstances of the state, and its relations to the federal government? — A. After our army had given up its arms and gone home, the surrender of all matters in controversy was complete, and as nearly universal, perhaps, as anything could be. Assuming the matters in controversy to have been the right to secede, and the right to hold slaves, I think they were given up teetotally, to use a strong Americanism. When you speak of feeling, I should discriminate a little. The feeling was that of any party who had been cast in a suit he had staked all upon. They did not return from feeling, but from a sense of necessity, and from a judgment it was the only and necessary thing to be done, to give up the contest. But when they gave it up, it was without reservation; with a view to look forward, and not back. That is my impression of the manner in which the thing was done. There was a public expectation that in some very limited time there would be a restoration to former relations; and in such restoration they felt great interest, after the contest was given up. The expectation was, and has been up to the present time, that there would be a speedy and immediate restoration. It was the expectation of the people that, as soon as the state was organized as proposed by the President, they would be restored to their former relations, and things would go on as before, with these two main issues given up wholly; that, with that as the result, there would be harmony,

* See above, page 24.

and that without it there would probably not be. I think there would be considerable revulsion of feeling if that is not so, as the expectation has been almost universal that that would be the result of reorganization. It is perhaps proper that I should say, in that connection, that a considerable apprehension has been felt lately. Texas being later in her reorganization than the other states, and having had an opportunity to witness the result in the case of the other states, considerable apprehension and some revulsion of feeling have already occurred; that is, a little terror lest such should not be the result of reorganization. My impression is, that the feeling, so far as feeling is concerned, is not as good as it was three or four months ago. I want to distinguish between feeling and judgment; for good feeling was returning as fast as human nature would admit.

Testimony of B. R. Grattan

B. R. Grattan was a Virginian who since 1844 had been the reporter of the State Court of Appeals. At the time of his testimony, he was a member of the state legislature elected while the Johnson plan was in force.

Mr. Howard: What is the general feeling among the secessionists of Virginia towards the government of the United States so far as your observation extends? — A. So far as I know, the sentiment is universal that the war has decided the question of secession entirely, that it is no longer an open question, and that we are all prepared to abide by the Union and live under it.

Q. You mean to be understood as saying that they suppose that the sword has settled the abstract right of secession? — A. Yes; we consider that we put it to the arbitrament of the sword, and have lost.

Q. What proportion of the legislature of Virginia are original secessionists, having in view the definition I gave? — A. I would suppose that there are few members of the legislature who are less able to judge of that matter than myself, for my acquaintance as a member is very limited; but I should suppose, from the general sentiments of the people of Virginia, that while probably a very large proportion of those who are now members of the legislature were not in favor of secession or a dissolution of the Union originally, yet nearly all of them went with their state when it went out. They went heartily with it.

Q. How have the results of the war affected the feelings of Virginians generally? What is the sentiment left in their hearts in regard to satisfaction or dissatisfaction with the government of the United States — love or hatred, respect or contempt? — A. I cannot undertake to say generally; my intercourse is very limited. I would rather suppose, however, that while the feeling against the government was originally very strong, that feeling has been very much modified; it is nothing like as strong as it was, and is gradually declining.

Q. You think that the feeling is gradually changing from dislike to respect? — A. Yes, I think so.

Q. Have you any reason to suppose that there are persons in Virginia who still entertain projects of a dissolution of the Union? — A. None whatever. I do not believe that there is an intelligent man in the state who does.

Q. In case of a war between our country and any foreign power, such as England or France, one that should put the government to the exercise of all its powers in order to secure its safety, and in case it should become apparent that there was a chance for secessionism to become a success hereafter, would you anticipate that any considerable portion of the people of Virginia would join the enemy? — A. No sir.

Q. Would there be many who would be likely to do so? — A. No, sir; I do not think there would be. You might find some boys who would do so. I think that the people have made up their minds to become a part of this union and to perform every duty connected with that relation. I speak with confidence on that subject, for while I was not an original secessionist, I am certain that nobody ever suffered more at its failure than I did, and I know what my own sentiments are, and judge other people by myself.

Q. What has been, in your judgment, the effect, in the main, of President Johnson's liberality in bestowing pardons and amnesties on rebels? — A. I think it has been very favorable; I think President Johnson has commended himself very heartily. There is a very strong feeling of gratitude towards President Johnson.

Q. Has that liberality in your judgment, increased or diminished the respect of these same persons towards the government of the United States? — A. It has increased it.

Q. Is that increase of respect towards the government, or is it especially towards President Johnson? — A. It is to Mr. Johnson, as representative of the government.

Testimony of Robert E. Lee *

Mr. Blow: In reference to the effect of President Johnson's policy, if it were adopted, would there be anything like a return of the old feeling? . . . — A. I believe it would take time for the feelings of the people to be of that cordial nature to the government that they were formerly.

Q. Do you think that their preference for that policy arises from a de-

* See above, page 29.

sire to have peace and good feeling in the country, or from the probability of their regaining political power? — A. So far as I know the desire of the people of the South, it is for the restoration of their civil government, and they look upon the policy of President Johnson as the one which would most clearly and most surely reestablish it.

Q. Do you see any change among the poorer classes in Virginia in reference to industry? Are they as much, or more, interested in developing their material interests than they were? — A. I have not observed any change. Everyone now has to attend to his business for his support.

Q. The poorer classes are generally hard at work, are they? — A. So far as I know, they are; I know nothing to the contrary.

Q. Is there any difference in their relations to the colored people — is their prejudice increased or diminished? — A. I have noticed no change. So far as I do know the feelings of all the people of Virginia, they are kind to the colored people. I have never heard any blame attributed to them as to the present condition of things, or any responsibility.

Q. There are very few colored laborers employed, I suppose? — A. Those who own farms have employed them more or less — one or two. Some are so poor that they have to work themselves.

Q. Can capitalists and workingmen from the North go into any portion of Virginia with which you are familiar and go to work among the people? — A. I do not know anything to prevent them. Their peace and pleasure there would depend very much on their conduct. If they confined themselves to their own business, and did not interfere to provoke controversies with their neighbors, I do not believe they would be molested.

Q. There is no desire to keep out labor and capital? — A. Not that I know of. On the contrary, they are very anxious to get capital into the state.

Q. You see nothing of a disposition to prevent such a thing? — A. I have seen nothing, and do not know of anything. As I said before, the manner in which they would be received would depend entirely upon the individuals themselves. They might make themselves obnoxious, as you can understand.

Part Four

THE PROBLEM OF NEGRO SUFFRAGE

11 TESTIMONY OF NORTHERNERS AND SOUTHERN UNIONISTS

Testimony of Stephen Powers

Stephen Powers was a reporter for the Cincinnati Commercial. *In the winter of 1865–66, he traveled in Florida, Louisiana, and Texas, where he had an excellent opportunity to observe conditions.*

Mr. Williams: Did you find that the Negroes in those states had any comprehension of the issues involved in the late war, and of the present condition of things in the country, so as to understand what was right and what was wrong in political matters? — A. Nine-tenths of the plantation Negroes are living in a state of brutish ignorance, and have very little comprehension of the issues of this war, beyond the mere fact that they were set at liberty and were set free. The house servants, the hotel waiters, and the residents of the cities are much more intelligent, and in many cases have exhibited a very commendable degree of information in regard to the issues of the war. I think I might say, however, that four-fifths of the Negroes in the South have no just comprehension of the franchises and privileges of a free citizen. But there has been much improvement in that respect since the Christmas holidays. I think I have never known of any more complete industrial and social revolution than was accomplished during those holidays. Up to that time the Negroes had been thriftless, gay, improvident, and relying on what they confidently expected, the division of their old master's property at that time. They were, however, sorely disappointed, and for a time were discouraged and desponding. But they very soon recovered, however, in consequence of their natural buoyancy, and have applied themselves to work for themselves and their families with a great degree of industry. They have by this time a pretty thorough understanding that it is necessary for them to provide for themselves, and they are setting about it in a rude, ignorant way, which is all that could have been expected of them. As for the right of suffrage, and in many cases the right to testify in courts, they have the most vague and shadowy ideas. I conversed with many of them, particularly the plantation Negroes, about the right of suffrage, and I found them afraid to speak of it, as though it was something which was not to be meddled with by them. The common remark among them was that they did not know anything about it, that "massa had never said anything to them about it." If they were led to the polls, I think the act of voting with them would be a merely physical act, and that it would be accomplished with very little appreciation.

Q. Have you seen the proposition laid before the Senate by Mr. Stewart? — A. Do you mean the proposition to grant universal amnesty for universal suffrage?

Q. Yes. — A. I have seen that proposition.

Q. In your opinion, what would be the action of the people of the three states of which you have been speaking if that proposition was submitted to them for adoption or rejection? — A. I think the people of the South generally would treat it with slight consideration. They understand pretty thoroughly that they already have, or will secure in the end, as much amnesty as is necessary; and they would consider it a bargain which it was not necessary for them to enter into. I think such a proposition would accomplish very little.

Q. What is your opinion of their views generally in regard to Negro suffrage? — A. I need not tell you that the Southern people are almost unanimously opposed to Negro suffrage. That opposition is founded upon the old prejudice which they have against the Negro, and upon their belief in his unfitness for the rights and privileges of citizenship; it is founded on nothing more reasonable than that. I think, however, indeed I am quite certain, that if it could be made positively certain to the Southern politicians that at or before the next apportionment they would lose upwards of twenty representatives in Congress unless they accorded to Negroes the right of suffrage, they would become pretty thoroughly convinced that it was a necessary and proper measure. The greatest opposition in the South to Negro suffrage would be found among the lower classes. I have generally found that when two classes are opposed in feeling, and unequal in power and influence, the dominating class is hostile to the inferior class just in reverse proportion as it is elevated above it. The poor whites of the South, knowing that the right of suffrage is the principal of the few slight barriers which separate them from the Negro race, will cling to that right with corresponding tenacity. And it will be they who will oppose, and insult, and oppress the Negro more than all others when he presents himself at the polls.

The wealthy land-owners of the South, however, have the most unbounded influence over the Negroes now, almost as much as they had when the Negroes were their slaves, and it seems to me that the proper approach to this castle of prejudice on the part of the poor, ignorant whites will be through the argument and persuasion of the politicians of the South. The Southern politicians have no insuperable prejudice against

Negro suffrage. And I am quite certain that if it is made plain to them that they will lose representation in Congress by consequence of not granting suffrage to the Negro, they will soon accede to the demand, and convince their followers, the poor people, that it is necessary and proper. I think that Texas will be the first of the late Confederate States that will grant suffrage to the Negroes. There are already three prominent newspapers in that state that openly favor Negro suffrage, or perhaps I should not say openly favor it, but whose editors are in favor of it, and who squint towards it at every opportunity when it is safe and expedient. One of those papers is the *Galveston Bulletin*, the organ of a large and intelligent class of people in and about Galveston. Another is the *Southern Intelligence*, in Austin, the organ of Governor Hamilton, and having a circulation of nearly 2,000 copies in the interior of the state. The third is the *San Antonio Express*, the organ of the German population that are to be found in and about San Antonio. There is also a strong sentiment tending in that direction in northern Texas, and it would only need the leadership of a few brave men, such as Governor Hamilton, Mr. Taylor, of the convention, and a few others like them, to carry that part of the state and the German population in favor of Negro suffrage.

Testimony of George R. Weeks

Dr. George R. Weeks was a physician from Ohio who had come to Arkansas as an army surgeon. Deciding to stay in the South after the war, he settled in Little Rock to practice his profession.

Mr. Boutwell: What is the feeling of the people in regard to conferring the elective franchise on Negroes or any part of them? — A. In Arkansas we are divided into two sections; those who have recently come there, and the original residents: of the latter class, I think two-thirds are opposed to Negro suffrage. Many who have been mustered out of the army have remained there; many of those are in favor of letting the Negroes vote. It is my opinion that generally there is a majority against Negro suffrage — a small majority.

Q. If the Negroes should be allowed to vote, any part or the whole of them, and if a question should arise involving the safety of the Union, the preservation of the government, on which side would the Negroes be likely to vote? — A. They would vote on the Union side, to a man. I think they are entirely reliable.

Q. Are there any of the adult male Negroes who are unable to understand the issues that were involved in the war between secession and

Union? — A. I think there are very few but that have an understanding of it, some more perfect than others. They all seemed to recognize the great fact of their liberation by the Northern forces. I was with General Sanburn recently, who has charge of the Negroes in the Indian territory, at Fort Smith. A Negro walked up to him and said, "Sir, I want you to help me in a personal matter." "Where is your family?" "On Red River." "Have you not everything you want?" "No, sir." "You are free!" "Yes, sir, you set me free, but you left me there." "What do you want?" "I want some land; I am helpless; you do nothing for me but give me freedom." "Is not that enough?" "It is enough for the present; but I cannot help myself unless I get some land; then I can take care of myself and family; otherwise, I cannot do it." They all seem to have a distinct idea that they are free, and that they are indebted for it to the North.

Testimony of James Sinclair *

Mr. Howard: Suppose the Negroes of North Carolina should be allowed to vote, how would the whites regard that? — A. I do not suppose there are 20 men in North Carolina who would not be opposed to it.

Q. What is your opinion of the general political effect in the state of allowing the Negroes to vote? I do not mean all of them, but a portion of them — those the most fit for it. Would it tend to give strength to the government? — A. Of course it would; there is no doubt about that.

Q. Would it tend to give prosperity and stability to the affairs of the state? — A. It is my opinion that it would. I am an advocate of impartial suffrage; to make no distinction on account of race or color.

Q. Would there be any liability on the part of the blacks to be led away to vote for secessionists or secession leaders? — A. There would be no danger, for this reason; next to the Lord Jesus Christ, and with many Negroes I am afraid a little higher, stands the name of President Lincoln. They are well aware of the existence and position of Sumner and such men. If candidates were put up tomorrow there for Congress, or for any other office, the Negro would not go to his old master to inquire about them, but they would come to me, or to you, or some Northern man upon whom they could depend.

Q. Suppose his old master should go to him and ask him to vote? — A. They would laugh at him. Long before the war they had got so they would not believe a word their masters said on some things. The reason the Presbyterian ministers are so down upon me is, that not one of the Negroes who formerly attended their churches will go to them now. But they will go and hear me, or any Northern minister, and they would come

* See above, page 18.

to us and ask us about their papers, or anything else that they desired to understand. Any Northern man in whom they have confidence can control them. If you confer universal suffrage upon them, I would like to have it that they should give their votes *viva voce,* in order that there might be no danger of changing their tickets by dishonest persons.

Q. Would not their votes in such case be influenced by fear of their masters? — A. Not at all.

Q. Would they have resolution enough to go against their old master's wishes? — A. Yes, sir; their old masters have not one particle of influence over them now; that is all gone. . . .

12 TESTIMONY OF SOUTHERN CONSERVATIVES

Testimony of Alexander H. Stephens *

Mr. Boutwell: What is the public sentiment of Georgia with regard to the extension of the right of voting to the Negroes? — A. The general opinion in the state is very much averse to it.

Q. If a proposition were made to amend the Constitution, so as to base representation in Congress upon voters, substantially, would Georgia ratify such a proposed amendment, if it were made a condition precedent to the restoration of the state to political power in the government? — A. I do not think they would. The people of Georgia, in my judgment, as far as I can reflect or represent their opinions, feel that they are entitled under the Constitution of the United States to representation, without any further condition precedent. They would not object to entertain, discuss, and exchange views in the common councils of the country with the other states, upon such a proposition, or any proposition to amend the Constitution, or change it in any of its features; and they would abide by any such change, if made as the Constitution provides. But they feel that they are constitutionally entitled to be heard by their Senators and members in the Houses of Congress upon this or any other proposed amendment. I do not therefore think that they would ratify the amendment suggested as a condition precedent to her being admitted to representation in Congress. Such, at least, is my opinion.

Q. It is then your opinion that at present the people of Georgia would neither be willing to extend suffrage to the Negroes nor consent to the exclusion of the Negroes from the basis of representation? — A. The people of Georgia, in my judgment, are perfectly willing to leave suffrage and the basis of representation where the Constitution leaves it. They look upon the question of suffrage as one belonging exclusively to the states; one over which, under the Constitution of the United States, Congress has no jurisdiction, power, or control, except in proposing amendments and not in making their acceptance and adoption by the states conditions of representation. I do not think, therefore, that the people of that state, while they are disposed, as I believe, earnestly to deal fairly, justly, and generously with the freedmen, would be willing to consent to a change in the Constitution that would give Congress jurisdiction over the ques-

* See above, page 22.

tion of suffrage; and especially would they be very much averse to Congress exercising any such jurisdiction without their representatives in the Senate and House being heard in the public councils upon this question that so fatally concerns their internal policy as well as the internal policy of all the states.

Q. If the proposition were to be submitted to Georgia, as one of the eleven states lately in rebellion, that she might be restored to political power in the government of the country upon the condition precedent that she should on the one hand extend suffrage to the Negroes, or on the other consent to their exclusion from the basis of representation, would she accept either proposition and take her place in the government of the country? — A. I can only give my opinion. I do not think she would accept either as a condition precedent presented by Congress, for they do not believe that Congress has the rightful power under the Constitution to prescribe such a condition. If Georgia is a state in the Union her people feel that she is entitled to representation without conditions imposed by Congress; and if she is not a state in the Union, then she could not be admitted as an equal with the others if her admission were trammelled with conditions that did not apply to all the rest alike. General, universal suffrage among the colored people, as they are now there, would by our people be regarded as about as great a political evil as could befall them.

Q. If the proposition were to extend [the] right of suffrage to those who could read and to those who had served in the Union armies, would that modification affect the action of the state? — A. I think the people of the state would be unwilling to do more than they have done for restoration. Restricted or limited suffrage would not be so objectionable as general or universal. But it is a matter that belongs to the state to regulate. The question of suffrage, whether universal or restricted, is one of state policy exclusively, as they believe. Individually I should not be opposed to a proper system of restricted or limited suffrage to this class of our population. But, in my judgment, it is a matter that belongs of constitutional right to the states to regulate respectively each for itself. But the people of that state, as I have said, would not willingly, I think, do more than they have done for restoration. The only view in their opinion that could possibly justify the war which was carried on by the federal government against them was the idea of the indissolubleness of the Union; that those who held the administration for the time were bound to enforce the execution of the laws and the maintenance of the integrity of the country under the Constitution. And since that was accomplished, since those who had assumed the contrary principle — the right of secession and the reserved sovereignty of the states — had abandoned their cause, and the administration here was successful in maintaining the idea upon which war was proclaimed and waged, and the only view in which they supposed it could be justified at all — when that was accomplished, I say, the people of Georgia supposed their state was immediately entitled to all her rights under the Constitution. That is my opinion of the sentiment of the people of Georgia, and I do not think they would be willing to do anything further as a condition precedent to their being permitted to enjoy the full measure of their constitutional rights. I only give my opinion of the sentiment of the people at this time. They expected as soon as the Confederate cause was abandoned that immediately the states would be brought back into their practical relations with the government as previously constituted. That is what they looked to. They expected that the states would immediately have their representatives in the Senate and in the House; and they expected in good faith, as loyal men, as the term is frequently used — loyal to law, order, and the Constitution — to support the government under the Constitution. That was their feeling. They did what they did, believing it was best for the protection of constitutional liberty. Towards the Constitution of the United States the great mass of our people were always as much devoted in their feelings as any people ever were towards any laws or people. This is my opinion. As I remarked before, they resorted to secession with a view of more securely maintaining these principles. And when they found they were not successful in their object in perfect good faith, as far as I can judge from meeting with them and conversing with them, looking to the future development of the country in its material resources as well as its moral and intellectual progress, their earnest desire and expectation was to allow the past struggle, lamentable as it was in its results, to pass by and to cooperate with the true friends of the Constitution, with those of all sections who earnestly desire the preservation of constitutional liberty and the perpetuation of the government in its purity. They have been a little disappointed in this, and are so now. They are patiently waiting, however, and believing that when the passions of the hour have passed away this delay in representation will cease. They think they have done everything that was essential and proper, and my judgment is that they would not be willing to do anything further as a condition precedent. They would simply remain quiet and passive.

Q. Does your own judgment approve the view you have given as the opinion of the people of the state? — A. My own judgment is very decided, that the question of suffrage is one that belongs, under the Constitution, and wisely so too, to the states, respectively and exclusively.

Q. Is it your opinion that neither of the alternatives suggested in the question ought to be accepted by the people of Georgia? — A. My own opinion is, that these terms ought not to be offered as conditions precedent. In other words, my opinion is that it would be best for the peace, harmony, and prosperity of the whole country that there should be an immediate restoration, an immediate bringing back of the states into their original practical relations; and let all these questions then be discussed in common council. Then the representatives from the South could be heard, and you and all could judge much better of the tone and temper of the people than you could from the opinions given by any individuals. You may take my opinion, or the opinions of any individual, but they will not enable you to judge of the condition of the State of Georgia so well as for her own representatives to be heard in your public councils in her own behalf. My judgment, therefore, is very decided, that it would have been better as soon as the lamentable conflict was over, when the people of the South abandoned their cause and agreed to accept the issue, desiring as they do to resume their places for the future in the Union, and to look to the arena of reason and justice for the protection of their rights in the Union — it would have been better to have allowed that result to take place, to follow under the policy adopted by the administration, than to delay it or hinder it by propositions to amend the Constitution in respect to suffrage or any other new matter. I think the people of all the Southern states would in the halls of Congress discuss these questions calmly and deliberately, and if they did not show that the views they entertained were just and proper, such as to control the judgment of the people of the other sections and states, they would quietly, philosophically, and patriotically yield to whatever should be constitutionally determined in common council. But I think they feel very sensitively the offer to them of propositions to accept while they are denied all voice in the common council of the Union, under the Constitution, in the discussion of these propositions. I think they feel very sensitively that they are denied the right to be heard. And while, as I have said, they might differ among themselves in many points in regard to suffrage, they would not differ upon the question of doing anything further as a condition precedent to restoration. And in respect to the alternate conditions to be so presented, I do not think they would accept the one or the other. My individual general views as to the proper course to be persued in respect to the colored people are expressed in a speech made before the Georgia legislature, referred to in my letter to Senator Stewart. This was the proper forum, as I conceive, to address them, and my utmost exertions shall be, if I live, to carry out those views. But I think a great deal depends in the advancement of civilization and progress, that these questions should be considered and kept before the proper forum.

Q. Suppose the states that are represented in Congress, and Congress itself, should be of the opinion that Georgia should not be permitted to take its place in the government of the country except upon its assent to one or the other of the two propositions suggested, is it, then, your opinion that, under such circumstances, Georgia ought to decline?

The Witness: You mean the states now represented, and those only?

Mr. Boutwell: Yes.

The Witness: You mean by Congress, Congress as it is now constituted, with the other eleven states excluded?

Mr. Boutwell: I do.

The Witness: And you mean the same alternative propositions to be applied to all the eleven states as conditions precedent to their restoration?

Mr. Boutwell: I do.—A. I think she ought to decline, under the circumstances and for the reasons stated, and so ought the whole eleven. Should such an offer be made and declined, and those states, should they be kept out, a singular spectacle would be presented—a complete reversal of positions would be presented. In 1861 these states thought they could not remain safely in the Union without new guarantees, and now, when they agree to resume their former practical relations in the Union, under the Constitution, the other states turn upon them and say they cannot permit them to do so safely to their interests without new constitutional guarantees. The Southern states would thus present themselves as willing for immediate union, under the Constitution, while it would be the Northern states opposed to it. The former disunionists would thereby become the unionists, and the former unionists the practical disunionists.

Testimony of Robert E. Lee *

Mr. Howard: How would an amendment to the Constitution be received by the secessionists, or by the people at large, allowing the colored people or certain classes of them to exercise the right of voting at elections?—A. I think, so far as I can form an opinion, in such an event they would object.

Q. They would object to such an amendment?—A. Yes, sir.

Q. Suppose an amendment should, nevertheless, be adopted, conferring on the blacks the right of suffrage, would that, in your opinion, lead to scenes of violence and breaches of the peace between the two races in Virginia?—A. I think it would excite unfriendly feelings between the two races. I cannot pretend to say to what extent it would go, but that would be the result.

Q. Are you acquainted with the proposed amendment now pending in the Senate of the United States?—A. No, sir; I am not. I scarcely ever read a paper. (The substance of the proposed amendment was here explained to the witness by Mr. Conkling.) † So far as I can see, I do not think the State of Virginia would object to it.

* See above, page 29.

† This amendment was an earlier version of what later became the Fourteenth Amendment. It had been reported to both Houses on January 31, 1866, and it provided that whenever a state abridged the franchise on account of race or color, all persons of such race or color were to be excluded from the basis of representation.

Q. Would she consent, under any circumstances, to allow the black people to vote, even if she were to gain a larger number of representatives in Congress? — A. That would depend upon her interests. If she had the right of determining that, I do not see why she should object. If it were to her interest to admit these people to vote, that might overrule any other objection that she had to it.

Q. What, in your opinion, would be the practical result? Do you think that Virginia would consent to allow the Negro to vote? — A. I think that, at present, she would accept the smaller representation. I do not know what the future may develop. If it should be plain to her that these persons will vote properly and understandingly, she might admit them to vote.

Mr. Blow: Do you not think it would turn a good deal, in the cotton states, upon the value of the labor of the black people — upon the amount which they produce? — A. In a good many states in the South, and in a good many counties in Virginia, if the black people now were allowed to vote, it would, I think, exclude proper representation; that is, proper, intelligent people would not be elected; and rather than suffer that injury they would not let them vote at all.

Q. Do you not think that the question, as to whether any Southern state would allow the colored people the right of suffrage in order to increase representation, would depend a good deal on the amount which the colored people might contribute to the wealth of the state in order to secure two things: first, the larger representation, and, second, the influence derived from these persons voting? — A. I think they would determine the question more in reference to their opinion as to the manner in which those votes would be exercised, whether they consider those people qualified to vote. My own opinion is, that, at this time, they cannot vote intelligently, and that giving them the right of suffrage would open the door to a great deal of demagogism, and lead to embarrassments in various ways. What the future may prove, how intelligent they may become, with what eyes they may look upon the interests of the state in which they may reside, I cannot say more than you can.

Q. Is there any sympathy felt in the South for those schemes of emigration to Mexico? — A. I believe that the masses of the people have not any sympathy with them. There are individuals who think that their interest would be benefited, and, indeed, that their prospects at home are so poor now that it is like losing their lives to remain. That feeling was stronger at the first cessation of hostilities than it is now. At this time it seems to be subsiding.

Testimony of B. R. Grattan *

Mr. Howard: Are you aware of the nature of the constitutional amendment now pending in the Senate of the United States in reference to the basis of representation? — A. Yes, sir.

Q. You know its effect? — A. Yes.

Q. It places the basis of representation upon numbers, including all classes and all races, but at the same time declares that in case any state shall exclude from the right of suffrage any portion of its population on account of race or color, the whole of the people of that race or color shall be excluded from the count, thus leaving the entire option with the states whether they shall exclude or include persons of color in the right of suffrage. I want to ascertain your opinion on that subject, whether you think the people of Virginia are likely ever to consent to let Negroes vote? — A. I should say not, sir, under no circumstances.

Q. Do you not think that the interests of the states would finally so operate as to induce them to take off the unkind proscription of the black race? — A. I do not think so. I would like to explain that. I, perhaps, ought not to undertake to express an opinion for the people of Virginia. My intercourse for years has been very limited. I have been confined very closely to my own duties as a lawyer, and I have mingled very little with the people. Perhaps I speak rather from my own sentiment and opinion. My own opinion about that is, that the very worst thing that can occur to the Negro (and I believe that will be the sense of the people), the very worst consequence to the Negro, will be the attempt to give him political power; and I believe that really the desire to preserve the Negro himself, to take care of him, and to prevent the consequences which will arise to him from such an effort would, of itself, preclude his admission to political rights.

Q. What, in your judgment, would be the consequences of such an enfranchisement: would it produce scenes of violence between the two races? — A. I believe it would. I have very great apprehension that an attempt of that sort would lead to their extermination, not immediately, but to their gradual extinction. It would set up really an antagonistic interest, which would probably be used as a power, because I have no doubt that the Negro vote would be under the influence of white people. You are to recollect that this is not simply a prejudice between the white and black races. It has grown to be a part of our nature to look upon them as an inferior; just as much part of our nature as it is a part of the nature of other races to have enmity to each other; for instance, between the Saxon

* See above, page 122.

Irish and the Celtic Irish, or between the English and the French. You must change that nature, and it takes a long time to do it. I believe that if you place the Negro on a footing of perfect equality with the white, it would actually increase the power of the white race, which would control the Negro vote; yet it seems to me that nothing can reconcile the white people to that short of equal political power, and I fear, therefore, very much the consequences of any attempt of that sort upon the black race in Virginia.

Q. Would not that prejudice become modified a great deal in case the blacks should be educated and rendered more intelligent than they are now? — A. You would have to change their skin before you can do it. I beg leave to say that, so far from there being any unkind feeling to the Negro, I believe that there is, on the part of the white race, towards the Negro, no feeling but that of kindness, sympathy, and pity, and that there is every disposition to ameliorate their condition and improve it as much as possible; but it is that difference which has existed so long in their obvious distinction of color and condition ——

Q. But suppose the condition of the Negro should change? — A. The condition is annexed to the color. We are accustomed to see the color in the condition.

Q. But the condition may be changed by education and enlightenment? — A. You are to recollect, as to that, that they are a people who now have no property, who are not accustomed, from their former condition, to any sort of providence for themselves; that they are not accustomed to take care of themselves; that they are a people who have always depended upon others; and, therefore, unless there is some power or person who is to give them wealth and to educate them, you can never expect that they will be in a condition to rise. They cannot educate themselves; they are not disposed to educate themselves. They live in the very lowest condition of life. They are not disposed to work if they can help it, as nobody else is, I suppose; so that I see no help or expectation that by their own exertions they are going to acquire that amount of property which will enable them to educate themselves. If they rise, it will be by the effort of the white race, among whom they live, to raise them.

Q. Is there a general repugnance on the part of whites to the acquisition and enjoyment of property by the blacks? — A. I do not know. I do not think there is. Far from it. We would be very glad to see them all doing well and improving their condition.

Q. Do you find a similar repugnance to the acquisition of knowledge by blacks? — A. No, sir; far from it; on the contrary, we are trying, so far as we can, to educate them; but we are too poor ourselves to do much in educating other people, and they are certainly too poor to educate themselves.

Q. You would, then, anticipate a struggle of races in case the right of suffrage was given to the blacks? — A. Yes, sir; I think so.

Q. You would not anticipate it in case the blacks should vote in the interest of the white race? — A. As I said before, I believe that if the blacks are left to themselves, if all foreign influence were taken away, the whites would control their vote. It is not in that the difficulty lies, but it is in the repugnance which the white race would feel to that sort of political equality. It is the same sort of repugnance which a man feels to a snake. He does not feel any animosity to the snake, but there is a natural shrinking from it; that is my feeling. While I think I have as much sympathy for the black race, and feel as much interest in them as anybody else, while I can treat them kindly and familiarly, still the idea of equality is one which has the same sort of shrinking for me, and is as much a part of my nature, as was the antagonism between Saxon and Celt in Ireland.

Q. You are aware that that state of feeling does not exist in Ireland, England, or Scotland towards the blacks? — A. No; because they never had them; because they never saw them in their constant condition. So that difference of alienation between Saxon and Celt does not exist here, but it exists in Ireland. It is where that has been the feeling operating for so long that it has become a part of our nature. It is not a simple prejudice, but it becomes part of the nature of the man, because a prejudice may be removed very soon.

Q. You have not much reason to expect that the legislature of Virginia will adopt this constitutional amendment in case it shall pass both Houses of Congress? — A. I cannot speak for others, but for myself I say certainly not. No political power would ever induce me to vote for it. That form is much more objectionable than even a proposition to make them voters. It is giving you all the advantages of numbers, while you are taking that from us which, according to the original constitution, we had — three-fifths of the slave population — and no political power will force me to consent to that.

Q. It will be left to yourselves to make up the number if you see fit. — A. But you leave us to do what you know we will not do, and then you deprive us of power. There would be more reason in an amendment basing representation upon voters.

Q. Have you any idea that the people of Virginia can elect either a legislature or convention that will impose restrictions on the right of suffrage among the whites, such as a property qualification, or the qualification of reading or writing? — A. I do not think so. I think these things never go backward, and I do not think there ever can be any such restrictions. However, perhaps I am as little competent to judge of these things as any intelligent man in Virginia.

Part Five

NEED FOR CONGRESSIONAL INTERFERENCE

13 TESTIMONY ON TERROR IN GENERAL

Testimony of Dexter H. Clapp

Dexter H. Clapp was a New Yorker who had served as a lieutenant colonel with the 38th U.S. Colored Troops. From July 1865 until January 1866, he was an agent of the Freedmen's Bureau in North Carolina. His testimony is illustrative of the impressions of radicals in the area.

Mr. Howard: What position have you been recently occupying in the service? — A. I was lieutenant colonel of the 38th United States colored troops. I am now located in Pitt County, North Carolina. I have been on duty in the Bureau of Refugees, Freedmen, and Abandoned Lands, in charge of twenty counties in the central part of North Carolina. I was on such duty from July 7, 1865, to January 15, 1866. . . .

Q. How are the Union troops treated down there by the secessionists? — A. As a general thing they are treated respectfully. The secessionists dare not treat them in any other way. There is a very wholesome fear of the federal soldiers. A lieutenant died at my house a short time ago, who attempted to make an arrest connected with a series of most outrageous murders. I can relate the circumstances if you desire it.

Q. Go on and give the narrative. — A. Some eight weeks ago several returned rebel soldiers, from Pitt County, went into the village of Washington and commenced shooting and beating Union men. Several assaults were made, and at least one Union man was publicly whipped in the streets, and some Negroes were wounded. One of the party was badly wounded by a person whom they attacked. On their return they met on the public highway a Negro. They first castrated him and afterwards murdered him in cold blood. These persons a short time afterwards went into the village of Washington and gave themselves up to the civil authorities and were placed in jail; but they soon escaped by overpowering the jailer. An order was issued by General Paine, commanding the eastern district, to the police of that county to arrest them. This was not done, and no effort whatever was made to arrest them. General Paine then ordered the chief of police, of Pitt County, to be tried by military commission for neglect of duty. General Paine was soon afterwards relieved from command, to be mustered out of the service, by an order emanating,

I presume, from the Secretary of War, but not connected with this matter. I think for some weeks no further action was taken in the matter.

Q. Where is General Paine from? — A. From Boston, Massachusetts. Meanwhile this party continued to commit outrages on freedmen and Union men. I know that several Negroes were shot by them, and it is reported to me that a large number were shot and otherwise maltreated by them. On the 25th of December the father of one of these parties, an old man named Kearney, was at the store of Church Perkins, in Pactolus, Pitt County, and left about two o'clock to go home. About that time an elderly man answering to the description of that man rode up to a plantation called the Ebon place, where two Negro boys, ten and twelve years old, were playing in the yard, no other persons being at the plantation. He ordered them to go before him on the road, threatening them with his double-barrelled gun. He took them a quarter of a mile down the road and then one mile direct into a swamp, and there he shot them, killing one instantly and wounding the other. The one who was wounded soon came back, and with his father and the mother of the one who was killed went to Pactolus and reported the matter to Lieutenant Smith. He went with them and found the body; shortly after that reports were made to the district commander at Newbern that this party was intending to "clean out" (that is the phrase they use) certain Northern gentlemen in that vicinity, and a party was sent by Colonel Wheeler, consisting of Lieutenant Kenyon, of the Twenty-eighth Michigan, and eight mounted men. They succeeded in arresting all but one of this party, but the prisoners escaped the same night. Two nights after, the soldiers returned to the house of this man, Phil Kearney, a man of considerable wealth, and, in endeavoring to make the arrest, Lieutenant Kenyon was shot. The gentleman living next to Kearney's refused to admit Kenyon into his house, although he was in a dying condition. He was brought to my room at Pactolus, and after about four days he died. A party of soldiers are now at that place endeavoring to arrest this man.

John Stanly, a nephew of Governor Edward Stanly, of North Carolina, the law officer of the eastern district under the provisional government, told me at the time of these transactions that it would not be safe for any person to express in any public place his disapprobation of these acts; that his life would be immediately the forfeit thereof.

Q. Is Stanly still in office? — A. No, sir; he went out with the provisional government; he would not stay in the country, and has gone to California.

Q. What is your opinion about the danger of any person expressing disapprobation of these atrocities? — A. Personally, I think he exaggerated a little, and yet at that time his remark was correct. I intend to live there, and I intend always to express my opinion; but things here look as if it might be dangerous. I am now living on a cotton plantation at Pactolus.

Q. How many persons do you suppose this gang was composed of? — A. About five. Of the thousand cases of murder, robbery, and maltreatment of freedmen that have come before me, and of the very many cases of similar treatment of Union citizens in North Carolina, I have never yet known a single case in which the local authorities or police or citizens made any attempt or exhibited any inclination to redress any of these wrongs or to protect such persons. The substance of this statement was made by me in correspondence with Governor Holden. That seems to me the worst indication of the state of society there — worse than the fact that these things take place.

Q. Do you suppose that the omission on the part of the authorities to interfere and enforce justice arises from their own fears of the ruffians, or from their sympathies with the ruffianism? — A. I think it comes from both causes; it would not be correct to assign either as a specific cause.

Q. How did Governor Holden demean himself towards such outrages; did he make any efforts as governor of the state to punish them? — A. I know of no such effort that he has made.

Q. Have these scenes been brought to his attention? — A. I cannot say that they have, but he must have known of them.

Q. Have they not been subjects of newspaper comments? — A. Yes, sir; I have known of several instances in which outrages were committed, and in which he exerted his influence with the military authorities to have them passed over. I can specify some particular instance.

Q. Do so. — A. A sergeant of the local police, Guion Earp, of Johnson County, brutally wounded a freedmen when in his custody, and while the man's arms were tied, by striking him on the head with his gun, coming up behind his back; the freedman having committed no offence whatever, that was shown.

Q. How is that military police organized; is it constituted under the state laws? — A. No, sir; it is constituted by the military authorities, and it was supposed that the best Union men were selected for the duty. This freedman lay in the hospital, which is under my charge, at the point of death, for several weeks. The sergeant of the police had searched his house previously for stolen meat, but did not find any. The same day he whipped another freedman, having searched his house and found no stolen property there. He whipped him so that from his neck to his hips his back was one mass of gashes, and so that after being untied he sank on the ground and lay there insensible all night, and was found there next morning. While Sergeant Earp was under my charge, and while I was investigating the matter, very many prominent citizens interested themselves to have him entirely discharged, he having been tried by a military commission and sentenced to one month's imprisonment. I was told by General Hardin, commanding the central district of North Carolina, that a large portion of the members of the constitutional convention interposed, first, with General Ruger for his pardon, and then by a petition to the President, to whom the proceedings have all been sent. I do not know whether any action has been taken by the President or not.

Q. Was Earp imprisoned on conviction? — A. He was paroled by General Ruger, awaiting the publication of his sentence. He had been imprisoned some six weeks.

Q. Are scenes like these which you have described of frequent occurrence in North Carolina? — A. They are, in portions of it, not immediately in the vicinity of military posts, but away from them.

Testimony of H. S. Hall

A lieutenant colonel of the 43d U.S. Colored Troops, H. S. Hall was Sub-assistant Commissioner for Freedmen in the northeastern district of Texas. His position gave him a good opportunity to observe conditions in the region.

Mr. Washburne: What have been your opportunities for learning the present condition and feeling of the people of Texas? — A. I have been thrown in contact with a great many of the most wealthy and influential planters, as well as professional men, of fifteen or twenty different counties in northeastern Texas, and have been intimately associated with them in matters of business.

Q. What did you find the state of feeling to be with the parties with whom you have come in contact, in regard to the restoration of the Union? — A. There seems to be a very general desire — an earnest wish — to be immediately admitted into the Union, which takes the shape of a demand of an absolute right. But there is no real love expressed for the government; on the contrary, there is an expression of hatred for the people of the North, and of Yankees generally, while the idea seems to be that they should at once obtain possession of the political privileges and powers which they once had. They seem to have the idea that they are entitled to all the rights under the Constitution which they ever had.

Q. What is the expression of their feeling toward the government, and toward those who control the government? — A. Their expressions are used more particularly in a party sense. They express a great deal of bitterness against the party which they term "the radicals" in Congress. Generally they are in favor of what they term the President's policy; but they denounce most bitterly the policy of the party which they term the radical party.

Q. What do they say about the Freedmen's Bureau? — A. They consider that an unmitigated nuisance. They think it can be much better dispensed with than not.

Q. What shape does their opposition to the Freedmen's Bureau take? — A. They give it no definite form, any more than expressions in words, generally.

Q. Has there ever been any interference with the operations of the Freedmen's Bureau? If so, to what extent? — A. There never has been any direct opposition to any of the officers or the men employed by the government in that bureau, in that part of Texas. There never have been any acts opposed to the operations of the bureau. In most instances they come forward and make contracts under the regulations adopted by the bureau, simply because they are under military jurisdiction, and are compelled to.

Q. What would be the state of the country in which you have been, should the military force be withdrawn, and the officers of the Freedmen's Bureau be also withdrawn? — A. Judging from the state of the country in counties where there is no military force, I can say there would be neither safety of person nor of property for men who had been loyal during the war; and there would be no protection whatever for the Negro.

Q. What would be the condition of the Negro under the circumstances, as compared with his former condition as a slave? — A. He would be, in many instances, forced to labor without any compensation, under some system of compulsion, nearly the same as formerly. He would be liable to worse treatment than ever before — to assaults in many instances, and even to murder. Frequent instances of murder have occurred in those counties where there has been no military force.

Q. Can you particularize some of those instances? — A. One case I can cite was that of a Negro woman named Lucy Grimes. She was taken into the woods in the month of December last, by two men, and there stripped and beaten until she died. These men — named Anderson and Simpson — were well known in the county. On the case being presented to the chief justice of the county, who was appointed by Governor Hamilton, he stated that he could not issue a warrant for their arrest on the evidence of a Negro, as there was no other evidence but that of the son of the murdered woman, and that he could do nothing whatever in the case. I made an effort to arrest the murderers, but they could not be found. They were secured and concealed by parties in the neighborhood.

Q. Do you state these matters from your own personal knowledge? — A. From my own personal knowledge. The case was brought before me. A complaint was made to me of the murder, in the first place.

Q. What were the circumstances attending or leading to the murder of this woman? — A. A child of this Negro woman had taken some money which was lying about some part of the house occupied by Mrs. Grimes, for whom she was working. The child had taken it out of the house and was playing with it. Mrs. Grimes accused the child of stealing the money, and required the mother to whip it; the mother declined doing so. Then Mrs. Grimes went and had an interview with these two men — Anderson and Simpson. Next morning they came and took away the Negro woman, Lucy, saying that they designed taking her to Marshall to present the case to me; instead of which, they took her to a piece of woods two miles from the house, and there stripped her and beat her. She lived till next morning. The son found her and reported the case to me, and I immediately sent out a surgeon with some cavalry. The body was found, and the facts were reported to me by the surgeon. No trace of the murderers could be found.

Q. State the condition in which the body was, and all the circumstances, as you learned them from the surgeon. — A. The body was found entirely naked, with the exception of a shirt. The back was very much beaten and bruised, apparently with some sort of whip or strap. Across the head and face there were several severe bruises, evidently made with a club; and, finally, there was a break in the skull, which the surgeon stated undoubtedly caused the death of the woman, made by a club.

Q. What were the antecedents of the murderers? — A. They were discharged rebel soldiers. Anderson was the son of a gentleman who was considered quite respectable in Harrison County. Simpson was a desperado, not a resident of that part of the country, but of Georgia or Alabama.

Q. Was the mistress of this woman examined by you? — A. She was not.

Q. What part did she take in the matter, so far as you could learn? — A. I could not learn of her taking any part, except conferring with Simpson and Anderson, requesting them to have this Negro punished in some way, simply because she refused to whip the child.

Q. How old was the child? — A. Ten or twelve years.

Q. Who came to see you about it? — A. A grown man; a Negro man twenty-one or twenty-two years of age; a son of the woman who was killed. He came to report the murder of his mother.

Q. You say the chief justice of the county court refused to issue a warrant? — A. Yes; the chief justice, who is now collector of internal revenue for that district, refused to issue a warrant because there was no testimony in the case but Negro testimony.

Q. What is the name of that chief justice? — A. D. B. Bonnefoy.

Q. What are his antecedents? — A. He has been considered an out-and-out Union man during the entire war.

Q. Do you think that his real motive for refusing to issue a warrant was his want of legal authority? — A. I believe it was, because he was firmly of the opinion that he had not the legal authority to do so.

Q. You think he acted honestly? — A. Yes, sir; I think he acted honestly.

Q. That is the law of Texas; is it recognized as being in existence yet? — A. Yes, sir; while that is the case, they at the same time punish Negroes under the same statute as they punish white men at present. They send them to the penitentiary and punish them in the same manner.

Q. Do you know of any other instances in which outrages have been committed on colored people? If so, state them. — A. During the month of November a young man named Webster fired upon a Negro woman who was in his employment for some language which he considered impudent. The ball struck her in the back of the head, resulting in a serious wound, but not causing death. For that offence he was arrested by the military authorities and tried, and fined $100. That was before I arrived at that post. The post was then commanded by Brevet Brigadier General Sheetz, of the Eighth Illinois Regiment of infantry.

Q. Is that the usual penalty imposed by military officers down there for shooting colored people? — A. That was the usual punishment in that part of the state. It had been for the reason that there were no other means of punishment in the hands of the military authorities. That portion of Texas has been considered as belonging to General Canby's department. I have never made any written communication to his headquarters, but I asked General A. J. Smith what I should do in case I succeeded in arresting men who committed murder, where there was no testimony but Negro testimony. His reply was that General Canby would not permit any citizen to be punished by military commission. That, of course, left the military authorities there perfectly powerless to punish adequately any offences upon Negroes. Another case of outrage was reported to me as having occurred at Navarro County. There is a family of Ingrahams there, very wealthy and influential. An unknown Negro came along and asked for work. A son of Hugh Ingraham, and son-in-law, said they would give him work. They armed themselves with revolvers, took the Negro a short distance from the house, in a piece of woods, and there tied him and flogged him to death.

Q. How do you know these facts? — A. This case was reported to me by a citizen of that county. His name I am not able to give; but it is on the records of the office.

Q. Did you take such testimony in the case as satisfied you of the truth of the statement that you now make? — A. Yes, sir; I applied to the commander of the post for a force to send out to arrest those parties. For two or three weeks I was unable to obtain it; the force there not being adequate. The gentleman who reported these facts further stated that he had designed to remove his family to Arkansas; that he had engaged a number of Negroes in the neighborhood of Ingraham's, and started them for a plantation in Arkansas; that his family had been stopped and taken back to his house, the house surrounded by citizens of that part of the country, and threats made that if he made his appearance there again they would take his life. I never was able to get a force of troops to send there, and am not able to give the result. The place is ninety-five miles distant from where I am stationed.

Q. Outside of the influence of the military, what was the condition of things? — A. Exceedingly disordered; no security for person or property, for white or black. I received a letter from Judge Simpson, chief justice of Upshur County, in reply to a communication of mine requesting him to collect the wages of some Negroes who complained to me of being defrauded of their wages. He replied that he was unable to act in the matter without a military force, and that it was impossible for him to arrest anybody or hold anybody accountable for acts committed against the Negroes. That letter I forwarded to Galveston to the assistant commissioner. I also received a letter from Chief Justice Priest, of Cherokee County, asking that an officer be sent there with a military force. There is a similar state of affairs in Panola County. In the month of December last four discharged United States soldiers, returning to their homes at the north, from San Antonio, were followed by a party of desperadoes and murdered in cold blood. The facts were reported to the military authorities at Shreveport, and a force of cavalry was sent out to apprehend the murderers. They passed through Panola County on their track, and reached the town of Henderson, in Rush County. The advance guard of four or five men entered the town, when the citizens gathered together, some with brickbats and some with revolvers, threatening them, and saying they could whip any number of Yankees that could be sent there. Their numbers continued increasing until the whole cavalry party, about twenty men, under the charge of an officer, came up, when they quietly slunk away. The officer who had charge of the party reported the facts to me on his return to Shreveport. He did not succeed in apprehending the murderers.

Q. What were the circumstances attending the murder of these soldiers? — A. As far as I was able to learn, it was a murder committed more for the purpose of robbery than for anything else.

Q. Disconnected with feelings of revenge? — A. I was not informed whether there was any feeling of revenge or spirit of bitterness against them because they had been soldiers.

Q. Of what had they been robbed? — A. Of very little except their horses. They were cavalry soldiers returning home with their horses.

Q. Do you know the names and regiments of the soldiers? — A. I am not able to give you that information.

Q. You are satisfied, from the evidence you had, that they were really murdered? — A. I am satisfied of the fact.

Q. Did you get any clue as to who the murderers were? — A. The name of the principal actor was reported to me, but I am not able to recollect it now. He had been a soldier in the rebel service, and had lost an arm.

Q. Do you know any other instances of violence committed there? — A. In the town of Jefferson, Marion County, Mr. R. H. Robinson, United States treasury agent, had seized some tithe-cotton; he was arrested by the civil authorities and indicted by the grand jury of the county, on a charge of swindling. The telegraphic communication between Jefferson and Shreveport was interrupted, and the despatch which he attempted to send to General Canby in New Orleans was not allowed to go. He was held in custody until he could report the facts to the commanding officer of the force at Marshall, who sent immediately an order to the chief justice, Judge Gray, to release him. Judge Gray refused to release him on the order of the commanding officer, who again sent another order requiring the judge to release him immediately or he would have him arrested and tried before a military commission. Before the second order reached, a file of soldiers, with a captain, which had gone into the town for the purpose of protecting the office there, went to the courtroom and released Mr. Robinson. This case was afterwards reported to General Canby, at New Orleans, and to Colonel Burbridge, the supervising special agent of the treasury. On the case being reported, the action of Mr. Robinson was fully approved, and he was not only relieved from any charge in the matter, but he was sent back to his district at Jefferson.

Q. How long was he held in confinement? — A. About three days. On Christmas Day two soldiers of the 46th Illinois, stationed there at that time, furnished with whiskey by the citizens of Marshall, and under their influence, murdered a Negro by shooting him. The two soldiers were at once arrested by Major Clingman, who was commanding the post. Charges were preferred against them, and a request was forwarded to General Smith for a military commission. The civil authorities, through the chief justice, issued a warrant for their arrest, and a demand was made on the major to turn over the soldiers to the civil authorities. The major very properly refused to comply with the request. No further action has been taken in the matter, but this simply shows the spirit of the civil authorities there.

14 TESTIMONY ABOUT THE MEMPHIS RIOT

Testimony of J. N. Sharp

Dr. J. N. Sharp was a physician from Iowa who had come to Tennessee with the army. Remaining after the end of the war, he became Acting Assistant Surgeon on the staff of the Freedmen's Bureau in Memphis. His testimony, like that of the witnesses who follow, was given before the Select Committee on the Memphis Riots chaired by Representative Elihu B. Washburne. Democratic Representative G. S. Shanklin sought to bring out facts which would support the Southern view of the riot.

The Chairman: What is your residence and business? — A. My residence is Memphis. I have been a surgeon in the army most of the time, and am now acting assistant surgeon, United States volunteers, connected with the Freedmen's Bureau. When the riot occurred I had been out of the service a couple of months.

Q. Where did you reside before you came here? — A. I came from Iowa. I have been here since August 1863, except three weeks in Arkansas.

Q. Did you go up to Arkansas to remain? — A. No; I went on business.

Q. What was the cause of your leaving there? — A. I had a business house there in which my partner remained, and I returned to Memphis and opened an office here. I have been practicing some little since then. My time now is mostly engaged in connection with the Freedmen's Bureau.

Q. Do you know anything connected with the late riots here? — A. Yes, sir. On the evening of the first I was down town, and went home, I think, about four o'clock. As I went up Vance Street I saw a large crowd near Vance and Causey. I did not go there. I saw a policeman I was acquainted with, who told me there was an outbreak of the Negroes. The crowd went out South Street. As I followed along I saw them firing and shooting every Negro they met. When I came to the Bayou bridge I saw another Negro in the bayou being chased. There were, I should think, thirty shots fired at him. He run up right among the crowd, and I saw several policemen shooting at him and beating him with their pistols and clubs. I then went round the corner and met a Negro running, the crowd firing at him. I jumped over into a backyard and went through in front on to Avery Street. There was a Negro lying there who had been shot through the shoulder. I went up to him. I heard that a number of citizens shot him, making the remark that they hoped every one of them would be killed. I saw my wife standing out on the street where we live, and went up and stood by her. About half an hour afterwards I saw another person go along there and kick him several times in the face. He then stepped back, pulled out his pistol, came up again, put it right over his breast, and fired. I went down shortly afterwards and rolled the Negro over. I found that he was pretty badly hurt. He was in the 3d Heavy Artillery last winter, and I knew him when I was at the post hospital. I got a Negro to carry him down home and I dressed his wounds. I went up and was standing in Dr. McGowan's office. A citizen came in there and said he hoped every Negro would be cleaned out. I told him that was riot, and that I thought it was the duty of every good citizen to discountenance such things. There was a Negro boy, who had been left there by Dr. Hood while he went to take care of the wounded. A burly Irishman came into the door half drunk and walked round this boy two or three times. Said he, "You damned nigger, what are you doing here? Why are you not out shooting round the corner like the rest of them?" Dr. McGowan said, "Let that Negro alone, I know him; he is a good boy." He turned to Dr. McGowan and called him a "low, dirty Yankee"; said that he was harboring "damned black scoundrels who were murdering white men." He swore "by God" that they did not want any damned Yankees here, and he be damned if they should stay in the country. I did not say anything, and Dr. McGowan said not another word. There was a large crowd around the door, and I knew if anything was said they would kill us. He called Dr. McGowan a liar, and abused him as an excited, drunken man would. This was after dark on Tuesday night. I started out and had gone about one hundred feet from the door, when somebody with a pistol halted me. I stopped. He said they wanted me; that they were not done with me yet. This was a citizen. He said to two policemen as they came up, "This is one of the men; I know him, by God." The same Irishman who was in the store put his pistol to my breast and said he would kill me. He pushed his pistol against my breast several times. A policeman, who had me by the arm, shoved him off. I appealed to him for protection, and asked him if he was going to stand still and see me murdered right under his eyes. He commenced hallooing for the captain of police. He came and ordered the policeman to let me go, and to let Dr. McGowan and the rest of them alone. I told him that I had not been connected with the mob at all, and, in fact, I had said very little. He told me to go along home. I told him I would not go unless he would give me protection; that I was afraid I would be shot in the back. He told a policeman to see me out of the crowd. The policeman went along with me for some distance. I then went home and staid at home.

Q. Do you believe it was the intention of the mob to kill you? — A. Yes, sir. I believe if the captain of police had not been there I would have been killed. I told Dr. McGowan not to open his mouth; that there were fifty men round the door, and that I had no doubt they intended to kill us. A policeman came to the door and said, "Come here. There is a God damned low Yankee who harbors the Negroes that are out shooting." Carter, the clerk, told him that McGowan had done no such thing. The policeman said, "You are a damned dirty liar; I will shoot you," and drew his pistol to shoot him.

Q. Do you know by whom the pistol was presented to you? — A. By an Irishman; I do not know whether he was a policeman or not.

Q. Have you ever seen that Irishman since? — A. No, sir; I do not know him at all.

Q. Whose wound had you been dressing? — A. Allen Summers's.

Q. How badly was he shot? — A. He was shot in the right shoulder. I thought he had been shot in the breast. He stated that a man stood right over him and shot him. There was a wound about the seventh rib, but when I came to examine it I found it was a stab.

Q. Was there any injury about his head? — A. He was struck over the eye, seemingly, by a policeman's club. The blow was a pretty severe one, and stunned him. He lay for about half an hour before he came to. I dressed the wounds that evening of several colored people. There was one man came to my office — I do not remember his name — who lived out in the country, and had come to town to do business for his employer. He ran into the mob before he knew it. There were two Negroes together, and as a policeman ran between the two he shot this Negro just below the knee. I have not seen him since that afternoon. I went also to see a colored woman the next morning who lived round on South Street. The mob came to her house about midnight, kicked in the door, and asked if there was any man there. She said no. They ordered her to get up and get a light, and while she was doing so someone — her daughter told me it was a policeman — stabbed her twice. I dressed her wounds. They told me the crowd were going round hunting colored men, and were going to "kill every damned nigger" they found. The next night when I went down to see her she was gone, and I have not seen her since.

Q. State the nature of the stabs. — A. The stab in front was just below the bulge of the short ribs and penetrated the cavity. The stab behind was about an inch from the spine.

Q. Was that fatal? — A. I think not; although she was suffering a great deal of pain. I think she was bleeding inwardly, although I did not consider her dangerous when she left. The incision was a small one, not more than a quarter of an inch wide, perhaps made by a pocket knife.

Q. How old was she? — A. She must have been about fifty years of age.

Q. What else did she say they did? — A. I believe that was all. They went from there to other houses. I asked her if she could identify the man who stabbed her. She said not. Her daughter thought she identified the policeman, but she did not strike a light, and could not see him distinctly. While I was standing near the corner of Elliott and Avery Streets, perhaps two hundred yards from South Street, a crowd of police and citizens passed. I saw a little Negro boy, I should think from his looks about twelve years old, come running down an alley to see what was going on. He stood about ten feet from the sidewalk, when a policeman came along, put out his pistol and shot. I saw the smoke of the pistol, saw the boy fall, and heard him cry out. He lay there a little bit, but finally got up and went off up the alley. I did not see or hear anything of him afterwards.

Q. Where was he shot? — A. I thought it was through the hips, judging from the range of the pistol and his walk when he went off.

Q. You do not know the boy's name, or the name of the man who shot him? — A. No, sir.

Q. Was he playing with other boys? — A. No, sir; he appeared to be running down the street to see what was going on.

Q. You have spoken of the wounds you dressed. Were there any others? — A. There were quite a number in the freedmen's hospital, at the head of Main Street, I attended to.

Q. Was Dr. Beecher with you? — A. Yes.

Q. Were they the same parties whose wounds Dr. Beecher saw? — A. Yes.

Q. Then you know nothing of any other cases Dr. Beecher could not testify to? — A. No, sir. I may perhaps remark that this Allen Summers was brought to the hospital.

Q. What did you see the next day? — A. The next morning I started down town, went by the hospital and saw Dr. Beecher. I saw citizens running up street. They said there was a mob up Causey Street. From there the crowd went over to what they call "Lickskittle," on the Overton property, where there were a great many Negro shanties. They then came around on to and up Main Street. I did not go anywhere near them at all; I kept out of the way of them that day. I did not leave my house. I stood at my door sometimes and could see them firing on Main Street. I could see the smoke of the pistols and could see the men, but it was too far off to identify anything.

Q. Are you a surgeon of colored troops? — A. No, sir; I have been for two years in the general hospitals of this city, until last winter, when I was ordered out to the post hospitals at Fort Pickering, where were colored soldiers.

Q. While you were in the fort, and the colored regiment was there, what was their conduct there? — A. Very good.

Q. Do you mean inside the fort or outside? — A. I mean inside.

Q. Do you know how it was outside? — A. I do not. I have heard some complaints of soldiers thieving, but I never saw anything out of the way. They were always polite and gentlemanly towards me.

Q. Do you know of their being riotous or being boisterous towards citizens? — A. I have never seen any of it since I have been in the city, and never saw any difficulty in reference to them until that morning, and then I saw no Negroes fighting or shooting at all. All that I saw were running or trying to get out of the way.

Q. From your knowledge, living here in Memphis and having opportunities to know, will you state what has been the conduct of the colored people in Memphis, those who are soldiers and those who are not soldiers? — A. As far as my knowledge goes it has been very good indeed.

Q. You have known, I suppose, of isolated instances of bad conduct on the part of Negroes? — A. Not more than you would find among the whites. You will now and then find a Negro who will get drunk, steal, break into houses, etc., be arrested and punished, but generally they will be very quiet and peaceable.

Q. What has been the conduct of the people towards colored persons? — A. I have not mixed much with the citizens, and know very little except what I have seen in the streets. When the police arrested a colored man they were generally very brutal towards him. I have seen one or two arrested for the slightest offence, and instead of taking the man quietly to the lock-up, as officers should, I have seen them beat him senseless and throw him into a cart.

Q. How many instances of this kind have you seen? — A. I saw one on South Street about a week before the mob. I was at Dr. McGowan's drugstore. I saw five of the police walking rapidly past. I went to the door and saw a Negro standing on the bridge. He had his arm up over a colored woman. I did not see that he was doing anything. I went back, and in a moment Dr. McGowan called me to the door. They had hold of the Negro pulling him along. The Negro was talking to them and wanting to know what they had arrested him for. They took him along right in front of the drugstore, and one of the policemen went up and struck him over the head from behind. They took him along as far as Causey Street, when he began to pull back. A policeman came up again, struck him over the head and knocked him down with his mouth in the mud. He lay there some time, just quivering, in the mud. They called a dray and put him on. That was the first time I heard any threats on the part of the colored soldiers. They said the man had just come out of the fort, and had not done anything. If they had had the opportunity, I think they would have used some violence. I advised them to keep quiet and let the police officers alone, for I had heard the Negroes say if ever the police came up again and arrested a Negro in that way they would resent it. It was about a week afterwards that the police came up and arrested this Negro that created the riot.

Q. Who was the Negro who created the riot? — A. I do not know, except what I have seen in the papers. I do not know how the thing was started at all. I have heard that a Negro was arrested, and that the Negro soldiers got after him and killed him.

Q. Did you see or hear any other acts of violence committed on the Negroes? — A. No, sir; nothing more. I have dressed the heads of a good many.

Q. How many Negroes' heads have you dressed? — A. When I was in the Gayoso hospital two soldiers came in, one shot through the shoulder and the other struck over the head by a policeman. There was a case last winter, when I was in the post hospital, of a Negro who was shot; I do not remember whether he got well or not; and another case of a Negro who had served in the rebel army, and who had been shot by a policeman on Front Street. He was shot through the brain, and another shot through the heart, and another through the back of the neck, breaking his spine — all three shots fatal.

Q. Do you know under what circumstances he was shot? — A. The Negro was employed on the bluff here by some men who owned cotton. After working all day he had gathered up a sack full of loose cotton, which his employer told him to take to his house. A policeman saw him on the way and accused him of stealing the cotton. The Negro explained how it was, but the policeman arrested him and commenced dragging him along and abusing him. He resisted the policeman, who pulled out his revolver and shot him. The first shot was fatal, and he fell instantly, but the policeman fired two other shots after he was down. The policeman was arrested, tried by a military commission, and, I think, sentenced to the penitentiary at Nashville for five years.

Q. How many of these cases altogether have you seen? — A. These five are all that I know of, or which have come immediately under my own observation. There are a great many many others I have heard of. I could give you no idea how many. There has been a great deal of it going on for the last two or three years.

Q. What has been understood to be the conduct of the police towards the Negroes generally? — A. Very brutal.

Q. Have you known the city authorities to punish a policeman found guilty of murder, assassination, or brutality towards a Negro? — A. No, sir; I do not know of an instance where they have taken any action in reference to this riot, so far. There have been no arrests made by the city or municipal authorities.

Mr. Shanklin: You spoke of having been engaged in business over in Arkansas — what kind of business have you been engaged in? — A. Mercantile and general supply business at Cotton Plant, Woodruff County.

Q. You spoke of an instance of what you conceived to be cruelty to a Negro by a policeman who arrested him about a week before the riot — will you state whether the Negro resisted the policeman in any way before he was struck? — A. Nothing more than to pull back. There were five policemen who had hold of him. They were pulling him along, and of course he pulled back. He was hallooing and talking very loud. I heard the policemen tell him several times to keep quiet, but he still kept pulling back, when the policeman who was behind him struck him.

Q. Then the cause was that he was resisting, and they were compelled by force to drag him along? — A. He did not resist all the time; he would walk along ten or fifteen steps and then stop and want to talk; he would want them to explain why he was arrested; then they would commence dragging him again. One policeman had him by the collar, dragging him when they struck him over the head.

Q. I ask you whether the soldiers in the fort have not been in the habit of coming down into the city in small groups of three or four, or more? — A. Yes, sir, very often.

Q. Will you state whether many of them have not been in the habit of frequenting drinking houses on South Street and in that portion of Memphis? — A. I could not give you an opinion, from the fact that I do not think I was ever on South Street before this riot.

Q. Have you seen them about drinking establishments in the city? — A. Very seldom. I have seen Negro soldiers quite drunk.

Q. Have they been, generally, when drunk, noisy and boisterous, talking loud and cutting up on the streets? — A. I have never seen a Negro on the streets drunk or boisterous. When they got drunk they would generally be arrested and brought back to the fort. It is very seldom you will see one on Main Street drunk. They are generally to be found, when drunk, on the back streets and alleys, where I do not often go. Last winter there were soldiers round all the time patrolling the streets, and when they would find one under the influence of liquor they would bring him in.

Q. Were there many brought in that way? — A. No, sir, not many.

Q. You spoke of threats being made by some Negro soldiers who saw this one arrested and brutally treated by the police — will you now state what language you then heard used? — A. I will tell you just as nearly as I can remember. When they started off with the Negro on the dray or cart, there were, perhaps, twenty-five Negroes standing there on the corner, and perhaps half of them Negro soldiers. As I came back I heard a Negro say that the police never came up on that street to arrest a Negro without arresting him in about that style — that they must fall upon him and beat him senseless before they could carry him away. As I remember, he said, "That is about played out," or something similar. Said he, "By God, if I catch a policeman arresting one of our men in that way again I will resist him." The man's name is Posey. I said to him, "You had better mind your own business. These men are officers of the law, and they have arrested that man for something you do not know anything about." I counselled them to let the police alone.

Q. What reply did they make? — A. I do not know that they made any reply. I went off and went on home. There was considerable excitement among them at the time. They were talking on the corners pretty loud, as Negroes will, denouncing these things, etc.

Q. Do I understand you to say you have never seen these Negroes upon the streets act rudely or discourteously towards the police or anybody else? — A. I never have. I have been here three years, and have never had a Negro insult me or crowd me off the sidewalk. They invariably get out of the way when I come along. I have never had a rude word from one of them.

Q. Have you never seen anybody else crowded off the sidewalk by them? — A. I never have. I think they have received credit for things they have never done. There has never been a robbery, theft, or burning, where the parties were not known, that has not been charged to the Negro soldiers here.

Q. Has there never been any charges of that kind made against white men in the papers? — A. Yes, sometimes, but that was where the parties were known. Arrests have been made of white men for stealing, murder, and drunkenness, but wherever there were houses burned or broken into at night, and the parties were not known, the Negroes had to bear the blame.

Testimony of Lucy Tibbs

Lucy Tibbs was the wife of a Negro member of a Mississippi River steamboat crew. She resided in Memphis and was one of the victims of the rioters.

The Chairman: Where do you live? — A. I have lived in Memphis very nearly three years.

Q. How old are you? — A. I do not know exactly. I suppose about twenty-four.

Q. Have you a husband? — A. Yes; my husband is on a steamboat. We came here from Jackson, Arkansas, when the rebellion broke out.

Q. Were you here during the riots? — A. Yes, sir.

Q. State what you saw. — A. Where I am living is where they had the best part of the fight. On Tuesday afternoon, when I first started on South Street, I did not see it. When I saw the crowd they broke and run in every direction, boys and men, with pistols, firing at every black man and black boy they could see. They shot them down as fast as they could come to them.

Q. How many did you see shot down on Tuesday? — A. I saw two. I knew one of them very well; he was a sergeant at the fort. Both of them belonged to the fort. They were killed dead about ten rods apart.

Q. By whom were they killed? — A. The first was killed by John Pendergrast.

Q. Is he a policeman? — A. No, sir; he keeps a grocery right there by my house. I was looking right at him when he shot the man. The soldier made an effort to get up the bayou. Mr. Pendergrast went to a policeman and got another pistol and shot him in his mouth.

Q. How near was he? — A. As near as you are to me. I saw him put his pistol right to his head. I cried out, "Look here; see John Pendergrast shooting down innocent men in that way." By this time another man came in sight, about one hundred yards off. They beat him and kept him down until they could load their pistols. They shot him three times, burst his head open, and killed him.

Q. How far were you from this? — A. About one hundred yards off.

Q. Were you near enough to see distinctly? — A. Yes, sir; I was near enough to know him. This Pendergrast is such a notable man I could not help but know him.

Q. Who killed the second man? — A. There were so many round I could not tell who killed him. Pendergrast was there. A colored man saw him fall over his dog in trying to get to him. I could not say who it was that killed him.

Q. What did they do after they left this second man? — A. They just broke back to South Street, shooting at every colored man they saw.

Q. How many other soldiers did you see them shoot at? — A. I could not tell exactly. Every man they saw they went after, and the men would get behind other houses and out of sight. I do not know whether they killed any more at that time or not. There were plenty of them killed on South Street; but I did not see them killed.

Q. How many dead colored people did you see on South Street altogether? — A. There were four who laid about two hundred yards from my house two days and nights. There was a colored girl burned up just a little way from my house. Her name was Rachael Hatcher.

Q. Did the four you mention include the two you saw shot? — A. Yes, sir; four in all. I saw Rachael when they shot her, and I saw her when she was burned up.

Q. What were the circumstances under which she was burned? — A. They burned down the schoolhouse that day, and at night they set the houses on fire. They barred up all the doors, then surrounded the houses and told the folks to stay in there.

Q. Is that what they told you? — A. Yes, sir; but I saw them surround the houses. The old man Pendergrast and his son set them on fire. I saw them when they set the houses on fire. When the fire got very hot I saw men, women, and children break out and run to the bayou. They shot at them as fast as they could while they were running. They wounded some of them, but did not kill any except that girl. When the house she was in was on fire she ran out, and just as she turned the corner they shot her in the mouth. She fell down between two houses, and both houses were burned. I saw her body the next day, and they took it away the same evening.

Q. Who took these bodies away finally? — A. They said the citizens took them away. I know the wagons went round that evening and took them up. It was white men that took them away.

Q. How long did the bodies remain before they took them away? — A. Some of them lay from Tuesday afternoon until Thursday or Friday before they were taken up. I took no notice of the date.

Q. Were there any threats made against you? — A. Mr. Pendergrast's boy, the one that has since run off, said to a yellow woman that if I said he killed the man across the bayou he would kill me.

Q. Who is this Pendergrast? — A. This young man run off about three weeks ago, but he dodges back and forth. The old man is still there, and one of his sons.

Q. Was it the young man or the old man you saw shoot? — A. It was the young man who run off. I saw the old man and his youngest son both in the crowd there.

Q. Did the old man have pistols? — A. The old man and his son both had pistols. Just where I live, when the greatest fight was going on Wednesday morning, there were, I should think, four hundred persons in the crowd. They were just firing at every colored man and boy they could see. They killed a colored soldier just above my house on Wednesday morning, about nine o'clock. The policeman Roach shot this man and wounded him in the leg. A man by the name of Galloway, a white drayman, was there. The policeman said, "Galloway, there is a damned rascal who was in the fray yesterday afternoon." There were two soldiers together; one of them ran and got away. They surrounded the other and kept him there. He said to them, "I was not in it at all; please don't kill me." They said, "Yes, you were," and policeman Roach fired and shot him in the leg. At this time he was rather leaning over a gate. Galloway walked up to him, put a pistol to his head and shot him down. He died before anybody could get to him. After Mr. Cash shot Charley Wallace, and they had searched his pockets, some women came up and bathed his head in water. He belonged to the 59th Regiment. I do not know the name of the other colored man who was shot.

Q. Where does this Mr. Cash live? — A. He is staying at Pendergrast's now.

Q. What does he do? — A. He is not doing anything. He got burned out some two months ago. I understood he bought another place a few days ago.

Q. I understand you to say, then, you saw four men killed under the circumstances stated, and that you know in addition of two others being killed, and that then you saw the dead body of this girl Rachael? — A. Yes, sir; and my brother got killed on Tuesday afternoon; who killed him I do not know.

Q. What was his name? — A. His name was Bob Taylor. He had been a member of the 59th Regiment, but was out of the service. On Tuesday afternoon when they were firing and going from house to house, I told him to try and get away if he could. He started to run away, but was found dead the next morning by the bayou just back of my house. He was older than I am. They robbed me that night of $300 of his money.

Q. Did they come into your house? — A. Yes; a crowd of men came in that night; I do not know who they were. They just broke the door open and asked me where was my husband; I replied he was gone; they said I was a liar; I said, "Please do not do anything to me; I am just here with two little children."

Q. Did they do anything to you? — A. They done a very bad act.

Q. Did they ravish you? — A. Yes, sir.

Q. How many of them? — A. There was but one that did it. Another man said, "Let that woman alone — that she was not in any situation to be doing that." They went to my trunk, burst it open, and took this money that belonged to my brother.

Q. Did they violate your person against your consent? — A. Yes, sir; I had just to give up to them. They said they would kill me if I did not. They put me on the bed, and the other men were plundering the house while this man was carrying on.

Q. Were any of them policemen? — A. I do not know; I was so scared I could not tell whether they were policemen or not; I think there were folks that knew all about me, who knew that my brother had not been long out of the army and had money.

Q. Where were your children? — A. In bed.

Q. Were you dressed or undressed when these men came to you? — A. I was dressed.

Q. Did you make any resistance? — A. No, sir; the house was full of men. I thought they would kill me; they had stabbed a woman nearby the night before.

Q. How old are your children? — A. One of them will soon be five, and the other will be two years old in August.

Q. What did they mean by saying you was not in a condition to be doing that? — A. I have been in the family way ever since Christmas.

Q. Who was this woman stabbed the night before? — A. I do not know. I heard a woman and a man who went over there and saw her talking about it.

Q. Was she violated too? — A. I suppose she was; they said she was. The next night they burned all those shanties down. Where they went to I could not tell.

Q. How many houses did they burn down? — A. Three or four.

Q. Would you know this man who committed violence upon you if you should see him? — A. I do not think I would.

Q. What countryman was he? — A. I could not tell.

Q. What countrymen did the crowd appear to be? — A. They appeared to be like Irishmen.

Q. How many rooms were there in your house? — A. Only one.

Q. And this took place in the presence of all these men? — A. Yes, sir.

Q. Have you stated everything you know? — A. They killed a woman's husband who lives next house to me. He lived a week. She was gone to the fort. The next day he said he would stay close in the house, and he did not think they would trouble him. They called him outside the house and shot him down. There was a crowd about, and I could not tell who shot him. They shot him three times, and one of them said, "Damn you, that will show you how to leave your old mistress and master." They took $25 from his pocket. I saw them when they shot him on Wednesday morning. His name is Fayette Dickerson.

Q. Then that makes five you saw killed? — A. Yes, sir.

Q. Did you know any one in this last crowd? — A. The old man Pendergrast and his three sons were all in the crowd. Mr. Cash was there and Charley Toler.

Q. Who is Charley Toler? — A. He is a young white boy, very nearly grown, who lives right there. I could not identify any of the others, except Charley Smith; I did not see him kill anybody or do anything. He said he had been in the Union army; he had been teaching school; I had been to school to him. I asked him if he would not come and stay at my house and protect it. He said he could not and could not tell me anything about it; that he was out with his gun the night before with thirty or forty others, and he did not know what they were going to do — that the Negroes started it, and that he would be ready for them. I believe he was put in jail.

Q. What for? — A. A woman who washed his clothes made complaint against him. His clothes were all bloody, and she supposed he brought a dead man's clothes there for her to wash. They were clothes he had never brought before.

Q. Do you know who he was arrested by? — A. He was arrested by the bureau and is confined at the fort.

Mr. Shanklin: Did you see the commencement of the fight, or had you heard shooting before you saw anything? — A. I did not see the commencement; I heard the first firing.

Q. Where is your house located? — A. Just the other side of South Street, on Rayburn Avenue.

Q. What time was it in the evening when you saw the first fighting? — A. I suppose about six o'clock, perhaps half an hour before sundown, when I saw the first man killed. I had heard shooting before that.

Q. How far from where you live was the first firing that afternoon? — A. It was right in sight of my house. I could not tell you how far. I suppose about two blocks.

Testimony of Marcus J. Wright

Marcus J. Wright was a Memphis lawyer who before the war had served as clerk of the city's Common Law and Chancery Court. After joining the Confederate army, in 1862 he became military governor of Columbus, Kentucky, and was promoted to the rank of brigadier general. After Appomattox, he retired to Memphis, where he resumed his law practice. Appointed by General Stoneman as a citizen member, he served on a commission to investigate the Memphis Riot. In later years, he collected Confederate documents and was one of the compilers of the Official Records of the War of the Rebellion. *His testimony is representative of the views of conservative Southern whites.*

Mr. Shanklin: Were you in the city during the recent riot? — A. Yes, sir.

Q. Will you state whether you saw any part of that riot, and what you did? — A. I saw no part of it; I was at my office daily, which was then on Second Street above Jefferson; there was no riotous proceeding in that vicinity, or in the vicinity of my residence.

Q. Did you see passing through the streets any of those mobs, so as to form an opinion as to the character of the people who constituted them? — A. I did not.

Q. Will you state, from your knowledge, or any information on which you can rely, what was the character and class of the mob who perpetrated the atrocities upon the colored people during the riots, and state, also, your sources of information? — A. The ablest source of information I have is the testimony of others who were present, and who stated to me that they saw different riotous proceedings, such as shooting citizens; that there were no citizens engaged in them, except such as the policemen, and the rabble who were with them were low people whom they did not recognize as citizens.

Q. From your intercourse, and from the opinions you have heard expressed by the masses of the citizens of Memphis, what is the state of feeling existing between those masses and the colored population in the city of Memphis since and previous to this riot? — A. I do not think there is any unkind feeling among the mass of citizens towards the Negro — certainly not among those who were the former owners of Negroes. I think their disposition is to be kind to them, and that they prefer them to new servants. I know of instances during these riots — at least I know from information — where the Negroes sought protection from their former owners; but I think there is a hostile feeling towards the Negroes entertained by some men of a low class who are engaged in business, and who regard the Negroes in the same business as their rivals. As a general rule, these men are foreigners, and are engaged in driving hacks and drays, and a very large majority of the draymen of the city are Negroes, and many of them have been doing business for particular houses for years — for many large houses will have so many draymen all the time — and these men will sometimes underbid them in draying, and not being able to get their business, would entertain bad feelings towards the Negroes. I think the bad feeling towards them is confined to this class, though there may be exceptions. I have heard no expression of unkind feeling towards the Negro uttered by respectable people.

Q. What are the feelings and sentiments of the resident colored people towards that better class of white people? — A. Very kind — exceedingly kind. They feel that they are their friends, and rely upon them in matters requiring advice or assistance, when they generally seek them out.

Q. State, so far as you have been able to learn it, from your intercourse with the businessmen of Memphis, property holders, and the fixed residents of the city, what is their sentiment in regard to this riot, and the outrages perpetrated upon the Negroes. — A. I have heard but one expression from that class, and that is condemnation of it. During the time the riot was going on, a good many persons who had been in the army with me (I had been in the Confederate army) came to me and said that outrages were being committed by a low class of people — that they were getting up a riot, and they wanted to put it down. They asked me what they should do; I said, nothing, unless General Stoneman called upon them. Their object was to suppress it, and they were willing to put it down; but I told them they were under parole, and they must take no step unless they were called upon by General Stoneman.

Q. Was that the common feeling among the paroled soldiers, as far as you know? — A. It was the entire feeling, as far as I know.

Q. Did they act upon your advice? — A. Yes, sir. Some of them were afterwards summoned by the sheriff, and they told him they must do nothing except upon the call of General Stoneman. This was to excuse themselves for not serving under the sheriff.

Q. I will ask if the effect and operation of the franchise law which has been in force for a year or two in Tennessee has been to throw the control of the city elections into the hands of what is considered here an inferior class of people? — A. That is my opinion, sir. The proof that was required to be made under the law at the last municipal and county elections (I am not familiar with the present law) was a certificate from two witnesses that he had always been an unconditional loyal man to the

United States; and there was a large number of men that went to the polls with certificates and proofs from two men that had not been here for the required length of time — six months — and probably the party whom they proved had not been here six days.

Q. Was the effect of that law to disfranchise a large portion of the citizens of Memphis? — A. Yes, sir; it disfranchised perhaps four-fifths of the property holders here. The businessmen here, with few exceptions, were almost entirely disfranchised.

Q. Is the effect of that law to place the control of the election in the hands of such men as constitute the police force, the hackmen, draymen, and men who work on the wharf? — A. I think so, sir. It put the power of election in the hands of those who have very little or no material interest in the city, and who had not been resident here for any long time, and were not known to the older businessmen of the city.

Q. Is it a fact that the police force was taken from that class — draymen, day laborers, hackmen, etc.? — A. I do not know; but I know from seeing the police mustered daily at the station-house, and from seeing them frequently, that a large majority of them are Irish. One or two have been here for some time; Garrett, chief of police, has been here a long time, but the larger portion are strangers to me. At one time I knew nearly everybody here.

Q. Is Garrett an Irishman? — A. No, sir; he is not.

Q. Will you state whether you were not selected by General Stoneman as one of the military commission to investigate this riot, and whether you acted on that commission? — A. Yes, sir; General Stoneman requested me in person to come. He said he intended to appoint a commission of officers of the army, and he would like to select one citizen of Memphis to act with them; as I had resided here a considerable length of time, and as he happened to know me personally, he said he would be glad if I would serve, and I did serve on the commission with General Runkle, Captain Allyn, and Captain Colburn, of the quartermaster's department.

The Chairman: What position did you occupy in the army? — A. I was brigadier general towards the close of the war.

Q. You stated that you were on this commission to examine into this riot? — A. Yes, sir.

Q. Did your commission make any report as to its judgment and conclusion? — A. No, sir; we only reported the facts. General Stoneman told me in the first place that he did not desire an opinion; he merely desired the facts. Afterwards General Stoneman requested the recorder of the court to inform us that he would like us to make up a report; but, as the proceedings will show, we asked to be relieved, as there would probably be two or three reports. General Runkle was anxious that it should be so, for, as chief of the bureau, he had a report to make to his superior officer, and he did not want to make two reports.

Q. To what conclusion did you come as to the nature, extent, and character of the riots? — A. I became satisfied, from the investigation, that the beginning of it was the arrest of some Negroes, who had been soldiers, by the police. They arrested some men, and had them under charge, when other Negro soldiers following after them, and probably under the influence of liquor, commenced firing on them. The fighting commenced between the police and discharged Negro soldiers, and there had evidently been strong feelings between the police and the colored soldiers. It was at first a sort of skirmish; then the police called for assistance, and gave notice to their different friends and the rabble, who have no particular property to be preserved, and who are always ready for a row, and it then assumed the proportions of a very considerable riot. I do not think that one-half or one-quarter of the people who went there went from anything but curiosity, but I have no doubt that many shot down Negroes without any cause in the world, and that they burnt schoolhouses, churches, and dwellings on Wednesday night, and robbed, and committed very many outrages of that sort.

Q. Was it deemed necessary to call in United States troops to suppress this riot? — A. Yes, sir.

Q. What do you think would have been the consequence if there had been no regular troops to rely upon in the emergency? — A. I think fifty good men could have checked it at any time.

Q. If there had been no troops here? — A. I think the sheriff could have selected a number of men who would have checked it. Such crowds are always cowardly; and I think they could have been checked. There were many men here ready to go.

Q. Do you think the mob would have been checked had it not been for the regular troops? — A. I think it would, sir, by the old citizens; I judge so from the expression of feeling on the part of the citizens.

Q. Did they make any attempt? — A. No, sir; I think they depended upon the troops.

Q. What do you think of the troops being here for the preservation of the peace? — A. I do not think that they are necessary. I think the Negro troops here have not tended to the peace of the place; the city has been more quiet since they left.

15 TESTIMONY ABOUT THE NEW ORLEANS RIOT

Testimony of Rufus K. Howell

Justice Rufus K. Howell was a prominent Louisiana Unionist, who, after having served since 1857 on the District and Probate Courts of New Orleans, resigned in 1864 to become a leading member of the convention which drew up Louisiana's first Free State constitution. In 1865, he was appointed Associate Justice of the State Supreme Court, and in 1866, acting as President of the adjourned 1864 convention, he tried to recall it in order to reverse the conservative trend of the time. The New Orleans riot was the result. Howell as well as the following witnesses testified before the committee to investigate the New Orleans riots chaired by Congressman Thomas D. Eliot. Democratic Representative Benjamin M. Boyer sought to bring out facts to strengthen the President's case against the radicals.

The Chairman: State your residence. — A. New Orleans.

Q. How long have you resided here? — A. I have resided in New Orleans since the fall of 1850, with an intermission of a few months in 1855 and 1856.

Q. State during that time what public offices you have held? — A. The first public office I held was that of school director; I held that some years. In April 1857, I was elected to the bench of the district court of the city of New Orleans, and was reelected in 1861, after the secession of the State of Louisiana. I held that office until March 1864, when I was transferred to another of the district courts, the probate court, and resigned that position in July 1864. The first of April 1865, I was appointed by Governor Wells associate justice of the supreme court of the State of Louisiana, which position I now hold. I was a member of the convention of 1864, elected from the seventh representative district of the city of New Orleans, while holding a commission as judge of the second district.

Q. What office in the convention did you hold? — A. I was merely a member. I was a defeated candidate for president. Judge Durell was elected president. At the second meeting of the convention, on the 26th of June, 1866 — a preliminary meeting held for the purpose of calling the convention together — I was elected president. Judge Durell had then left the city, having notified the convention previously of his intention so to do.

Q. State what steps you took for calling the convention. — A. I simply drew up a call under the direction of that preliminary meeting, composed of some forty-five members, and published it. The call was issued on the 8th. . . .

Q. Pursuant to this call what took place? — A. Some twenty-five members of the convention assembled in answer to their names on the 30th of July, a few minutes after twelve o'clock. There being so small a number present, a motion was made to take a recess of an hour to give the sergeant-at-arms an opportunity to go out and notify members known to be in town that we were assembled and would await their attendance. Some five or six members came in immediately. It took some little time for the sergeant-at-arms to select his messengers to go around to the different places and notify members. We had information that there were sixty or over in town. There were some fifty members residing in town, and some ten or fifteen in the country who had come in. While the sergeant-at-arms *pro tem* — selected for the occasion — was selecting his messengers, we heard music in the direction of Canal Street, and the report of a pistol, as well as we could distinguish from that distance. A few minutes afterwards a band of music appeared in the middle of the street, coming up from Canal Street, attended by a flag and followed by an indiscriminate crowd, filling the entire street. I could not estimate the number — it was not a very large crowd. It passed from beyond my view from the side window in the building where I was standing. I went down to the governor's office. I had received a message that the adjutant of General Baird was there and desired to see me. As I went down this flag was carried up into the hall. I had an interview with General Baird's adjutant as to the character of the crowd and the prospects of the convention. Captain Caziark, I believe, was the adjutant's name. He asked me when we were going to meet. I told him that we had already met and adjourned. He said, "Don't you meet at six o'clock?" I replied that we would not; that if we were to assemble so late in the afternoon it might encourage some disposition to disturb us; that we would not sit later than three o'clock; that we expected to assemble again about half past one o'clock, and before three would adjourn till the next day. The crowd by this time was increasing in front of the Mechanics' Institute building, but Captain Caziark and I parted under the impression that there would be no disturbance at all. He said the object of his mission to me was to know whether there was likely to be any disturbance at the Institute. I immediately returned to the hall upstairs, but had scarcely got into the room when the firing was renewed just in front of the building, and apparently continued for two or three minutes. A good deal of consternation appeared in the room where we were. The room was about one-third full, I suppose. I determined to go to the governor's office and see if we could devise any means to prevent the disturbance from extending. I went through the back way, and as I passed the platform I saw the corpse of a Negro lying on the opposite side of the street. When I got into the front room occupied by the governor's private secretary, the street was entirely clear in front of the building down nearly to Canal Street. There was a mass of persons who seemed to be kept back by a line of policemen, while in the other direction on my left was another crowd headed apparently by a larger number of policemen than on my right. The governor was not there; he had left at eleven o'clock. I sat down to write to General Baird informing him of what was going on; but I had scarcely written three lines when this crowd on my left began to move simultaneously on the building, and commenced firing into the windows. They seemed to be shooting into the side as well as at the front windows. I moved from there, of course, and the crowd from below at this moment began to move up. There was general confusion and excitement. I was advised by the governor's son to take my position with some others in his father's room, which occupied the lower floor, immediately under one side of the hall. He remarked that if they saw me in there they would certainly shoot me. I was not an eyewitness to anything more that occurred after that as to attacks in the building. I remained in the governor's parlor during the whole day. Missiles of various kinds, brickbats, bullets, etc., pretty frequently came into the room where we were. There was an open lot just at the side of the building, and I could occasionally see, through the curtains, what was going on there. There was an almost uninterrupted firing and yelling in that lot for some time. The lot, I learned afterwards, was occupied by a family of Negroes.

Q. How long did you remain in the governor's room? — A. From one o'clock until after four. Seeing then that the military were apparently in possession of the city, I thought it safe for me to attempt to get home. I knew that my family were anxious. As I went out into the private secretary's room, a police officer standing there, inquired how I got into that building. I replied that I had been there all day. He then said, "You are my prisoner," and ordered me to go with him. Just at that moment three officers of the army, whom I had seen approaching, came to the steps, and one of them asked me if I was a member of the convention. I told him I was, and asked him if I should accompany this policeman. One of them replied he knew nothing about it. The policeman, who had released me and stepped back when the officer spoke to me, again stepped up, took me by the collar, jerked me out, and blew his whistle for help. The military sentinels who had possession of the street let a policeman through, and he came to the assistance of the one having me in charge, both drawing their revolvers. I remarked that it was unnecessary to make such demonstrations; that I should certainly not attempt to make my escape, and prevailed upon them to let go of me. I walked along, and they with me. After they knew who I was, they were exceedingly abusive all the way to the station of the first district, where they conducted me. They were only restrained when I told them that I was in their power, and they could of course say what they pleased. Occasionally, as we passed along, some of the crowd would use offensive language, but there was no active violence. They stated that their object in keeping their pistols in their hands was to keep the crowd off, but the crowd of citizens was pretty well dispersed by that time. It was nearly five o'clock when I arrived at the police station, where I was locked up.

Q. How many police were out at that time? — A. I did not see many as I was going to the police station.

Q. How long did you remain at the police office? — A. I was in the cell about half an hour, I suppose, when General Baird sent to Colonel Crosby to have me released. While I was waiting for the turnkey to let me out, the mayor and Lieutenant Governor Voorhees came up, and said they had just heard of my arrest, and proposed to release me on my parole, and I was let out with the understanding that if my services were needed during the night to repel any disturbance, they would call on me. The lieutenant governor proposed to walk with me towards my residence, and protect me from the crowd on the streets. He did accompany me several squares, and until we had gone beyond where there was anything like a collection of persons, and I then walked home alone. I remained in my house pretty closely for two weeks. After a few days my attention was called to the movements of an individual who seemed to be hanging around the house, and watching it. He proved to be Lucien Adams, of the mayor's secret corps. I learned indirectly that his motive was to see that I did not assemble the convention in my residence. Whether that was true or not, I do not know. He was round my house every morning and night for about two weeks. I was out the next day after the riot to call upon several who had been wounded or hurt.

Q. Can you state how many were wounded or killed on the 30th? — A. I know of but one member of the convention who was killed — Mr. Henderson. Dr. Dostie was killed, and the Rev. Mr. Horton. They were the only white persons who were killed to my personal knowledge.

Q. How many Negroes were killed? — A. That is problematical. My belief is that the specific number will never be ascertained.

Q. How many to the best of your judgment? — A. To the best of my judgment, between fifty and one hundred — probably as many as one hundred.

Q. How many were killed or wounded excepting those who were friendly to the convention, if any? — A. I have heard of but one who was killed on the opposite side. Some eight or ten were wounded, as I learned from hearsay. That one was killed in the yard of the Medical Institute.

Q. What was his name? — A. Cenas, the son or nephew of Dr. Cenas.

Q. Are you able to state how that man was killed? — A. I am not, from my personal knowledge.

Q. Can you state whether any arrangement of any kind had been made by members of the convention to resist by force any attempt to arrest members of that body? — A. On the contrary, I know it was the general understanding of those with whom I conversed that we would submit quietly to an arrest, if attempted by any proper authority. It was talked over freely before the meeting.

Testimony of Charles W. Gibbons

Before the war, Charles W. Gibbons had been a free Negro in Louisiana. After an unsuccessful effort on the part of the Confederates to enlist him in a black unit, he joined the Union army and became a captain in the black Louisiana Native Guards. Because of the prejudice against Negro officers, he was forced to resign but reentered the service to repel General Richard Taylor's forces. An eyewitness of the riot, he held views common among the educated blacks in Louisiana.

The Chairman: State where you live. — A. 290 Gravier Street, New Orleans; I have lived here ever since I was born; I am about twenty-eight years of age.

Q. Were you in the city on the 30th of July last? — A. I was.

Q. Did you witness any of the disorders on that day? — A. I did.

Q. State, beginning in the morning and going through the day, all that you saw and heard in connection with the riot. — A. On the evening of Friday previous to the riot there was a man by the name of Tasspot who went to the meeting, and fell dead there. We were invited on Sunday to go to his funeral, which was on the Sunday evening previous to the riot. When on the corner of Custom-house Street I stepped into a little grocery, and overheard two policemen talking. I heard one of them say, "By God, we are going to hang Dostie and Hahn." The other policeman said, "Do you think so?" The first one said, "Yes, we are going to shoot down all these God damned niggers." I think the numbers of these policemen were 41 and 42; I took the numbers, and as I am nearsighted, and to be positive, I got some of my friends to get the numbers so as to be sure. There were two policemen and a citizen together; one policeman was larger than the other; the smallest policeman made the remark, "You cannot do that; there are too many troops here." The citizen said there were not many troops here, only a few companies of the Eighty-first up by the cotton-press. The policeman asked if there were not some up at

Camp Parapet and some at Fort Jackson. The citizen said, before there would be time to bring them up they could exterminate the niggers. They did not see me at the time; I was in the grocery store; the moment they saw me they stopped. I mentioned what I had heard to Captain Jourdan, and he said I had better go and take the numbers of these policemen, which I did, and got some of my friends also, to be sure that the numbers were correct. The next morning, which was Monday morning, I made out a statement in writing of what I had heard, though, by the advice of a friend, I did not sign my name. I took it to Dr. Dostie's house; he was not in. I gave the letter to the servant, and asked her to give it to Dr. Dostie when he came in. The servant said she would; that she expected Dr. Dostie would be in soon. I said I would call back. I went back and found Dr. Dostie in. I told him I came to warn him of the danger about to happen to him. He made the remark to me, "I am going unarmed; I know they want to take my life, but I think it is a good cause to die in; if they want to take my life they can do so." Said I, "You can do as you please; I thought it my duty to call and tell you, as in your remarks at the meeting on Friday night you told the people to come out and attend the convention." He said on that night, "Go home — go quietly — go orderly — behave yourselves, and if there is anybody, white or black, that disturbs you, protect yourselves." These were the remarks he made. After that I bade him good morning, and then went home; and at half past eleven o'clock I went to the convention; a friend went with me, a Creole. As we were going along he said to me, "Captain, there is a procession coming up." It was coming up Dauphin Street, and I went over there with him; there were, perhaps, forty or fifty persons in the procession. They had an American flag, which I believed belonged to the First Native Guards. We turned up Burgundy Street to Canal Street with the procession. As we got there I was right behind the band. A man in citizen's clothes, having a blue ribbon in his buttonhole, stepped out and ordered the procession to halt. No one would halt for him. Then he fired. Whether he hurt anybody or not I do not know. With that the procession became somewhat confused.

Q. Where was this first shot fired? — A. It was right on Canal Street, near Dryades Street. He then turned and ran towards the levee. A part of the procession ran after him. Then they came back, formed into line, and marched to the hall. After we got into the hall (I was up there about ten minutes), if I am not mistaken, the flag was taken up to the stand. I am not positive about that. During the time that I was there I noticed a detective, who seemed to be noticing what he could see or hear. I made the remark that there was going to be something squally. By and by I heard firing outside. I went to the door, and came up Dryades Street towards Common Street. There was a policeman about ten feet from me, who said, "There goes one damned nigger captain, the son of a bitch; kill him." He fired at me. Then two or three of them ran out together. I ran with the friend who was with me until we were midway on the block from Common Street. I said to him, "Let us turn round, and we may have a chance to dodge the balls." I had done that when I was in the army. We turned round and retreated about ten steps backwards, when my friend said, "I am shot; I believe I am killed." He put his hand to his side and fell. I turned and ran. When I reached the corner of Common and Dryades, two men grabbed me and said, "What are you doing here?" Said I, "Doing nothing." Said he, "You God damned black son of a bitch, go 'way, God damn you." I went to the corner of Baronne, and there I was arrested. They carried me about twenty steps. There were others with me. I stepped aside without their noticing me, and got away from them. That is all I know of it.

Q. Where did you go then? — A. I went home.

Q. What was the name of the man who was shot? — A. I do not know. He was in the same regiment with me; but I did not know his name.

Q. Where did you join the procession? — A. At the corner of Conti and Dauphin Streets.

Q. Who fired that first shot? — A. I do not know the gentleman.

Q. Was he a policeman? — A. I cannot say; he had a blue ribbon tied in his buttonhole.

Q. What had the procession been doing that made him call upon them to halt? — A. Nothing; they were marching down peaceably. The band was playing "Yankee Doodle."

Q. Was that procession armed, so far as you know? — A. Not to my knowledge.

Q. What was the object of the procession? — A. The object was merely to go there and hear the proceedings of the convention; that is all the object they had, to my knowledge. . . .

Q. At the time you left, when the firing commenced on the street in front of the Institute, had any of the police then gone upstairs into the convention room? — A. No, sir; as I came downstairs, the policemen, a majority of them, were at the corner of Dryades and Canal Streets. As I came there, three of them who were ahead of the others came out, and one of them said, "There is that damned nigger captain; kill the black son of a bitch."

Q. Did they shoot at you? — A. They did.

Q. How many shots? — A. I do not know; they were shooting at me continually until I got out of their way. I could not count the shots.

Q. Who was it that shot at you? — A. The police; no citizens, to my knowledge.

Q. Did you say they called you captain? — A. Yes, sir; they knew me.

Q. Had you been a captain in any other service than in the United States service? — A. Never; I have been a free man since my infancy. At the time the rebellion broke out, they called on all the free people to do something for the Confederate government; and if they did not do it, a committee was appointed to look after them, and they would be robbed of their property, if not killed. I was against the rebellion until the last moment. There was a policeman by the name of Robinson, who came to me and said I had better go into the service; if I did not, they would take me and lynch me. Under that advice I enlisted in Captain Jourdan's company, but I did not stay in it longer than I was absolutely compelled to. At the time I got out I tendered my resignation, and it was accepted, though it is the first time I have heard of tendering a resignation as a private.

Q. What did this policeman say to the citizen besides what you related, when he said they were going to hang Hahn and Dostie? — A. I did not hear them say anything. The only thing I heard else was when he referred to the troops.

Q. What time was it when you heard that conversation? — A. It was, I think, about four and a half in the afternoon.

Q. Could you tell that citizen now if you were to see him again? — A. No, sir; I do not think I could identify him. . . .

Mr. Boyer: Were there not colored men in the city of New Orleans who did not enlist in the Confederate service? — A. There were plenty of them.

Q. What necessity was there, then, for you to do otherwise than they did? — A. Because I was free. A majority of the population of the city of New Orleans had to do the same thing in order to save themselves; if they did not they would have been hung or driven out of the country. We did not go with the intention of fighting for the rebels; we said among ourselves that the moment "we saw the flag, we were going to drop our arms; that we would not fight"; but we had to enlist to save ourselves.

Q. Do not you know of any free people in New Orleans who did not join the Confederate service? — A. I do.

Q. Are there quite a number of them? — A. That is more than I can say.

Q. Those who did not choose to join the Confederate service did not lose their lives, did they? — A. No, sir, not to my knowledge. Nobody ever lost his life, for we never went into any engagement.

Q. Then why could you not have done as the others did, and not volunteered in the Confederate service? — A. Because of the warnings I received.

Q. You volunteered then, you did not wait to be conscripted? — A. There was no conscription in the state, at that time.

Q. So you were a volunteer in the Confederate service? — A. Yes, sir, in order to save myself, as a majority of us had to do it in order to save ourselves. But the moment General Butler arrived, several of us wrote him a petition asking his authority to raise a company. I assisted first in raising a company to fill up a company for the Second Regiment. Then I recruited a company for the Third Regiment, of which I [was] captain.

Q. How long were you in the Confederate service? — A. About two weeks.

Q. Did you state all the circumstances, in your opinion, that compelled you to join the Confederate service? — A. Yes, sir.

Testimony of Andrew S. Herron

Andrew S. Herron was the Attorney General of Louisiana at the time of the New Orleans riot. A former secessionist, he was actively involved in the measures that led to the disturbances. His testimony sheds light on the attitude of the law-enforcing agencies of the state.

ANDREW S. HERRON, whose name was given to the committee by Lieutenant Governor Voorhees, as one whose knowledge would enable him to state facts of value to the committee, being duly sworn, testified as follows:

I was not present at the riot of the 30th of July last, nor near it, but was, during the morning and until three or four o'clock in the afternoon, at the first district court. I was at that time, and am still, attorney general of the State of Louisiana. My attention had been called to the preceding meeting of the convention of 1864 by the call for its reassembling, issued by Judge Howell, acting as president of the convention; also by the proclamation issued by the governor of Louisiana to fill vacancies in that convention. The proposed meeting of that convention was brought before the grand jury. The convention was said to have met, and I believe the official proceedings of one of its caucuses or secret meetings were published in one of the papers of the city, though the meeting was professedly in secret and with closed doors. I believed that the proposed meeting of the convention on the 30th, for the purposes proposed in the call of the president, or rather of the gentleman acting as president, would be a violation of the laws of the State of Louisiana. I brought the matter before the grand jury on the day that the convention met, and evidence was received by the grand jury, showing that certain persons claimed to be members of the convention, and an indictment was found against them, drawn up by myself, indicting them as being guilty of making and assisting at an unlawful assemblage, which is a misdemeanor under the laws of the State of Louisiana. That was the only offence which, under the statutes of the state, I thought these parties were guilty of. Several days previous to the meeting of the convention fears were entertained that a collision and riot would occur. I used every effort in my power to see that every necessary step should be taken to avoid that result. Some few days before the meeting of the convention I saw Mr. Monroe. He called at my office and we had a conference in regard to the proposed meeting of the convention, and, I think, in that conversation he stated to me that he had had a conference with General Sheridan, and that he had made an appointment for himself, myself, and General Sheridan to confer upon this subject; but in consequence of General Sheridan's absence from the city no conference was held between Mr. Monroe, General Sheridan, and myself in regard to that convention. The object I had in view in desiring to see General Sheridan at that time was to ascertain to what extent the military could be used in supporting the civil authorities. It was my intention then to prefer an indictment against these parties, for they were claiming to be a constitutional convention — claiming for themselves the powers of a constitutional convention — claiming the power to alter the fundamental laws of the state, and that, under the circumstances under which they must necessarily meet, would be a violation of the law. There might possibly be a difference of opinion as to whether the offence was committed by their meeting without any positive action being taken on their part, but my opinion was that the offence was committed on their meeting, and I expected to indict them on their meeting, and I wished to know how far the military would support them. That conference, however, did not take place. Mr. Monroe afterwards, as I learned, addressed a letter to General Baird upon the subject, which letter was published. In this letter General Baird stated that he would interfere to prevent the arrest of members of the convention. On Saturday morning the papers reported a meeting that was held at the Mechanics' Institute the previous evening, at which incendiary speeches were reported to have been made. On Saturday morning Lieutenant Governor Voorhees and myself telegraphed to the President of the United States the fact that General Baird would not only not assist in arresting these parties under civil process, but that he would prevent their being interfered with. A despatch was received sometime either on Saturday night or Sunday morning — but your memory, gentlemen, will enable you to recall the contents of that despatch better than mine can supply it, for it has probably been before you; the purport of it was that the military would be expected to assist, and not oppose, the civil authorities. General Baird came to the conclusion, as reported to Lieutenant Governor Voorhees, and upon that report I acted, viz: that those members of the convention who were indicted, he would not allow to be arrested by the sheriff. Being anxious to prevent any collision between the military and the civil authorities here, I at once acquiesced in General Baird's decision that no attempt was to be made on the part of the sheriff to arrest the members of the convention; that they might be indicted, but that, instead of going to the convention to arrest them, the sheriff should go directly to General Baird, who would endorse upon the order his objections to allowing the sheriff to proceed in the execution of his duty under the laws of the state, and then that the whole matter should be forwarded, as I understood, by telegraph to the President of the United States for his instructions in the premises. In the meanwhile the civil authorities were to abstain from interfering in any way whatever with the members of the convention. As to the riot which took place on the 30th of July last, I am unable to give any direct testimony, as I was not there; but I think it was on the evening of Monday, the 30th, and after the indictment had been found by the grand jury, that the sheriff did call on General Baird, and he did endorse on the documents authorizing the arrest of these parties his order that, for the present, the sheriff should abstain from making any arrests under it. That matter, together with other information, was, I think, telegraphed to the President on either Monday evening or Tuesday morning.

In answer to that despatch giving the information, there was a despatch received, directed to Lieutenant Governor Voorhees and myself, from the Adjutant General's office at Washington. In answer to that the facts were telegraphed to the President, briefly, as they had to be. The same facts were embodied in a communication of greater length by Lieutenant Governor Voorhees, and signed by him and myself, and this we despatched to the President by mail. I received a despatch from the President telling me that General Sheridan would afford me such assistance as would be necessary to enforce the civil process; that the military were expected to cooperate with the civil authorities, and not to thwart them. I think it also contained something about the fact that this convention had no right to meet, and that no convention would be authorized here except it was a convention fresh from the people. The only portion of that despatch that I considered as having anything to do with the discharge of my duties was that portion authorizing me, in case I should think it necessary, to call upon General Sheridan for troops in carrying out the orders of the civil authorities. That despatch was immediately after communicated to General Baird, who had in the meantime issued his orders not to arrest those parties. General Baird's response was, that he did not doubt the authenticity of the despatch, but that he was not disposed to alter his order till he himself had received instructions from the President or the Secretary of War. I am under the impression that that conversation between General Baird and myself took place on Tuesday, the day after the riot; it may have been as late as Wednesday, but I think it was Tuesday. General Sheridan was absent, and did not return until the next day. Not desiring to be or appear to be officious, and not desiring to intrude myself upon the military commander, I remained, after General Sheridan's return, till late in the evening, or possibly till the next morning. I then started with the intention of seeing General Sheridan, to ascertain if he had revoked the order. Martial law had been proclaimed to a certain extent. On my way to find General Sheridan I met General Baird, and he told me at the City Hall that he would revoke his order to the sheriff, and allow them to arrest the members of the convention who had been indicted by the grand jury, which was done that night or the next morning, and the sheriff, I think, arrested about twenty members of the convention without any trouble or difficulty. I felt the greatest anxiety that no collision should take place, and that no violation of law should occur, and that no riot or anything of that kind should grow out of the meeting of this convention. I attended a meeting of gentlemen at the mayor's office on Saturday night before the meeting of the convention, at which several prominent citizens, some few lawyers, and prominent merchants, probably some twenty or thirty, were present, intending to ascertain if possible what was best to be done to prevent trouble or collision growing out of the meeting of the convention. At that meeting it was agreed to issue a proclamation calling upon the people of the city not to be brought into collision, or to go about in numbers, so as in any way to invite such a result. It was also suggested, and I think carried out, that the city papers should call upon the citizens to abstain from meeting in unusual numbers, or from going about in the streets in such a way as might incidentally lead to a collision. I felt supremely anxious myself to avoid anything of the sort, and from the expressions of opinion made at that meeting, from the tone of the papers, and the mayor's proclamation, and from the general feeling of the citizens who were interested in preserving the peace, I was inclined to think that there would be no trouble or collision of any kind.

Mr. Boyer: Is there any statute law in force in the State of Louisiana within the provisions of which the assembling of the convention of the 30th of July would be embraced in the definition of an "unlawful assemblage"? — A. I was under the impression, and still believe, that the act relating to riots and unlawful assemblages is in force, and embraces such a meeting as the convention of the 30th of July.

Q. Can you furnish us with a copy of that statute? — A. Yes, sir.

Q. Were those engaged in that convention indicted under the statute to which you have alluded, or under the common law, or both? — A. They were indicted under the statute to which I have alluded. By the provisions of our state law, and under the decisions of our courts, nothing is an offence unless made so by statute. That class of cases which, under the jurisprudence of some of the states, can be prosecuted under the common law, are not punishable under our system, as interpreted by our supreme court, unless they are embraced in some statute expressly providing a punishment for the crime.

Q. How far back does that date? — A. As far back as 1803. There are a large number of our statutes that date back as far as that, but I am not certain as to the date of the one I refer to.

Q. Is there any subsequent legislation which has superseded that? — A.

I think not, sir. I would state that, in 1855, the legislature of this state adopted *de novo*, and afterwards embodied in what we call the revised statutes of the state, the laws previously passed, which, to be binding, must be contained in the act of 1855; but in the act of 1855, everything pertaining to crimes and offences in relation to riots, routs, and unlawful assemblages, is left out; but as there is nothing else relating to riots, etc., in the act, our supreme court had decided, in analogous cases, that unless there was some legislation upon the same subject-matter the original statute was still in force and not repealed.

CONCLUSION

Whatever the bias of the Congressional fact-finders, the three investigations showed that there was a considerable feeling of insecurity in the South. Unionists believed themselves discriminated against, if not physically threatened; Negroes were not only deprived of elementary rights but were little removed from conditions of slavery; and former Confederates still held to their opinions of state sovereignty and racial exclusiveness. Despite its appeal to conservatives, the Johnson plan, it appeared, had not succeeded in restoring national harmony. Although black suffrage was rejected by most Southerners, it was clear that the freedmen were perfectly capable of sensibly exercising the franchise if it were given to them. It was evident that they would sustain the Republican party in the South, and that it would be impossible to maintain the gains of the Civil War without some measure of enfranchisement of the blacks. Nor could there be any doubt that outrages had been perpetrated, not only in Memphis and New Orleans, but in other places as well.

Congress drew the necessary conclusions. The Joint Committee of Fifteen submitted the Fourteenth Amendment to Congress, which passed it in slightly altered form in June 1866. Providing, among other things, for Negro citizenship, the protection of civil rights from state interference, and the reduction of representation for states denying the right to vote to male citizens over the age of twenty-one, the Amendment might have been a way out for both the President and the South. But Johnson opposed it, and encouraged by his resistance, every Southern state except Tennessee failed to ratify it. The result was that after the great radical victory in the mid-term elections in the fall of 1866, the Republicans broke completely with the President. Seeking to shackle him by the enactment of the Tenure-of-Office and Command of the Army Acts, they proceeded to remake the South in accordance with radical concepts. They enacted four Reconstruction Acts that reestablished military rule in the South and provided for new elections based on universal suffrage limited by Confederate disfranchisement. The voters who met the acts' qualifications chose conventions and legislatures that ratified the Fourteenth Amendment, wrote new state constitutions, and reformed the eleemosynary and educational institutions of the South. If, as has so often been asserted, some of them were caught up in a welter of corruption, they were not substantially worse than many contemporary state governments in the North, then being disgraced by corruptionists like William Marcy Tweed. The Gilded Age was beginning.

After the election of Ulysses Grant as President, the Fifteenth Amendment, prohibiting disfranchisement on the basis of race, color, or previous condition of servitude, was also passed and ratified. But in the long run, it proved impossible to defend the freedmen against the onslaught of the entrenched forces of privilege in the South. The radicals passed from the scene; force and violence helped restore white supremacy in the old Confederacy; and in 1877, as a result of the compromise which gave Rutherford B. Hayes the Presidency in return for economic and political concessions to Southern conservatives, the last Federal troops were withdrawn from the reconstructed states.

Nevertheless, the testimony taken in 1865 and 1866 had not been totally useless: it had helped to establish the political climate in which the Fourteenth Amendment could be ratified. And while for years the amendment was used merely to protect great corporations, during the twentieth century the courts again relied upon it for the protection of minorities. Thus one hundred years after the era of Reconstruction, the radicals' labors bore fruit. The witnesses had not pleaded in vain.